DATE DUE

DEMCO 38-297

LITERARY MONOGRAPHS · *Volume 5*

LITERARY MONOGRAPHS

Volume 5

EDITED BY

Eric Rothstein

Published for the Department of English by

THE UNIVERSITY OF WISCONSIN PRESS

Published 1973
The University of Wisconsin Press
Box 1379, Madison, Wisconsin 53701
The University of Wisconsin Press, Ltd.
70 Great Russell Street, London

First printing

Printed in the United States of America

ISBN 0-299-06310-0; LC 66-25869

Publication of this volume has been made possible in part by a gift to the University of Wisconsin Foundation from the estate of Beatrice T. Conrad, Davenport, Iowa.

PREFACE

The Department of English of the University of Wisconsin continues with this volume a series of monographs in English and American literature. The series was inaugurated in 1967 to serve scholars whose work might take a form too lengthy for journals but too brief for a separate book.

For future volumes of *Literary Monographs* we invite works of high quality, scholarly or critical, that contribute materially to English or American literary studies. We welcome not only conventional literary essays but also those involving experimental critical theories and methods whenever they are eloquent and persuasive. And we will be flexible enough to welcome monographs involving comparative literature or comparative aesthetics, so long as they significantly illuminate literature in English.

The editorial board of *Literary Monographs* would like to express its appreciation to the University of Wisconsin Foundation for making possible the publication of this volume through a gift from the estate of Beatrice T. Conrad, Davenport, Iowa.

Eric Rothstein

Madison, Wisconsin
November 1972

NOTES ON SUBMISSIONS

Manuscripts should be from 15,000 to 35,000 words in length. They should be submitted, with return postage and self-addressed envelope enclosed, to

> The Editor
> *Literary Monographs*
> Department of English
> Helen C. White Hall
> 600 N. Park Street
> University of Wisconsin
> Madison, Wisconsin 53706

Manuscripts should follow the *MLA Style Sheet,* with a few exceptions or amplifications included in the specific instructions given below.

1. Paper should be 16-pound or 20-pound weight bond in normal quarto size; do not use highly glazed paper (sold under such trade names as "Corrasable"). To make satisfactory photocopying possible, the paper should be white and the typewriter ribbon black. Handwritten corrections may be made in pencil or washable ink; avoid ballpoint pen. Leave margins of 1 to 1 1/2 inches on all sides.

2. Manuscripts should be double spaced throughout, including notes and all excerpts, prose or verse. Do not indent prose excerpts, but mark them with a pencil line along the left margin to the full length of the quotation and allow an extra line of space above and below.

3. Brief references should be inserted in the text (see *MLA Style Sheet,* Sec. 13f). In notes, first references should be cited in full. Succeeding references to books should use short titles rather than *"op. cit.";* e.g., Taylor, *Problems,* p. 12. Short references to journal articles should use author's name, journal name, volume, and page; e.g., McKerrow, RES, xvi, 117.

As can be seen from this volume, *Literary Monographs* reserves the use of footnotes for information that is needed in order to follow the argument of the text or to understand a system of in-text citation. Endnotes supply documentation, or they may extend or parallel the text discussion. Contributors are requested to organize their manuscripts so that endnotes and footnotes are on separate pages, with separate numbering sequences.

CONTENTS

CHAUCER'S BROCHE OF THEBES:
THE UNITY OF "THE COMPLAINT OF MARS"
AND "THE COMPLAINT OF VENUS"

Rodney Merrill

Since the time of F. J. Furnivall, editors of Chaucer's minor poems have printed "The Complaint of Mars" and "The Complaint of Venus" as two entirely separate poems.* In doing so they have turned away from an editorial tradition which was firmly founded on the testimony of every reliable manuscript containing the complaints. The first purpose of this essay, therefore, must be to examine the arguments which have led to this practice, to show that outmoded and uncritical ways of reading Chaucer's poems and of understanding their genesis are mainly responsible for it, and by doing so to put the burden of proof on the shoulders of those who would continue to separate the two complaints. In this task I shall be following in the footsteps of Aage Brusendorff, Haldeen Braddy, and G. H. Cowling, whose arguments lend persuasive support to viewing the poems as a sequence, at least in terms of the circumstances of their composition.[1] If their findings have had almost no effect, the reason may lie in the indifference with which most readers approach works of such small compass, outwardly considered, in the range of Chaucer's productions.

My second and more important aim, therefore, will be to show why the reunion of the two complaints has important consequences for an enriched understanding of a work which yields to no other of Chaucer's in subtlety, and which exceeds many in concentration. In the course of these two tasks, I shall also attempt to show that the title by which the poem was known to some of its early readers, *The Broche of Thebes*, is suited to it in

* They are printed under these titles in Geoffrey Chaucer, *Works*, ed. F. N. Robinson (Boston, 1957), pp. 529-533, 537-538. Hereafter I shall refer to them respectively as the "Mars" and the "Venus." Furnivall's reasons for separating them are most fully expressed in the headnote to the "Venus" in his *Parallel-text Edition of Chaucer's Minor Poems* (London, 1879), p. 411.

3

such interesting ways as to deserve restoration. Here also I am interested more in the literary ramifications of the title than in proving that Chaucer himself knew the poem exclusively by that title. In any event, barring some discovery as important as a holograph manuscript, such proof would be impossible, just as it would be impossible to demonstrate that he never considered either of the components as a separate poem.

I. THE UNITY OF THE POEM

Indeed this latter problem requires some clarification at the outset. To say that the two parts form an indissoluble unity would be to expect an external structural coherence which cannot be found and need not be looked for. Yet the separation of the two complaints has proceeded largely on the assumption that poems should form a unity in an almost classical sense, or else they should be considered as distinct wholes. According to such thinking, of course, *The Canterbury Tales* is simply a collection of fragments strung together, more or less successfully, by a "framing narrative" (which itself is far from perfect). Similar assumptions bedevil the discussions over the "unity" of Malory's "Works"—or his "hoole book." I shall argue that the "Mars," with its narrative introduction, *may* have been composed first (perhaps under the title of *The Broche of Thebes*) and that the "Venus" *may* have been composed and even conceived later, but that the latter nevertheless develops in crucial ways the issues raised in the former, and carries the discussion, as it were, to its conclusion.

Brusendorff has argued for this sequence of composition, but he considers only the scandalous events which may have provided the occasion for the poet's activity, and he does not consider the poems as a sequence from a more strictly literary point of view. He bases his apparent belief that the poems are to be separated on the fact that John Shirley, the scribe who is responsible for the meager information we have concerning these events, seems to think of them as distinct poems. This conclusion is drawn from the rubrics which Shirley, in accord with his general habit, attached to the poems in his manuscript, now Trinity College Cambridge MS R. 3, 20.[2] At the head of the "Mars" Shirley writes:

Loo yee louers gladeþe and comforteþe you of þallyance entrayted betwene / þe hardy and furyous Mars þe god of armes and Venus þe double goddesse of loue made by Geffrey Chaucier at þe comandement of þe renomed and excellent Prynce my lord þe Duc Iohn of Lancastre.

At the end of the complaint:

Þus eondeþe here þis complaint whiche some men sayne / was made by my lady of York doughter to þe kyng of Spaygne / and my lord of Huntyngdoun some tyme duc of Excestre. and filowing begynneþe a balade translated out of frenshe in to englisshe / by Chaucier Geffrey þe frenshe made sir Otes de Grauntsomme knight Savosyen.

This "balade" is the "Venus," and following it Shirley writes:

Hit is sayde þat Graunsomme made þis last balade for Venus resembled to my lady of York. aunswering þe complaynt of Mars / and here filoweþe a balade made by Chaucier of þe louer / and of Dame ffortune (*Fortune*, Robinson ed., p. 535, follows).

We shall have to consider these rubrics at more length, but at this point a few remarks should suffice. In the first place, even Shirley speaks about the connection between the poems: he thinks the original of the "Venus" was written by Grandson as an "answer" to the "Mars." Moreover, his belief that the "Venus" is a translation is probably based on the last lines of "Lenvoy" to the "Venus":

> And eke to me it ys a gret penaunce,
> Syth rym in Englissh hath such skarsete,
> To folowe word by word the curiosite
> Of Graunson, flour of hem that make in Fraunce.
>
> ("Venus," ll. 79-82)

In fact, the "Venus" is not at all an exact ("word by word") translation; Chaucer is engaging here as throughout "Lenvoy" in *ironia*, and his "word by word" actually amounts to an invitation to his readers to see how much, and in what respects, he has modified the "curiosite / Of Graunson."[3] Shirley apparently did not know the "original" (which is spoken by the male lover), and, taking Chaucer literally, concluded that Grandson's poem itself consisted of Venus' "answer" to Mars' complaint. Once we become aware of the subtlety and creativeness of Chaucer's adaptation, we will no longer be inclined to consider it the mere translation of an independent poem, but rather a deliberately crafted continuation of *The Broche of Thebes*.

Thus, insofar as Shirley's rubrics would suggest the independence of the two parts, it is because of a mistake concerning translation. His failure to include them under a common rubric doubtless stems from this error; but in any case Brusendorff himself has ably demonstrated that the textual authority of Shirley's manuscripts is much inferior to that of almost every other copy of the poems.[4] Shirley apparently liked to copy poems or parts of poems on the basis of his rather imperfect memory. He was not overly concerned to maintain the integrity of the texts which were the means of his livelihood. What he did care about was sales, and Brusendorff points out that his rubrics often read like a modern publisher's blurbs. This commercial purpose can likely be seen in the gossip suggesting the "human interest" of such poems as the "Venus"; and both Brusendorff and Braddy have pointed out that Shirley's sources might well have been the poet's own family, Thomas Chaucer and his daughter Alice, the wife of the Duke of Suffolk. Thus what Shirley says is at least as reliable as modern speculations as to the "identity" of Mars and Venus. We must not rest any crucial conclusions upon it, but we can accept it provisionally without in the least implying that the scribe is an important authority in determining textual questions.

Since all significant manuscripts support the linking, any argument in favor of the original separateness of the two complaints needs to maintain that some scribe, acting entirely on his own authority, combined them and gave them the titles they carry in most of the sources, and that from this combination descend all the complete versions which we possess. Such a theory, unlikely as it is, becomes even more so when we consider that the two parts are deliberately linked in the authoritative manuscripts of two distinct traditions, as set forth in the standard editions of these poems.[5] In other words, to suppose them originally separate is to postulate at least two copies of the orginally distinct complaints which, however differing in other respects, agree in viewing them as a sequence. It is to presume that an anonymous scribe had an inspiration which will appear more and more interesting when we look closely at the sequence from a literary point of view. And it is to claim that the authentic tradition is lost, only this late and erroneous combination surviving.

In all good manuscripts, then, the complaints are joined: manuscripts in which either is found alone are clearly unacceptable as evidence.[6] The "Mars" occurs by itself in Harley 7333, where it breaks off unfinished (two leaves have been torn from the volume immediately following this fragment). Longleat 258, written probably in the early sixteenth century—much later than the complete versions with which it is textually associated, those in Fairfax 16 and Tanner 346—contains another fragmentary copy, lacking the first six stanzas. The "Venus" occurs alone in MS Ashmole 59, a Shirley MS: it is even less reliable than Shirley's other redaction of the complaint (in MS R. 3, 20), as it is very late, omits an entire stanza (the second of the second balade), and attributes the poem to Thomas Chaucer. (Shirley himself, we have seen, provides the more credible attribution to the elder Chaucer in MS R. 3,20.) Finally, Cambridge University Library MS Ff. 1. 6, dubbed the "Findern Anthology" by R. H. Robbins, contains another copy of the "Venus": but this anthology seems even less trustworthy than Shirley. Hammond, p. 343, describes it as follows: "In many hands, all latter XV century if not later, and all slovenly, current, and untidy. . . ." Robbins' list of the contents of the MS shows (p. 614) that this complaint follows two other excerpts from Chaucer's works, Anelida's Complaint from *Anelida and Arcite* and the Story of Thisbe from *The Legend of Good Women*. This fact alone does not prove that the "Venus" is an excerpt, but it certainly disposes of any argument for separation which might be based on the version here. It can also remind us that though the "Venus," like Anelida's Complaint, may be read in detachment, its original context may extend and even change our understanding of its meaning.

I think we may conclude that there is not one iota of evidence in the manuscript tradition which would justify separating the poems. On the contrary, such separate versions as appear result from the tendencies of scribes to excerpt (Ashmole 59, the "Findern Anthology") or simply not to reach the end of the poem (Harley 7333). Brusendorff's account of the way these poetic miscellanies were compiled, from several smaller booklets in the possession of the scriptorium, makes fragmentation seem a far likelier eventuality than creative combination.[7]

If the parts were written and printed from the beginning (or at least since the completion of the "Venus") as a sequence, it remains to define what sort of unity they possess. The final answer to this question must await a reading of the poem, but a few preliminary suggestions can be made which may put to rest some editorial arguments for printing the parts separately. In the first place, they may have been composed months or even years apart. We cannot hope to know conclusively whether the poem was the gradual realization of a full-blown original idea, or whether it is the product of a creatively incremental mode of writing (Malory offers the same problem, though the second is more likely in his case). Medieval writers could entertain a liberal notion of a "unified" structure, just as medieval masons were quite ready to adapt the design of a single cathedral to changing needs and stylistic expectations.

In the present case, however, Chaucer may have had the additional stimulus of external events to make him push his comic exploration of *fol amour* one step further. And here we must touch on the question of Chaucer's adaptation in the "Venus," a subject which will receive more attention below. This poem, moreover, is hardly the only one in which Chaucer included "translations" and "original" parts in the same work. But here the circumstances are special: and some of Chaucer's fun may derive from the very fact that the "Venus" is in fact a "translation." A

short discussion of the so-called "personal allegory" of the poem will show
why.

Building upon the indications furnished by Shirley in the rubrics quoted
earlier, scholars have reconstructed the series of events which may have
suggested the two parts.[8] Shirley suggests that the poems refer to the love
affair between John Holande, Earl of Huntingdon, sometime Duke of
Exeter, the half brother of Richard II, and Isabel Langley, Duchess of
York, daughter of Pedro, King of Castile.[9] According to Shirley, John of
Gaunt commanded the poem from Chaucer; and Furnivall notes that
Gaunt obtained a pardon for John Holande after the latter had incurred
disgrace by stabbing the heir to the Earl of Stafford in July 1385. Brusen-
dorff, Cowling, and others have pointed out that Holande's notorious
ferocity accorded well with the "cruelte, and bost, and tyrannye" which
Venus "forbad" Mars ("Mars," ll. 36–37), and have considered that Mars'
isolation, mentioned in ll. 65–67, might refer to Holande's disgrace.
Gaunt's intervention was apparently caused by the fact that his daughter
Elizabeth had been seduced by Holande; as a result Elizabeth's betrothal
to the Earl of Pembroke was annulled, and she married Holande. In June
1386 Gaunt made his son-in-law the constable of his forces in the Castilian
expedition. We can understand, in such circumstances, that Gaunt might
have taken an interest in Holande's behavior and therefore requested
Chaucer to provide a gentle suggestion about the folly of his actions.

Cowling suggests that Chaucer's poem referred to Holande's liaison
with Elizabeth, rather than Isabel; he maintains that Chaucer would not
dare to reflect publicly on the honor of the Duke of York and his wife,
even at the request of the Duke of Lancaster. But Cowling also sees the
poem's fiction as an apology, dignified and poetic, for the "inauspicious
marriage" of Elizabeth and Holande. Even a superficial glance at the
poem would show how far from dignified the fiction is; and it is apologetic
only in suggesting that the folly it portrays is a general human failing.[10]
The story has wider reference to the famous account of the love affair of
Mars and Venus and its punishment by Vulcan, the outraged husband. It is
a story of humiliation, and if nobles were as sensitive as Cowling believes,
Gaunt could hardly have been happy to see his own daughter in the title
role. The husband's honor, moreover, is not centrally in question. Vulcan
is never mentioned, while Mars is humiliated (and feels himself to be so) in
the poem itself. If the poem had been an "exposé" dangerous for its
author, the ferocious Holande would certainly have inspired as much fear
as York.

What seems more likely is that Chaucer could expect his audience to
enjoy a well-contrived joke. Even Gaunt, whose love life hardly provided

an example of married chastity, would have been "attainted" by the implication of Chaucer's satire. This poem, like Pope's *Rape of the Lock,* nourishes the good humor upon which it depends for its success. The poet's urbane sense of the ludicrous never allows him to forget the universal implications of his fictions; and even particular objects of wit can feel the sympathy in his portrayals of them.

If we accept Shirley's account, cloudy as it may be, we can go on to consider how these facts may be connected with the composition of the "Venus." For this same Isabel of Spain seems also to have been the "lady" of Oton de Grandson: Shirley, in fact, says that Grandson "made þis last balade for Venus resembled to my lady of York. aunswering þe complaynt of Mars." Grandson could not have intended "þe frenshe" to be spoken by Venus, since his speaker is a man. But Haldeen Braddy has argued persuasively that Grandson was indeed known as an admirer of Isabel of York; the "Isabel" acrostics which occur several times in his poems probably refer to her.[11] (Needless to say, such acrostics do not necessarily imply a passionate relationship.) Thus we can see another way of reading Shirley's rubric. Grandson perhaps dedicated his poem *to* Venus "resembled to my lady of York." Even Shirley's confusion as to "aunswering" may be justified in a way, since Grandson's poem could have been a "response" to the "Mars." Grandson almost certainly knew Chaucer, as both were in the service of John of Gaunt. Thus, when the latter shows John Holande as Mars making a complaint which refers to Isabel of York as Venus, Grandson may "answer" with a series of balades dedicated to the same lady: Mars' complaint is in five parts, Grandson's composition is *Les cinq balades ensuivans.* Then the final stroke of wit would be for Chaucer to adapt the first, fourth, and fifth of Grandson's balades as a complaint to be put in the mouth of the lady herself. For initiates, the point would be driven home in "Lenvoy," where the poet refers to Grandson as "flour of hem that make in Fraunce," pretends to be following him "word by word," and finally, perhaps, dedicates the whole poem to the "Princesse" whom Venus represents.

Such a sequence of events would explain how Chaucer might have decided on a continuation of *The Broche of Thebes.* Having told, under fictional cover, of the adulterous love affair between Grandson's ideal "lady" and the unruly Holande, Chaucer shows the same lady turn Grandson's tribute to her into a declaration of devotion to Grandson's rival. Thus "real life" and fiction are entangled in several ways. The pressure toward ideal sexual devotion expressed in the fiction of Grandson's original *Cinq balades ensuivans,* as well as in both the "Mars" and the "Venus," is shown to be self-defeating, first by the "action" of the entire *Broche of*

Thebes, next by the "real-life" events which it "allegorizes," and finally by
the treatment of Grandson's poems to suggest his "betrayal" by his "lady."
The prominence of Jealousy increases from Grandson's original to Chaucer's adaptation; and we can hardly wonder, considering the rivalries
which may be in question. Moreover, even if the sequence of events
(composition of "Mars," response of *Cinq balades ensuivans,* addition of
"Venus") is inaccurate, there seems to be an ironic relationship between
Grandson's original poem, in which his lady is presented as supremely
virtuous, and Chaucer's adaptation of it to express that lady's illicit love
for Holande-Mars.

This speculative history of an *amour* (or of several *amours*) is not
brought forward as a "proof" that the two complaints are linked, but
rather as a guess about the circumstances of the continuation. It also
provides a positive way of looking at two features of the poem which have
been used as objections to its unity: the absence of any linking narrative
between the two complaints, and the fact that the second complaint is a
"translation." As to the first point, Chaucer might have spoiled some of
the fun and weakened the poem if he had tried to provide an explicit
transition between the two parts, presumably by causing the " foule" who
sings the "Complaint of Mars" to do the same thing for Venus. The later's
complaint, as we shall see, is intensely private, unlike that of Mars; and
Chaucer may well have preferred that it come to us direct from her
"remembraunce" as she puts that "remembraunce" into words. It would
be foolish, however, to base a claim for the poem's unity on its outward
smoothness; but if it shows a flaw in construction, it is in the sense that the
"missing links" of *The Canterbury Tales* are flaws.

The objection on grounds of translation has already been sufficiently
discussed. It suffices in summary to point out once more that Chaucer not
only is willing to use "translations" in original works wherever they fit his
purposes, but also that in this case he deliberately refers to the "curiosite"
of his original and to its author. Thus he provides a clue to his literary
game and hints that the very fact of "translation" may be part of the
poetic meaning.

Critics who object to the traditional linking of the complaints need
naturally to explain away the title of the second one, which seems so
obviously to connect it with the "Mars." This Skeat does when he says
that "The Complaint of Venus" "is not suitable for Venus, unless the
'Venus' be a mortal; neither is it a continuous 'Compleynt,' being simply
the linking together of three separate and distinct balades."[12] The second
part of this objection may be dismissed as simply the result of a failure to
read the poem. Both Grandson's *Cinq balades ensuivans* and Chaucer's

adaptation of it form quite obviously continuous wholes—though, as is often the case with medieval works, their parts can also be taken as wholes in themselves. And of course Chaucer himself, in "Lenvoy," refers to the poem in the singular. The first part needs a bit more discussion: it depends on A. Piaget's remark that "Dans ce poème [the "Venus"], il n'est question ni de Vénus, ni de Mars"; and Paget Toynbee agrees that the title is a misnomer which he, following Piaget, thinks was derived from Shirley's rubrics.[13] There is not the slightest evidence that the title has anything to do with Shirley. It is found in manuscripts of quite distinct and much more authoritative traditions; and it goes far beyond editorial license to assume "contamination" in the case of texts with a superior claim to authority, simply because the editor is not able to understand the reading. In fact, it seems quite certain that Shirley is himself trying to explain the title, insofar as the "Venus" is concerned; he strangely calls the poem a "balade" (singular), despite the fact that both Venus (l. 71) and the poet (l. 73) label it a "compleynt." This being the case, the title becomes a strong argument in favor of the linking; for to the casual observer—or to the average scribe—there is nothing in the poem considered by itself which suggests that Venus says it.

Indeed, the reactions of Skeat, Piaget, and Toynbee are just such as would be expected of unimaginative readers, for in the poem Venus addresses Love, complains of the sorrow Love causes, and in general talks as if she is subject to Love, not sovereign over it. Needless to say, this is precisely the point, one which was always implicit in the myth of Mars and Venus—the Goddess of Love feels the pains of her own tyranny, as it were. It is a point, moreover, which is brought out fully in the narrative of *The Broche of Thebes* and even more in Mars' complaint. In the latter Mars calls his lady " the verrey sours and welle . . . Of love and pley," and yet can exclaim, "Alas! that ever lovers mote endure, / For love, so many a perilous aventure!" (ll. 174, 178, 198-199), and can mourn that his lady "Is in affray, and not to whom to pleyne" (l. 214). Such paradoxes are so woven into the entire poem that it is simple literary obtuseness to use them as grounds for taking Venus' complaint out of her mouth. In one respect Skeat comes close to the truth, for Venus, like Mars, is not so divine that she cannot represent the sorrows of a mortal. Yet since the appropriateness of the title appears only after some understanding of the poem, it seems hardly possible that anyone but the author himself could have assigned it—unless it be the same inspired scribe who joined the two poems and imposed his judgment on his successors.

The title of the "Venus" and the unity it implies were accepted without question by the scribe of Fairfax 16, where the whole poem is headed

"The Complaynt of Mars and Venus." Moreover, the poem enjoyed sufficient esteem to inspire a splendid miniature which serves as frontispiece to
the manuscript, and which can afford us a rare and valuable opportunity
to see how an artist living not long after the poet undertook the practical
task of representing some of the work's meaning in visual terms. (The
miniature has been reproduced by Brusendorff, facing p. 264, and by
Wood, fig. 14.) Though it does not prove the unity of the poem, it bears
directly on the question of the kind of unity we should look for. The
miniaturist does not feel at all bound by the literal narrative, nor does he
try to reproduce the astrological machinery. And while Chauncey Wood's
discussion of the iconography (pp. 130-141) demonstrates that the artist
must have been aware of the conventions, we can also use his findings to
point out how boldly traditional materials are manipulated to make them
respond humorously and intelligently to the poem.

The most striking formal feature of the miniature as a whole is its
division into three panels, two vertical and one above, transverse; each is
strongly framed, yet all are contained within an outer frame which is itself
surrounded by floral decorations. Thus the tripartite unity-in-diversity of
the poem is visually adumbrated; moreover, the three main figures, while
having independent aesthetic existences in differing landscapes, interact
with one another. From his grassy spot Mars waves to Venus, who waves
back at him from the water in which she stands amid trees and rocks;
while above, Jupiter stands in the Sun, cloak outspread against the sky,
and glances toward Mars. The three parts of the poem—narrative, Mars'
complaint, Venus' complaint—are similar in their independence and their
essential interrelations. But we shall find that the principle of triplicity
extends a good deal further into the poetic form, expecially in the two
complaints; and it ultimately points to a Trinity in which power, knowledge, and love are perfectly united.

As Wood remarks, the presence of Jupiter instead of "Phebus"—who is
mentioned six times in the narrative—seems curious; and one might be
inclined to agree with his suspicion of a mislabeling, except that this
figure's beard and spear are much more appropriate to Jupiter than to
Apollo.[14] Perhaps Wood is right in suggesting that Jupiter would appropriately rebuke the disturbers of Olympian domesticity, thus figuring the
Christian God rebuking adultery. But Mars himself speaks of "him that
lordeth ech intelligence" as having wrought him and brought him hither
"for certeyn effectes" ("Mars," ll. 164-166); and the climax of his complaint is an effort to blame "the God that sit so hye" (l. 218) for his
suffering. Presumably Jupiter is the nearest pagan equivalent to this high
God, even if he is himself a planet. At any rate he seems to be presiding

over the whole drama, making a gesture of command and pointing his spear toward Mars. It seems appropriate, then, that Jupiter and the Sun should be so closely associated: the latter discovers the "conjuction" which the former, as ruler of the planets, ordains. What seems at first sight to be a mistake turns out to be an ingenious symbol of the identity of power and knowledge in God.

Even more curious than Jupiter is the condition of Mars' dress—or rather half dress. He is fully armed, except that his left arm and his right leg are bare. Wood's speculation "that the artist knew of some convention in which lecherous gentlemen are so depicted" (p. 133; he notices only the bare leg and cites pictures by Titian and Michelangelo as possible parallels) accords well with his emphasis on moralizing both poem and illustration. What seems more likely (and more amusing) is that the artist has chosen this way to suggest the haste of Mars' arming, and his subsequent helplessness ("Mars," ll. 92–112), as he watches Venus disappear. Chaucer's narrative does not mention such forgetfulness, but it insists on the feebleness. Mars' forlorn state is emphasized also in the woebegone expression on his face and in the transformation of his conventional wolf (which in *The Knight's Tale* is described as eating a man; cf. Wood, p. 132) into a blunt-nosed puppy snarling up at him, reminding us how "tame" ("Mars," l. 278) he has become.[15]

But the artist is not trying to capture a single moment from the episode, whether the greeting (as Wood thinks) or separation (as seems more likely, considering Mars' unhappy state); insofar as he is concerned about temporal sequence, he telescopes it as nonchalantly, and as skillfully, as any medieval artist. This treatment of time has a special significance in relation to this poem, however, because the astrological machinery makes the story into a series of cosmic events which will be repeated as long as the heavens last—a planetary analogue of the unceasing human movement from desire to deprivation. Thus, though the naked Venus appears as distressed as Mars—the overall comic realism causes even the water where she conventionally stands to suggest physical discomfort—she is represented in full iconographic panoply, with doves, nimbus, and conchshell, as the inspirer and symbol of desire. Above her stands a comic pageboy Cupid, aiming his arrow straight at Mars' eyes, while in the opposite corner Vulcan, bald, white-bearded, and stooped, makes something on his anvil; in his complaint Mars refers to the baneful "worcher" of the Broche of Thebes (ll. 259–262), though he conveniently neglects the actual name. Thus the awakening desire and the retribution for consummated adultery are evoked together. The visual parallel between Cupid's arrow and the spear which, just above, Jupiter points at Mars' heart suggests that Cupid and "so juste a kyng" ("Mars," l. 231), though not perhaps the same, are ultimately allied. Mars cannot resist the arrow of desire, yet he will inevitably feel the pains of separation ordained by the ruler of the planets. His complaint is much concerned with the apparent conflict between divine justice and the pains arising from love.

Nor are the human dimensions of the poem neglected: behind Mars kneel two figures with hands upraised, either to express their devotion to the God of War despite his unwarlike condition, or to respond to his plea to "hardy knyghtes of renoun" to "have som compassioun / Of my disese" ("Mars," ll. 272–277; cf. Wood, p. 133). Venus will make Mars' reputation for "gentilesse" the major justification for her love ("Venus," balade I). More delightful yet is the transformation of the Three Graces, which often accompany Venus, into three decidedly unattractive devotees of the Goddess of Love.[16] One of these naked ladies, eyes bent to the earth, seems to be obeying Mars' injunction to "pleyne" for "your honour and your emperise" ("Mars," ll. 285–289), while the other two, hands upraised, seem to beseech her aid. Thus is suggested the human confusion about the Love Goddess, who is supposed to give nothing but pleasure (cf. "Mars," ll. 174–181) but in practice brings as much grief as she is shown here to suffer.

In sum, the picture works much like the poem, by casting traditional mythological and conventional elements into human terms, so that their symbolic value is illuminated by the comic realism. In this respect the miniaturist's wit seems worthy of Chaucer himself: it should alert us, as it did the original readers of the Fairfax manuscript, to the fascinating complexities of the poetic achievement. For *The Broche of Thebes* has the concentrated significance which could be attained only by the most able practitioners of miniaturization.

II. THE TITLE

The title of the "Venus," I have suggested, is justified precisely because it seems inappropriate to the superficial view. The same sort of consideration favors the restoration of *The Broche of Thebes* as the title of the whole poem; but here the evidence is far less conclusive, for this title is indicated in only a few of the early versions, with an explanatory addition or as an explanation itself.[17] Harley MS 7333, where, as has been noted, only the first 178 lines of the "Mars" appear, has the heading "The Broche of Thebes as of the love of mars and venus." But Hammond notes that this rubric apparently headed the more authoritative version in Pepys 2006,

Hand B, before it was trimmed for binding. Finally, the first printer of the poem, Julian Notary, has as colophon "Explicit the compleyces of Maris and Venus / and of the broche of Thebes." (His heading is "The loue and complayntes bytwene Mars and Venus.") The only other indication is that provided by Lydgate in the list of Chaucer's works included in the Prologue to *The Fall of Princes:*

> Off Anneleyda and of fals Arcite
> He made a compleynt, doolful & pitous,
> And off the broche which that Vulcanus
> At Thebes wrouhte, ful dyuers of nature,
> Ouide writith, who theroff hadde a siht,
> For hih desir he shulde nat endure
> But he it hadde, neuer be glad nor liht;
> And yiff he hadde it onys in his myht,
> Lich as my maister seith and writ in deede,
> It to conserue he sholde ay lyue in dreede.[18]

Brusendorff points out that these last lines refer to the fourth tern of Mars' compaint, and he takes the title as referring only to what Robinson prints as "The Complaint of Mars." And though this may have been the case at first, the inclusion of "The Complaint of Venus" does not at all invalidate the title. On the contrary, as we shall see, it fulfills its deepest sense. The completed poem would then include the bird's proem, the narrative, Mars' complaint, Venus' complaint, and "Lenvoy."

It is not essential to my argument to insist that the poem was known to all of its earliest readers as *The Broche of Thebes;* but we are at least entitled to ask why, from a literary point of view, that title should ever have been given it. A superficial examination of the poem shows why scribes may well have been so puzzled by the title that they either dropped it or in effect explained it away; for the Broche of Thebes itself is the subject only of a few stanzas, used in rhetorical illustration of a point Mars is making in his complaint. But we would be equally puzzled if Lydgate, who must have known Chaucer's work as well as any man of his age, should have chosen that aspect of the poem to indicate the whole, if Chaucer himself had not pointed to its central significance by assigning that title. Indeed, *The Broche of Thebes* could appropriately be called a *difficilior lectio.* Its very "darkness" justifies it against the easier headings assigned by the men of small literary acumen who copied the poem, and who needed a title which would point out to potential readers or buyers what the poem was "about."[19]

In his complaint, Mars uses the Broche of Thebes as a historical *exemp-*

lum to clarify and support his argument that love, pleasant as it seems, is responsible for much suffering, in desiring, possessing, regretting the loss of the beloved. The Broche is well suited to fulfill such a function, as its description in the *Thebaid* of Statius makes clear.[20] But Neil C. Hultin has written persuasively of the importance of the Broche in a much more intimate connection: it came into being because of Vulcan's desire to revenge himself on Mars and Venus; it was given to Harmonia, the daughter of the lovers, and caused her destruction and, subsequently, a chain of baleful events throughout the history of Thebes.[21] By speaking about the Broche, Mars inadvertently directs our attention to the offended husband and to the illegitimate offspring of the affair, and above all to the calamitous consequences for Harmonia and others of Mars' adulterous love for Venus. Thus, says Hultin, Mars' reference to the Broche "points back to his responsibility in engendering Hermione [Harmonia] and thus precipitating the vengeance of Vulcan, and it points forward to the effect of courtly behavior upon others" (p. 66).

Mars is not really "in medias res," and in mentioning the Broche, he creates what might be called the literary equivalent of an optical illusion, a configuration of references which changes its very being according to the way one chooses to see it. If we see Mars as a contemporary, addressing the "hardy knyghtes of renoun" and the "ladyes" (ll. 272, 281) of the court of Richard II, we see that in his reference to the Broche as a historical object he has suppressed many important details: who its "worcher" was, why he made it, what the large consequences of possessing it were. But if we consider Mars as he appears in the narrative, we must conclude that the Broche does not yet exist. For the narrative leads us to believe that we are hearing about the very inception of the celebrated affair, that Phoebus is even now discovering them, and that Vulcan is yet to be informed, let alone to make the trap for the two lovers; while Harmonia is unborn, and the Broche is years in the future. Mars is drawing on his own future history for an object to illuminate his present sorrow.

The Broche thus points immediately to the stubborn self-deception of Mars, the foolish lover, in spite of his failure to mention that aspect of the matter. Statius makes it clear that the Broche is Vulcan's last resort, so to speak:

The Lemnian [Vulcan], so they of old believed, long time distressed at Mars' deceit and seeing that no punishment gave hindrance to the disclosed amour, and the avenging chains removed not the offence, wrought this for Harmonia on her bridal day to be the glory of her dower.

(Thebaid, II.269-273)

Now this has the highest relevance to Mars as we see him in both narrative and complaint. The narrative turns around the discovery of Mars and Venus by the Sun, and the comic distress of their separation, while in the complaint Mars himself discourses on the pains which result from love. And yet he gives not the slightest sign that he has "learned his lesson," that he will relinquish his pursuit of his lady. Indeed, he points to the very thing, the Broche, which will revenge his mad persistence.

Moreover, Mars is either ignorant of these implications, or else he conceals them for the sake of his argument. The definition of *exemplum* as it appears in the handbook of rhetoric formerly attributed to Cicero, *Ad Herennium,* points to his omissions: "Exemplum est alicuius facti aut dicti praeteriti cum certi auctoris nomine propositio," "the citing of something done or said in the past, along with the definite naming of the doer or author."[22] For Mars is here concerned (ll. 259-261) with "the worcher" as the ultimate author of his woes; but he neglects to mention that "the worcher" is Vulcan himself. To do so would undoubtedly "spoil his case." But not to do so spoils it for us, his understanders, beyond any possible recovery. His self-deception and obstinacy in the wrong appear strongest at the very moment when he is trying hardest to seem plausible and humble, to prove that he does not complain "folily / And causeles." Thus we see yet another apparent paradox. The attempt to assert and defend reasonableness, when exercised in the wrong cause, brings to light the deepest irrationalities.

The symbolism of the Broche will become richer as we increase our understanding of the whole poem, including "The Complaint of Venus"; but its importance should be clear enough for a beginning. Some readers might nevertheless question the power of such an allusion, and a short discussion may be helpful. In the first place, the poem obviously makes great demands on the literary sophistication and learning of its readers: the astrological intricacies, the complexities of form, the use of mythological contexts, the "personal allegory" and its implication in the literary "game" with Grandson, all presuppose literary responses of a high order. In the second place, while the allusion is primarily to Statius' *Thebaid,* one of the favorite books of the Middle Ages, Hultin points out that the Broche is mentioned elsewhere in the books Chaucer and his audience would have known—Virgil, his commentator Servius, Ovid, Dante, and the mythographers, including Boccaccio and Pierre Bersuire (the medieval references are based on Statius). Third, I agree with Hultin that the prominence of the Broche in Lydgate and in Harley 7333 (he mentions neither Pepys 2006 nor Notary's edition) shows that "more than ordinary importance was attributed to it in reading the poem" (p. 64); I differ from him mainly in believing that the poet himself pointed to this importance by using the Broche as his title, raising what might otherwise be a casual allusion to the central place in the reader's attention. The effect would be remarkably like the modern novelist's use of a title, *The Scarlet Letter*, *The Golden Bowl*, to underline a controlling symbolism. Finally, we have concrete evidence of one reader's response in Lydgate's reference to the poem, which points almost as a matter of course to its "worcher," Vulcan, thus connecting it with the subsequent history of the affair whose beginning we witness in the narrative.[*] Though this connection is all that is really *essential* for understanding the comic paradox of Mars' rhetorical use of the Broche, our pleasure grows as we know more of the specific context of the allusion (for example, the magic of the Broche, the disasters it caused, the fact that it was Vulcan's "last resort"). This entirely legitimate pleasure is simply taken for granted with respect to later poems of an allusive nature: nobody would reproach a reader of Pope or Eliot with "oversubtlety" for bringing his full literary consciousness to bear on an allusion.

The use of *The Broche of Thebes* as the title is justified, then, on sketchy but significant external grounds, the rubrics and Lydgate's reference, and even more by the intrinsic importance of the Broche to the mythological setting, to the portrayal of Mars' folly, and to the elucidation of the central theme, the dynamics of desire. One final consideration relates again to the problem of unity. The Broche of Thebes, "so ful of rubies and of stones of Ynde," is a complicated jewel, and so is the poem it names. Though the various "gems" of which the latter is composed do not all refract the "light" of the reader's understanding in the same way, their existence side by side enhances the significance of each part while it constitutes a rich and varied whole: rather as the juxtaposition of "rubies and . . . stones of Ynde" sharpens the sensuous apprehension of each separate stone as it makes the whole jewel more splendid than the sum of the splendors of its isolated parts. We shall see that the central meaning of the poem depends on our willingness to look for another sort of unity than that found, for example, in the perfectly rounded finish of *Pearl*, the better-known jewel of fourteenth-century English literature. If we con-

---

[*] Lydgate shows that, as Hultin suggests (p. 64), ". . . if it is known at all to the contemporary reader it is known as an instrument of retribution for adultery."

ceive the entire poem as a "broche," a jewel which gains its effect by the juxtaposition of brilliants, we shall be prepared to savor the peculiarly Gothic pleasure of unity achieved through contrast and congruence, and to accept the absence of explicit transitions and other conventional devices for structuring our response to the poem.

III. THE POEM AS A JEWEL

Perhaps a good way into the poem itself is to consider how complicated a jewel it is simply in terms of artifice. I have already discussed the social situation, the "chain of events," to which the *Broche* might almost be said to be a pendant (ME *broche*, L *monile*), and which it transforms and illustrates. Another aspect of its intricacy, the astrological references, has been elucidated by earlier scholars, notably Manly and Skeat; the notes in the latter's Oxford edition are extremely detailed. Robinson's notes provide summaries of their discussions. The meeting between Mars and Venus is the witty transcription of a planetary conjunction, and Chaucer exploits a technical vocabulary to considerable effect in the narrative portion of the poem. Manly asserts that "the poem is so packed with astrological allusions and conforms so closely to astronomical relations and movements that it can hardly be regarded as anything else than a mere exercise of ingenuity in describing a supposed astronomical event in terms of human action and emotion."[23] This "supposed astronomical event," says J. D. North, really did occur in 1385, and he shows in detail that Chaucer's transposition of it in the "Mars" is more accurate than the surviving almanacs he might have used.[24]

Gardiner Stillwell has ably argued that this astronomical framework provides an ironical comment on love's mischances and on the illusion of free choice. Love, Chaucer seems to say, has more to do with destiny than choice.[25] In an interesting article arguing for the derivation of the medieval love complaint—especially the "Mars"—from Ovid's *Heroides*, Nancy Dean carries this point even further: "What better example could there be of the ultimate destiny of love to change than the projection of Mars and Venus as planets, turning by necessity in destined paths at destined rates? ... The blame is not on Mars and Venus. The planets must follow certain courses...."[26] The problem of moral responsibility under conditions of emotional determination is finally resolved, as we shall see, only in "The Complaint of Venus." Hultin maintains against Stillwell (his argument bears even more against Dean, whom he did not know) the freedom and thus the responsibility of Mars and Venus insofar as they are portrayed as human: their sin, he says (pp. 66–67), lies in their will, in that they assent to "set a stevene" in order to further their own pleasure. Though he is undoubtedly right in seeing culpability in their wilful succumbing to concupiscence, his insistence on an Augustinian dualism tends to empty the situation of its problematic interest in something of the way that Dean's wholehearted determinism would do, though from the opposite direction. Dean ignores the probable resonance of the story in the "real world" of John Holande and Isabel of Spain and maintains that Mars and Venus are only Chaucer's example which he uses to discuss the nature of love; if such were the case, the psychological subtlety which is manifest in both complaints would seem to be superfluous. Hultin's heavily moralistic view of the poem almost as a tractate against *fol amour* would also militate against the positive interest in the working of a lover's mind as he seeks to come to terms with his love and his suffering. We shall see that Chaucer wants not merely to condemn foolish love but to show how it drives the lover himself—even the pagan Mars or Venus—to discover the central problems of worldly existence.

The astronomical conjunction, we may conclude from these discussions, is an economical and vivid way of representing the irresistible force of sexual feeling which is a central theme of medieval love poetry; against it may be seen the complexity of psychological response and moral evaluation. But the question of determination is also present in another way. Hultin has shown that the fact that the conjunction happens in Venus' house, Taurus (cf. "Mars," ll. 85–86), predisposes those who are born under it to lechery and fornication, and brings about epidemics, diseases, evil winds, injuries to plants and animals. It is not necessary to take a stand on Chaucer's serious belief in astrological influences to agree with Hultin that this circumstance, like the Broche itself, points to "the consequences of the love upon others only tangentially involved" (p. 67). If the "originals" of the lovers are indeed Isabel, daughter of a foreign king and wife of a powerful duke, and John Holande, the son and brother of kings and son-in-law of another powerful duke, such "tangential" consequences might be extremely serious, worthy of both the astrological predictions and the Theban parallel.

Even if we do not follow every detail of the celestial revolutions, we can sense in them the overriding order and natural harmony which produce the "music of the spheres"—though the music comprehends such discords as the suffering of Mars and Venus. This music provides the metaphysical justification, so to speak, for the comedy of Chaucer's treatment, and it corresponds on the cosmic scale to the bird's song, whose cheerfulness takes into itself such melancholy events. The "optical illusion" of Mars' reference to the Broche of Thebes is resolved by the cyclic universality implicit in the astrological machinery. As the amorous affair of Mars and Venus is repeated indefinitely, in 1385 as in mythical antiquity, so the Broche pertains at once to the future and to the past. But this resolution functions also on the level of significance. The meeting, love, and anguish of Mars and Venus are not merely representative of such affairs; they are part of the fabric of the universe, of an overriding structure of action and reaction, sin and retribution, which encompasses all particular times. In *The Broche of Thebes* Chaucer has created an image of Boethian Fate. We shall see later how the reader rises from this image to perceive in it the operations of Providence.

Another immediately apparent feature of the poem's technical achievement is the intricacy and variety of the narrative stances to be found in it. If we are not careful, we shall feel this variety merely as confusion; but here, as elsewhere, much enjoyment is to be gained from looking at the matter in a more positive way. The poem opens with an exclamation directed first to "foules" and then to human lovers; and we learn that this speaker is himself a bird only in the brief narrative interjection, presumably by a human speaker, in ll. 13–15:

> Seynt Valentyne, a foul thus herde I synge
> Upon thy day, er sonne gan up-sprynge.
>
> Yet sang this foul . . .

The "I" of l. 13 will reappear at the end of the "Venus" as an ironically self-deprecating poet, grown old and dull; for the moment we need to know only that we are hearing not exactly a bird's song but the report of one, addressed to Saint Valentine. This intervention of a "reporter" between "song" and "listener" is important: for the bird-narrator shows a consciousness which is paradoxically both birdlike and human. As a bird, he partakes in the purely natural and uncomplicated joys of love, so that he can say, "Gladeth, ye foules, of the morowe gray!" and urge his fellow fowls to "cheseth yow your make" (ll. 1, 17). Yet his song also constitutes a warning to those human lovers "that lye in any drede" to flee, "lest wikked tonges yow espye" (ll. 5–6). The same unresolved attitude appears in the fact that he intends to sing a song about love's woes "for the worship of this highe feste," St. Valentine's Day, which is presumably dedicated to exalting the joys of love.[27] Moreover, despite the self-deprecation of "in my briddes wise" (l. 23), he clearly wants his song to have an epic elevation which we hardly expect of a love celebration, or listen for from one of nature's innocents. The "firy torches rede" of Phebus (l. 27), the *periphrasis* of "the thridde hevenes lord" and "hevenysh revolucioun" (ll. 29, 30), the *interrogatio* of ll. 43–46, the apostrophe of ll. 106–112, are all clear examples of the high style. The narrator of this mock epic believes in himself and his task; yet by his attempt to raise and dignify the episode, he unwittingly points out to us its essential comedy. After Mars is awakened, for example,

> He throweth on his helm of huge wyghte,
> And girt him with his swerd, and in his hond
> His myghty spere, as he was wont to fyghte,
> He shaketh so that almost hit towond.
> Ful hevy was he to walken over lond;
> He may not holde with Venus companye,
> But bad her fleen, lest Phebus her espye.
>
> (ll. 99–105)

The "arming of the hero" is not only fruitless, it is an actual hindrance in these circumstances; and in the context of medieval romance (one thinks of episodes from the story of Lancelot and Guinevere) Mars' humiliation appears even more abject. Such bathos, of which the bird-narrator seems unconscious, occurs also after the bird's heartfelt apostrophe in l. 141:

> Now God helpe sely Venus allone!
> But, as God wolde, hyt happed for to be,
> That, while that Venus weping made her mone,
> Cilenius, rydinge in his chevache,
> Fro Venus valaunse myghte his paleys se,
> And Venus he salueth and doth chere,
> And her receyveth as his frend ful dere.
>
> (ll. 141–147)

We are not allowed to mourn "sely Venus" very long. Even if Stillwell goes too far in suggesting that Venus has found a new lover, he is right in noticing how drastically these lines affect our response to Mars' complaint.[28] We are prepared for that response here, where we see how the bird's excessive ambitions as a narrator highlight the absurdity of the events he would glorify.

If the whole "Mars" consists of the report of a bird's song, Mars' complaint is in turn reported by the bird. Moreover, Mars' stance toward his audience is at least as complicated as the bird's. As the latter sought to glorify love by inflating the adventures of two prominent lovers, so Mars seeks to prove the reasonableness of his own complaint by "rehearsing" "the ground and cause of al my peyne" (l. 160). I have already remarked on Mars' pseudorationality; but it is important to notice that here he connects it with "The ordre of compleynt" (l. 155) itself. His ultimate motive will be to win the sympathy of a specific audience: in the last three stanzas he appeals to "hardy knyghtes of renoun" and to ladies "that ben true and stable" to mourn for him and his mistress, thus pointing out how far from "hardy" he is at the moment, and how far from "true and stable" his mistress is in relation to her own husband. This ironic appeal reaches its climax when, after probing deeply into the pains caused by love, he attributes nothing but generosity, humility, graciousness, honor, and gentleness to his lady, the Goddess of Love. Such contradictions are the fruit not only of his confusing emotions, his "troubled wit" (l. 161), but also of his immediate persuasive aims with regard to his audience; we shall look more closely at these matters later on.

As has been noted, the lack of transition to "The Complaint of Venus" gives us the impression of being confronted directly with the lady's own words; and it is not until afterwards that the poet appears (in "Lenvoy") as intermediary, so to speak—and there his concentration on the technical side of his performance undercuts the verisimilitude in a way rather different from the narrative intermediaries of the "Mars." Moreover, at the beginning of the "Venus" no attitude to an audience is stated; Venus' consciousness is of "creatures" at large, of "every wight" (l. 8). It is as if she were attempting to judge, or rather to justify, herself according to the standard she imputes to the world at large, as she meditates in private on her conduct and desires. If we see her utterance in this way, we can surely not blame the poet for showing this other dimension of the love condition, however we may wish for a more conventional transition.

I have suggested that "Lenvoy" modifies our reception of Venus' complaint *post factum*, so to speak; but the poet has a very characteristic stance of his own:

> Princesse, receyveth this compleynt in gre,
> Unto your excelent benignite
> Direct after my litel suffisaunce.
> For elde, that in my spirit dulleth me,
> Hath of endyting al the subtilte
> Wel nygh bereft out of my remembraunce;
> And eke to me it ys a gret penaunce,
> Syth rym in Englissh hath such skarsete,
> To folowe word by word the curiosite
> Of Grauson, flour of hem that make in Fraunce.
>
> (ll. 73–82)

Earlier I pointed to the sustained irony of these lines, part of which may have to do with the very particular audience, the "princesse," to whose "benignite" it appeals—and Isabel's "benignite" may well have been put under some strain by such a joke. More important is the way the outward humility of "Lenvoy" points to the best qualities of the poem. I have only begun to explore the enormous "subtilte" with which the whole poem is written, and the irony of the claim implicit in "word by word"; in Chaucer's departures from his model appears some of the greatest "subtilte" of all. Since in fact the poem is not what he says, it cannot have been a "gret penaunce"—but rather its reverse, showing in every line a superabundant joy in literary creation. The age of its maker, whether youth or "elde," could not have dulled his spirit. As for the "skarsete" of "rym in Englissh," we should notice that Chaucer uses only two rhymes in these ten lines, and that one of them, in -aunce, appears also in two of the three balades and in "Lenvoy" (a total of 16 out of 82 lines). This is "skarsete" of a different sort, perhaps, than a naïve reader would expect; for we usually connect this cliché about English (as compared with French or Italian) with the difficulty of finding enough words of the *same* rhyme to carry through the scheme of a whole balade, for example. Chaucer is clearly having a little joke at the expense of this standard complaint.

Such extreme self-consciousness on the part of the "poet" should not surprise us after what we have seen of the bird, of Mars, and of Venus. It reminds us, moreover, of another aspect of the poem's artifice: it is dazzling in its structure, or rather in its structures. Each of the three main parts of the poem—narrative, Mars' complaint, Venus' complaint—uses a different stanza form, and this differentiation of parts points out the three main stages of the poetic experience, from fast-moving action through persuasive discourse to private meditation. The Troilus stanza was never better utilized to shape our response to a narrative. We may consider its use in the stanzas quoted earlier as examples. In the first of these (ll. 99–105) the bravado of the arming gives way, in the fifth line, to a notation of Mars' helplessness; the rhyme scheme defines the pivot (which occurs on the second *b* rhyme, "Ful hevy was he to walken over lond"). In the second (ll. 141–147) we see "sely Venus allone" at first, and finally as the "frend ful dere" of Cilenius. Here also the rhyme scheme defines the modulation between the two sets of circumstances: "allone" rhymes with "mone," the other aspect of Venus' woe, while the interweaving *b* rhymes, "be," "chevache," "se," are all connected with her potential rescue, and the *c* rhymes, "chere" and "dere," sum up her situation after she is rescued. In general, the story flows smoothly enough to throw bathetic effects strongly into relief (for example, l. 73, "There is no more, but unto bed thei go"), yet each of the stanzas has its own subject matter and shape, like a miniature chapter of a novel.

Chaucer's formal control becomes yet more resplendent in Mars' complaint, where the nine-line stanza (*a a b a a b b c c*) is a coherent and flexible expansion of the Troilus stanza (with doubled *a*-rhymes) and shares with the latter a movement toward a summary or concluding couplet on a new rhyme. In this respect it differs markedly from Chaucer's other extended stanzas, which show a greater concern for integrating the last lines.° Yet the continuity in form between narrative and complaint does not prevent this nine-line stanza from conveying quite a different overall feeling, one fully suited to an argument which proceeds by expository stages and is shaped by emotional and apologetic ends. For Mars is delivering a miniature oration according to the Ciceronian model of a judicial speech, with exordium, narration, confirmation, or "fides," and peroration, in order to defend himself against possible accusations of folly ("Mars," ll. 155–163).[29] We shall see below how complex this task becomes: Mars' "troubled wit" (l. 161) appears as much in the lapses and inconsistencies in his rhetorical strategies as in his own direct remarks.

The form of the oration not only helps us to find our way through Mars' often contradictory intentions, it also throws into relief the ternary structural principle, which was not made entirely clear by the nineteenth-century division into a proem and five terns. The exordium (the Proem) consists of nine lines divided into three parts of four, one, and four lines: the middle line, "And causeles, alas! that am not I" (l. 159), makes the major personal statement of the stanza even as it effects the transition from the general characterization of "The ordre of compleynt" (l. 155), to Mars' own intention "to declare my ground of hevynesse" (l. 163).† The narration (Tern I) has three stanzas, each tripartite in varying ways (see below). The confirmation (Terns III–V) contains three terns, and again the three stanzas of each tern are usually divisible into three parts, even if not always in symmetrical fashion. The peroration (Tern V), like the narration, has three stanzas, effecting an overall tripartite symmetry for the main

---

° In *Womanly Noblesse* Chaucer uses a nine-line stanza *a a b a a b b a b* and an envoy *a b a b a a*. The Complaint in the *Anelida* uses two stanza forms, a nine-line one *a a b a a b b a b* and a sixteen-line one *a a a b a a a b b b b a b b b a* (the latter with varied line-lengths); the most important stanza form in *A Complaint to his Lady* is a ten-line one *a a b a a b c d d c*. See Robinson ed., pp. 533, 306–308, 528–529. The same point applies to the balade stanza (*a b a b b c b c*) used in the *ABC*, the *Monk's Tale*, and of course various balades, including the *Fortune*; the stanza in the "Venus" is *a b a b b c c b*.

†Robinson's punctuation unnecessarily obscures both thought and structure; if we must punctuate, a stop after "folily" would rescue "causeles" from its redundant (cf. l. 157) and grammatically doubtful adverbial usage and make it a proper and necessary adjectival modifier (through "that") of "I." We should remember that the original state of the MSS. would have left it to the reader to decide such questions.

body of the speech (*narratio, confirmatio, peroratio*). All the while Chaucer maintains the forward movement mentioned above, exploiting all the resources of syntax and thought-rhythms to paint a convincing picture of a mind in motion.

A closer look at the *narratio* (Tern I) should suffice to indicate Chaucer's art in using the nine-line stanza. The first stanza (ll. 164–172) consists of a single sentence, whose articulations as defined by the rhyme scheme fall into three main parts, a temporal clause, a main clause, and a result clause which is itself dependent from a relative clause modifying "her":

> The firste tyme, alas! that I was wroght,
> And for certeyn effectes hider broght
> Be him that lordeth ech intelligence,
> I yaf my trewe servise and my thoght
> For evermore—how dere I have hit boght!—
> To her that is of so gret excellence
> That what wight that first sheweth his presence,
> When she is wroth and taketh of hym no cure,
> He may not longe in joye of love endure.

Each of the parts includes subordinate clauses which help define the symmetry of the stanza: to "him that lordeth ech intelligence," l. 3, corresponds "her that is of so gret excellence" in the rhyming l. 6, while another relative clause in l. 7, which has the same rhyme, dominates the last tercet and introduces a hypothetical person whom Mars seems thankful not to be. Thus the three clauses succinctly define Mars' sense of his situation; while an exclamatory interjection—"how dere I have hit boght"—divides the stanza into two equal sections and begins the movement toward the rather negative conclusion. These final lines show how the rhyme scheme can be used to maintain forward movement, as the "excellence-presence" rhyme in ll. 6-7 links the final tercet firmly with the preceding line. By such smooth management we are almost beguiled into passing over the strange fact that Mars sees arbitrary suffering as the consequence, and thus the proof, of his lady's excellence. On one level this is an ironic glance at astrological determinations, of course; but it adumbrates a major tension in Mars' psychology.

Having noted Venus' potential cruelty, Mars passes to a celebration of her bounteous nature in stanza two. Here the anaphoras on "Of . . ." in the middle five lines point out another kind of tripartite symmetry, 2(*a a*)-5(*b a a b b*)-2(*c c*); in terms of meaning, the first and last parts signal Mars' overall assertiveness about his lady, though they flow into and from the specific gifts named in the middle:

> This is no feyned mater that I telle;
> My lady is the verrey sours and welle
> Of beaute, lust, fredom, and gentilnesse,
> Of riche aray—how dere men hit selle!—
> Of al disport in which men frendly duelle,
> Of love and pley, and of benigne humblesse
> Of soun of instrumentes of al swetnesse;
> And therto so wel fortuned and thewed
> That thorogh the world her goodnesse is yshewed.
>
> (ll. 173–181)

The anaphoras are far from monotonous: they include a series, an inter-jected exclamation, a relative clause, an internal anaphora, and a triple use of "of" in three different senses.

The third stanza returns to the divisions of the first, though with greater syntactical definiteness, giving the whole tern a tripartite symmetry:

> What wonder ys it then, thogh I besette
> My servise on such on that may me knette
> To wele or wo, sith hit lyth in her myght?
> Therefore my herte forever I to her hette;
> Ne truly, for me deth, I shal not lette
> To ben her truest servaunt and her knyght.
> I flater noght, that may wete every wyght;
> For this day in her servise shal I dye.
> But grace be, I se her never with ye.
>
> (ll. 182–190)

The definiteness of the division corresponds to the strength of Mars' affirmation of service. The rhetorical question of ll. 1–3 takes in the suffering of stanza one and the pleasures of stanza two—"wele or wo"—but Mars seems hardly conscious of the capriciousness he has ascribed to Venus in stanza one as he goes on to make a ringing affirmation, in the middle three lines, concerning first the past and then the future. Though the humor of these lines depends partly on our knowing that astrological "deth" will come to Mars when he is in conjunction with the sun, we are even more impressed by the "wo" of such a conclusion to his "servise," undertaken in the hope of "wele."* Mars can hardly avoid a glimmering of

---

* Technically speaking Mars will be "combust," but I think the mention of death here and elsewhere—cf. "Mars," ll. 90 (where Venus exclaims, "Alas, I dye!"), 108, 126, 270—is a rhetorically heightened reference to the temporary "destruccioun" of the planet's influence, accurate but ironical: Mars deserves neither praise nor blame for this "death," and our sympathy is much qualified by the certainty of his "resuscitation."

this stiuation in the last three lines, repudiating the notion of flattery, characterizing himself as one who has not long endured "in joye of love."

Clearly any valid attempt to deal with form in detail must illuminate the entire poetic achievement. But these remarks should give some idea of the closely worked artistry of Chaucer's jewel. It is most important that we realize how much of the aesthetic effect depends on precise details; such exquisitely wrought miniatures as those in the nearly contemporary *Très Riches Heures* of Jean Duc de Berry are quite comparable. The media differ, but the attitudes which produced them are similar. We do not expect an illuminated manuscript to make its appeal in the same manner as a wall-sized tapestry; and as we seek the pleasures proper to the miniature, so must we be sensitive to the concentrated effects of the short poem as against expansive narratives like the *Troilus*.

This little homily applies with even greater force to "The Complaint of Venus," for here Chaucer has undertaken that apex of medieval lyric form, the balade; moreover, while making each balade distinct in form and thought, he interrelates the whole series of three in most beautiful ways. But the love balade is altogether a difficult form for us: it renounces almost every obvious and "colorful" poetic effect in the service of a consummate orchestration of the emotions as these appear in apologetic discourse. Indeed, a rigorous French practitioner of the form might conceivably chide Chaucer for the broad effect in Venus' l. 33, "Jelosie be hanged be a cable!"—an unladylike exclamation at best. Chaucer's mastery of the form is nevertheless beyond doubt; even if his achievement here presupposes the *Cinq balades ensuivans* of Oton de Grandson, it is so creative as to be an original poem.

The form of a balade cannot be properly understood apart from the meaning, and the frequent mistake of critics has been to eliminate the latter by simplifying or overschematizing the former. The basic rhyme scheme, *a b a b b c c b* (longer stanzas are quite common in French), is capable of infinite variations in syntactical and rhetorical development, while the crucial feature of the balade, the changing relationship between the refrain and the various stanzas, exploits every sort of grammatical, logical and emotional configuration. Beyond these general remarks, I should point out that the "Venus," comprised of three balades of three stanzas each, allows the inner formal principle its fullest expression— appropriately, since the movement into private (though still apologetic) discourse takes us closer to the roots of psychological experience. Thus the external differences in the two complaints are offset by the importance of the number 3 as a structural determinant: "triune triplicity" governs each of Mars' terns and the whole of Venus' complaint. The numerical relationship appears also in the number of lines; Mars speaks 144, Venus 72. It can hardly be a mere accident that the number of the Zodiac should enter by way of such significant multiples into both complaints, along with the number of the Trinity. The internal continuity between the complaints, as we shall see, extends to the meaning: Venus does not echo Mars, but her complaint is profoundly relevant to his; it extends and completes it.

Thus the whole poem is a jewel which expresses unity in diversity, the division of celestial music (Mars and Venus are planets moving through the skies) resolved into the three-in-one of the God who is beyond the comprehension of the participants. A full understanding of the *sentence* must wait: here we can conclude that Chaucer was never truer to his complicated vision of the world than when he invented the varied formal riches of *The Broche of Thebes*.

IV. THE SENTENCE: "THE COMPLAINT OF MARS"

Our reward is not merely the pleasure of artifice: it includes psychological insight and religious exaltation. But it should be clear by now that we shall never attain these deeper meanings if we are not prepared to grasp and follow up the hints which are provided. In saying this I appeal not merely to the medieval love of hidden meanings, though this is relevant in the most immediate way to such sophisticated poems, but also to the perennial right of a great poet to direct his poems toward those who have ears to hear and eyes to see, not toward readers who are suspicious of all but the most obvious meanings. We may of course argue about these inner significances; nobody is a god in his perceptions. But the critic must proceed on the assumption that they exist.

The first of these hints comes in the bird's proem, where the bird is warning "lovers, that lye in any drede" to flee. In consoling them he says,

> Taketh your leve; and with seint John to borowe,
> Apeseth sumwhat of your sorowes smerte.
> Tyme cometh eft that cese shal your sorowe:
> The glade nyght ys worth an hevy morowe!
>
> (ll. 9–12)

Hultin compares the last line with Psalm 29:6, "Ad vesperum demorabitur fletus: et ad matutinum laetitia," and points out that Augustine and Rabanus Maurus interpreted the morning as the day of judgment which will be received with joy by the faithful. By reversing the notion, Hultin suggests, "the bird's consolation establishes the aube lovers [that is, those who "lye in any drede"] as part of those who cannot endure the light of truth" (p. 61). Up to a point, this is probably accurate; but the moralism which was noted in connection with the astrological references also appears here, for this psalm is a song of thanksgiving to God for his mercy, and it tends much more to the consolation than the condemnation of sinners who have provoked God's anger:

> Exaltabo te, Domine, quoniam suscepisti me, nec delectasti inimicos meos super me.
> Domine Deus meus, clamavi ad te et sanasti me.
> Domine, eduxisti ab inferno animam meam, salvasti me a descendentibus in lacum.
> Psallite Domino sancti eius, et confitemini memoriae sanctitatis eius.
> Quoniam ira in indignatione eius, et vita in voluntate eius. Ad vesperum demorabitur fletus, et ad matutinum laetitia.°

We may indeed not be able to accept the bird's kind of consolation; but scriptural reminiscence points beyond his own ignorance to another kind which is supremely acceptable.

I think we can be even more definite in establishing a religious context for the opening of the poem. Though the use of "seint John" as a pledge is colloquial,[30] it is especially appropriate here, since the writings of the Apostle John are preeminently those which are devoted to the "tyme" that "cometh eft." As Evangelist, he records Christ's great discourse to the apostles gathered at the Last Supper, consoling them for His imminent departure, evoking not only His own Second Coming but also the sending of the Holy Spirit as Comforter. Ultimately His words look toward the great final day: "Amen, amen dico vobis, quia plorabitis et flebitis vos; mundus autem gaudebit. Vos autem contristabimini, sed tristitia vestra vertetur in gaudium" (John 16:20). As the visionary of Patmos, John tells of a "morowe" which is much heavier than any "glade nyght" could justify: and yet this is also the time when sorrows will cease for those who have believed and repented of their sins. As Evangelist and letter-writer, John is the major authority on quite another kind of love than that known to the bird, a merely natural creature. Saint John as a pledge may not work in mundane terms, but he is most infallible as a guide to the God who is love, forgiving and comforting. Only this high love can resolve the anguish which results from seeking the innocent satisfaction of birds in their natural mating, and yet finding the guilt, frustration, and deprivation

---

° *Biblia Sacra Vulgatae Editionis,* ed. cura et studio Monachorum Abbatiae Pontificiae Sancti Hieronymi in Urbe Ordinis Sancti Benedicti (Marietti, 1965), Psalm 29:2-6. Subsequent biblical quotations are drawn from this edition.

which men must suffer in their love. This distinction between nature and man becomes even more poignant when the bird commands his fellow "foules" either to choose a "make" or to renew their "servyse." We are reminded of the impossibility of obeying his injunction, "Confermeth hyt perpetuely to dure" (l. 20), with respect to human loves, even as we recognize it as an ideal to which nature unmediated by man (the listener of ll. 13–15) would never think of aspiring.

It is just the anguish of this contradiction between the ideal wish and the mortal possibility which the narrative and Mars' complaint describe, and which Venus' complaint acts out, as it were, in a lover's mind. We shall see that the urgency of the problem is both intensified and illuminated by these lovers' total ignorance of the one kind of "servyse" which may perpetually endure, the one consolation which could reach beyond their "hevy morowe." This context of Christian ideas will operate along with the other frames of reference which help us understand the lovers' situation. As pagan god and goddess, Mars and Venus are defined by a mythological background, especially operative, as we have seen, with reference to the Broche. As planets, they are located according to astrological lore, which operates especially in the narrative but is important throughout. As representative human lovers, they gain resonance and particularity from the worldly scandal which their love affair "allegorizes"; of course this last context cannot have the force for us that it had for the original readers.

In the light of the Christian doctrine evoked in the Proem, then, our laughter at the predicament of Mars and Venus is qualified by an awareness of the deeper issues at stake: we see that their sorrow is justified by a pagan ignorance of what "seint John" says. Chaucer's bird-narrator also makes us able to sympathize with the lovers in a more positive way. Venus' influence makes Mars gentler and more capable of feeling the pains of others, less inclined to "cruelte, and bost, and tyrannye." The God of War himself is well aware of the ridiculous figure he cuts in his "tamed" state. Yet the undeniable universality of his condition ("The proudest of yow may be made ful tame," l. 278) wins our sympathy, as does his concern for his beloved's sorrow, even if the one seems to violate his warlike nature and the other is rendered superfluous by the "rescue" of Venus.

In the complaint, moreover, we see how Mars' sorrow, together with his attempt to defend its reasonableness, drives him to explore the problem of enduring love at ever-deepening levels. We should keep both sides of the fictional motive in mind. On the one hand, we must try to see how the emotion itself applies pressure to the utterance, causing Mars to follow

certain lines of thought in his attempt to gain solace. For in spite of the
disclaimer in his Proem (1. 162, "not for to have redresse"), Mars like all
distressed lovers seeks relief from his pain. The questions at the beginning
of the *confirmatio*, the second tern, thus indicate a need which is inherent
in the very act of complaining:

> To whom shal I than pleyne of my distresse?
> Who may me helpe? Who may my harm redresse?
> Shal I compleyne unto my lady fre?
> Nay, certes, for she hath such hevynesse . . .
>   (ll. 191–194)

On the other hand, we must be aware of his persuasive purpose, his desire
to defend himself from charges of irrationality and folly. Perhaps we
cannot always distinguish the calculations required for the second end
from the spontaneous outcry of the first. Certainly the "troubled wit" of
Mars himself could not. But our sense of psychological verisimilitude
depends on keeping both aspects of the utterance in mind. For example,
the four lines quoted above seem quite consciously rhetorical, amplified
interrogatio incorporating *repetitio* (or *anaphora*), "shal I . . . pleyne,"
"Shall I compleyne," "Who may . . . ," "Who may," with elaborate alliter-
ation especially in the second line, ending with *ratiocinatio* (argument by
question and answer).[31] Since these lines show, in effect, that he can hope
for "redresse" from nobody, the questions serve a rhetorical purpose both
in justifying his complaint and in winning sympathy; and they are well
suited to begin the *confirmatio*. But to see them only as artifice is to
deprive them of their very reason for being. In Mars' utterance the poet
makes us see how private emotion enters the public realm of persuasive
discourse.

The Proem, as the exordium, is intended to win the attention of the
audience, and this it does in two steps, as we saw above. First, Mars
recognizes an "ordre of compleynt" and the need of having a cause to
support it. Thus, he acknowledges the community's right to judge. Second,
he places himself with regard to that "ordre," demands pity on grounds
which he will seek to demonstrate.

We have already looked at the first tern, the narration of the circumstances, and seen how it suggests the tensions in Mars' self-justifying
effort. Our knowledge of the myth enables us to supply some important
aspects of the situation, such as the fact that Venus has a husband, which
Mars omits to mention. And even as we are impressed by the psychological ambivalence in Mars' praise of his lady's excellence, we are compelled

to humorous assent by our recognition that her qualities are indeed those of the astrological Venus. The two exclamations noticed earlier draw attention to his doubts:

> I yaf my trewe servise and my thoght
> For evermore—how dere I have hit boght!—
> (ll. 167-168)
> My lady is the verrey sours and welle
> Of beaute, lust, fredom, and gentilnesse,
> Of riche aray—how dere men hit selle!—
> (ll. 174-176)

The interruptions are accounted for by rhetorical theory as *admirationes,* exclamations of astonishment concerning the facts being narrated.[32] But there is a further effect of which Mars must not be aware: they seem to belong together, so that the dear purchase apparently consists of "riche aray." This is Chaucer's joke, of course; but it links Mars' distress with the more down-to-earth pecuniary woes which befall mortal lovers. If such rhetorical exclamations seem to go against his immediate purpose, to demonstrate and justify his love for Venus, they are more successful, in a comic way, in winning our sympathy for his woes.

The tension between the two sides of his effort continues in the next tern, where the *Confirmatio* begins. Almost at once Mars passes from a consideration of his and Venus' particular woes to a general commentary on the sorrow of love. Psychologically, this movement results from the impasse described above. Mars can obtain no relief from his lady, and even to think of doing so reminds him that she is in an equally bad situation. Our knowledge that she is not underlines the subjectivity of Mars' notion about his plight, but it does not invalidate his response to that notion. Rhetorically, generalizing his case will justify his sorrow on broader grounds: all true lovers suffer, why should not Mars be entitled to? He also "proves" obliquely that he *is* a true lover, since if he were "fals," he would have "his ese" (l. 208). When he returns from his "long sermoun / Of aventures of love" (ll. 209-210), the movement is once more twofold. He has gotten outside his own sorrow enough to say he feels greater woe for his lady than for himself:

> The poynt is this of my distruccioun:
> My righte lady, my savacyoun,
> Is in affray, and not to whom to pleyne.
> O herte swete, O lady sovereyne!
> For your disese wel oughte I swowne and swelte,
> Thogh I non other harm ne drede felte.
> (ll. 212-217)

This represents a genuine advance away from the narrow self-concern of the opening, and as such it is not invalidated by Mars' false estimation of his lady's "disese." But it is mediated in the most important way by the persuasive purpose. Auditors will be more impressed by a show of unselfishness than by the loudest lamentations for his own sorrow.

For his rhetorical purposes, Mars had in effect labeled as a digression his excursion into general truths about love. The third tern, nevertheless, takes him much further along the same path. Again we perceive the emotional pressure behind his movement: to recognize his lady's plight "availeth" as little in bringing relief to her (or to her lover) as did the "long sermoun" itself. But the basic emotions are becoming yet more entangled with rhetorical exigencies. Mars has just reminded us that he could do nothing at all for his lady, and a glance at the narrative will suggest what sorts of guilt and frustration he must feel over his helplessness:

> And yet therto ys double thy penaunce,
> For she that hath thyn herte in governaunce
> Is passed half the stremes of thin yen;
> That thou nere swift, wel maist thou wepe and crien.
>
> (ll. 109–112)

And in the complaint itself he says, as if with some hint of Venus' real situation, "But were she sauf, hit were no fors of me" (l. 197). Thus another aspect of Mars' psychological situation makes itself felt in his rhetoric. He needs to divert from himself the shame and even guilt he feels (or should feel) over the supposed distress of his mistress. What better way of relieving himself of his obligatory discomfort ("*oughte* I swowne and swelte") than by directing attention away from the particular circumstances to the general conditions of his love? The consequence may be to cast strong doubts on the wisdom of his determination to "die" in the service of love. But Mars will also suggest a resolution for this conflict which he himself cannot attain.

In effect, his rhetorical gambit consists in blaming God for his love and his pain. But the blame comes in the form of questions, and these will raise other echoes in our minds than the ones he looks for.

> To what fyn made the God that sit so hye,
> Benethen him, love other companye,
> And streyneth folk to love, malgre her hed?
> And then her joy, for oght I can espye,

> Ne lasteth not the twynkelyng of an ye,
> And somme han never joy til they be ded.
> What meneth this? What is this mystihed?
> Whereto constreyneth he his folk so faste
> Thing to desyre, but hit shulde laste?
> (ll. 218–226)

If Mars has shifted grounds—he had previously made his own lady "the verrey sours and welle ... of love"—he has recognized, as even mortal lovers must, that the lady who rouses his love is not the ultimate cause of it. But he has also recognized, as a pagan god, that there is a God above the gods; and as planet he has pointed out that there is a First Mover beyond all the motions of the spheres. For Mars this deity is a supreme Necessity which acts on "his folk" whether they will or not. He had already suggested something of the sort in the opening lines of his complaint, where he spoke of "him that lordeth ech intelligence." But then he had gone on to talk as if he himself had been acting from completely free will, and as if he were still so acting:

> Therfore my herte forever I to her hette;
> Ne truly, for my deth, I shall not lette
> To ben her truest servaunt and her knyght.
> (ll. 185–187)

These lines have ironic implications: Mars as planet will "die" when he is in conjunction with the sun, and so his statement here simply gives the facts—this astronomical "deth" will not prevent him from continuing his celestial motions. But he wishes to attribute free and noble will to himself, in deciding to continue as "her truest servaunt and her knyght." When, later on, he disclaims this will ("streyeneth folk to love, malgre her hed"), we recognize in his rhetorical confusions another stage of that question which occupied the Christian Middle Ages, and which has already been raised in the astronomical references of the narrative: how far, and in what respect, can men be said to be endowed with free will, if God is omnipotent and omniscient?

Thus, if Mars' questions arise from a combination of psychological and rhetorical exigencies, they embody genuinely philosophical probings. He represents for us the manner in which men rise from their preoccupations with immediate pleasures and pains to a large-scale questioning of universal conditions; and if this process is comic in part, it is also deeply moving. As he goes on in the next stanza, we begin to catch a hint of the answer:

> And thogh he made a lover love a thing,
> And maketh hit seme stedfast and during,
> Yet putteth he in hyt such mysaventure
> That reste nys ther non in his yeving.
>   (ll. 227-230)

Though Mars the pagan god cannot know it, rest is just what Christ promises in the great sermon which has already been evoked:

> Pacem relinquo vobis, pacem meam do vobis; non quomodo mundus dat ego do vobis. Non turbetur cor vestrum, neque formidet.
>   (John 14:27)

> Haec locutus sum vobis, ut in me pacem habeatis. In mundo pressuram habebitis; sed confidite, ego vici mundum.
>   (John 16:33)°

The sort of "reste" which is in the "yeving" of this God is the fruit of His love, a love which Mars cannot understand:

> And that is wonder, that so juste a kyng
> Dothe such hardnesse to his creature.
>   (ll. 231-232)

The God who is God of intelligence and justice cannot meet the demands which human desire makes on him: indeed he seems to be hostile:

> Hit semeth he hath to lovers enmyte,
> And lyk a fissher, as men alday may se,
> Baiteth hys angle-hok with som pleasaunce,
> Til many a fissh ys wod til tgat he be
> Sesed therwith; and then at erst hath he
> Al his desir, and therwith al myschaunce;
> And thogh the lyne breke, he hath penaunce;
> For with the hok he wounded is so sore
> That he his wages hath for evermore.
>   (ll. 236-244)

In this figure, which includes characteristics assigned by *Ad Herennium* to the *similitudo* and the *imago*, Mars is seeking not to explain himself but to

---

° See also Paul's discussion of entering into God's rest in Hebrews 3:18-4:11, especially 4:3, where he says, "Ingrediemur enim in requiem qui credidimus."

persuade others; technically he is engaging in *expolitio,* refining, "dwelling on the same topic and yet seeming to say something ever new" (*Ad Her.,*IV.xlii.54). Thus the picture of the fish tempted by the bait and "sesed" by the hook is to rouse his listeners' pity by putting the lovers' plight vividly before their eyes (*Ad Her., similitudo per conlationem,* IV.xlv.59–xlvii.60). And the comparison of God to a fisherman is to make listeners censure him for his cruelty (*Ad Her., imago,*IV.xlix.62). But Mars has chosen an image about which his audience of fourteenth-century Christians knows more than he, and their reaction will be correspondingly larger and more complex than the simple agreement he looks for. Hultin (pp. 70–73) has described the double tradition of fishhook images which would qualify this reaction. Some writers, including Ovid, Cicero, Isidore, and Andreas Capellanus, use the fishhook to signify the lure of "pleasaunce" and especially sexual pleasure by which men are caught. Hultin quotes a moralizing poem from the Vernon Manuscript which develops the image and says "Wommon is worm, þer heo is wikke," and men had better let her alone.[33] On the other side is Christ's saying to Simon Peter and Andrew, "Venite post me, et faciam vos fieri piscatores hominum" (Matthew 4:19) and the medieval commentaries which, says Hultin, generally interpret this "as referring to the clergy who lure men to their salvation" (p. 72). Augustine distinguishes the two kinds of hook, and Andreas Capellanus agrees with him that the hook of God is recognizable by the fact that nothing God gives rise to can harm men.[34] Hultin concludes from his reference that Mars is quite simply wrong in accusing God of dangling the baited hook: ". . . he has been lured, not by God as he insists, but by a force which seeks his 'distruccioun' " (p. 72).

But Mars is not wrong according to his lights, which are those of a pagan; and insofar as philosophy informs them, his Christian readers must agree with him. For no Christian would dare to deny that God is responsible either for the beauty of the world, including its lovely women, or for the desire in us which responds to that beauty: we have already seen how the problem of emotional determination is present throughout the poem, especially in the implications of the astrological background. The danger of Manichaean dualism, implicit in Hultin's "force which seeks his 'distruccioun,' " is psychological as well as doctrinal: a man's desires are not bad in themselves; his freedom lies not in choosing whether to love, but in deciding what to do, how to respond to his desires with his will. Vergil sums it up in the *Purgatorio:*

Onde pognam che di necessitate
Surga ogni amor che dentro a voi s'accende,
Di ritenerlo è in voi la potestate.°

Chaucer's humanism and his Christianity alike transcend the moralistic
reduction of the human situation to the bleak choice between asceticism
and damnation. The possibility of rising to a higher understanding of the
emotional predicament is present in the very pain Mars feels, even in his
attempt to alleviate that pain rhetorically by raising the question of God's
responsibility. Gerard Manley Hopkins, as profoundly Catholic and hu-
manistic a poet as Chaucer, could still ask the question five centuries later,
and his answer would be very similar:

To what serves mortal beauty—dangerous; does set danc-
ing blood. . .
What do then? how meet beauty? Merely meet it; own,
Home at heart, heaven's sweet gift; then leave, let that alone.
Yea, wish that though, wish all, God's better beauty, grace.[35]

The perception of "God's better beauty, grace" is not to be confined to
philosophers or monks, nor is it to be attained simply by refusing "heav-
en's sweet gift" which causes such pain, but by owning it and passing
beyond it.

The question of emotional determination and free choice will come up
again and be finally resolved only when we consider "The Complaint of
Venus": for the unity of the poem appears most urgently in the solution to
its central problem. Here we must consider how a Christian perspective
transforms Mars' image. In it we have the perfect paradigm for the
transformation of the world by the Light which shone in our darkness: for
the Ovidian hook of sexual pleasure *becomes* Christ's hook to draw us to
salvation. We certainly think of the pain and frustration caused by the
"angle-hok," but we also see that Mars' opening question, "To what fyn
. . .?" is answered. God the fisherman wants to stir men up by acting upon
their desire, to rouse them out of their satisfaction with their single
existences. Yet He wants also to show them that merely earthly objects of

---

° Dante Alighieri, *Opere,* ed. E. Moore and Paget Toynbee (Oxford, 1963), *Purgatorio,*
canto XVIII, ll. 70-72; all citations of Dante refer to this edition. Vergil goes on to say that
Beatrice means this noble power, "nobile virtù," by free will, "lo libero arbitrio," and to
warn Dante to keep it in mind when she speaks of the subject. See also, on this point, canto
XVI, ll. 67-105; canto XVII, ll. 91-139; the lines in canto XVIII (16-69) leading up to those
quoted in the text; and the discussion of "The Complaint of Venus," below.

"pleasaunce" cannot fulfill the desires so roused. This unfulfilled desire, this aching thirst for "reste," is the "line" of love by which God may "catch" his fish. Man's desire for the fleeting things of the world leads to suffering; but this "myschaunce" may be the very best fortune possible, if it causes him to seek more lasting goods. This is a Christian commonplace: in Mars' complaint we are made to see the psychological realities upon which it is based.

Yet we must not simplify: the danger remains, the hook may indeed result in damnation. The situation is exactly characterized by the double inscription over the gateway to the garden in *The Parliament of Fowls:* the dreamer is puzzled to find that it leads both to "the welle of grace" and to "the sorweful were / There as the fish in prysoun is al drye" (Robinson ed., p. 312, ll. 129, 138-139). Even Mars can take limited account of the real danger in his final lines, which Hultin (p. 71) rightly considers as recalling Romans 6:23, "Stipendia enim peccati mors, gratia autem Dei vita aeterna, in Christo Iesu Domino nostro." Characteristically, Hultin, like Doctor Faustus in the first scene of Marlowe's play, quotes only the first part of this sentence, and thus turns what is intended as consolation into a sentence of condemnation. Mars does not know of the grace of God, and in speaking of what happens "thogh the lyne breke," he cannot see that the "lyne" represents God's loving grace as it operates through the mortal emotions. But the Christian can easily see how the "breaking" of that line would cause complete loss. The "wound" of the hook, love for the things of the world, remains unto eternal death, "forevermore," unless the "fish," the suffering mortal, submits to being "drawn in" by the "fissher." For the Christian, then, Mars' figure will clarify God's purposes (as *similitudo*) and rouse praise of his wisdom (as *imago*). Mars' rhetoric at once defeats his immediate purposes and satisfies the deeper thrust of his probings. His quest is so urgent that it comes very near sucess, despite his folly and his ignorance. Seeing him, the Christian will learn gratitude for the Light which shows him the Way.

I have already commented on the fourth tern as a rhetorical *exemplum;* but not we can see how it comes as the climax of an effort which began in emotions of distress and was elevated by a rhetorical purpose to a philosophical disquisition, which, for the Christian reader, has crucial religious implications. It still retains the urgency of the woe and the apologetic nature of the oration: we have seen how much Mars leaves out of his description of the Broche. But the other side of the question is even more interesting. The Broche is the bait on the "angle-hok" considered in relation to the more complex perception and response of intelligent beings:

> The broche of Thebes was of such a kynde,
> So ful of rubies and of stones of Ynde,
> That every wight, that sette on hit an ye,
> He wende anon to worthe out of him mynde;
> So sore the beaute wolde his herte bynde,
> Til he hit had, him thoghte he moste dye;
> And when that hit was his, then shulde he drye
> Such woo for drede, ay while that he hit hadde,
> That well nygh for the fere he shulde madde.
>
> And whan hit was fro his possessioun,
> Then had he double wo and passioun
> For he so feir a tresor had forgo;
> But yet this broche, as in conslusioun,
> Was not the cause of his confusioun;
> But he that wroghte hit enfortuned hit so
> That every wight that had hit shulde have wo;
> And therefore in the worcher was the vice,
> And in the covetour that was so nyce.
>
> (ll. 245-262)

Simply as an epitome of the human predicament in time, these stanzas could hardly be excelled. For the Broche stands for any object of human desire; its magically disastrous properties point to that apocalyptic "hevy morowe" mentioned earlier. Thus, it symbolizes the world itself as it is present to man's cupidity. When we consider the power it possesses, we cannot wonder that Mars looks beyond it to its "worcher." Moreover, the problem of free will is given a new setting. No longer is a blind response to the "pleasaunce" on a fishing hook in question. The "covetour" shares the "vice" with the "worcher."

In the last stanza of the tern Mars returns once again "to speken of my peyne":

> So fareth hyt by lovers and by me;
> For thogh my lady have so gret beaute
> That I was mad til I had gete her grace,
> She was not cause of myn adversite,
> But he that wroghte her, also mot I the,
> That putte such a beaute in her face,
> That made me coveyten and purchace
> Myn oune deth; him wite I that I dye,
> And myn unwit, that ever I clamb so hye.
>
> (ll. 263-271)

Mars' attempt to exonerate his lady is equivocal, to say the least; for it implies that it would be better for Mars if she had not been created—or at least not created so beautiful. But his "unwit" appears, for a Christian, as the necessary prelude to conversion: for only by climbing so high, and discovering that to desire such an object brings "adversite," can most men be persuaded of the need to climb yet higher, to the Worker himself. Mars cannot know this; but the Christian lords and ladies, to whom he appeals for justification of his "unwit," have been taught by "seint John." They know that the alternative to coveting one's own death is to desire eternal life. Warned by the destructive future which is latent in the Broche of Thebes, they can choose a future in which their sorrows will cease.

If Mars began by trying to persuade us that his love was not foolish, he has now given up the attempt. His love is "unwit," instead of reasonable devotion; and he goes on to admit by implication that the complaint itself must seem ridiculous, as in his peroration (the fifth tern) he beseeches "hardy knyghtes of renoun" to "take hit [my disese] not a-game." He has nevertheless proved far better than he can know how much "ground and cause" he has for his "peyne." Ignorant of the redeeming Christ, Mars can only look forward to an eternity of desire and frustration. In one respect this is merely the comic transformation of the astronomical cycle which governs him. But human lovers who are not bound to an endless repetition of their allotted spans may take from him a serious warning with regard to the limits of the lower passion which he laments. When he asks them to complain for him and his beloved, they will respond with a lament for all earthly love, for all "beaute, fredom, and manere" (l. 294) beneath the changeful moon (l. 235).

Above all, they will be reminded by Mars' final stanza of another Lady who reaches and exceeds his praise in ways which Venus never could:

> Compleyneth eke, ye lovers, al in-fere,
> For her that with unfeyned humble chere
> Was evere redy to do yow socour;
> Compleyneth her that evere hath had yow dere;
> Compleyneth beaute, fredom, and manere;
> Compleyneth her that endeth your labour;
> Compleyneth thilke ensample of al honour,
> That never dide but al gentilesse;
> Kytheth therfore on her sum kyndenesse.
>
> (ll. 290–298)

Anybody with a sense of the mythic context must see in this stanza sheer infatuation, when the qualities it lists are attributed to Venus "þe double goddesse of loue," especially since Mars himself has called attention to her potential cruelty as a proof of her "excellence." Vulcan and Dido are just two of the unfortunates who would contradict one aspect or another of Mars' effusions, and Chaucer's own *Legend of Good Women* narrates many "Veneris monumenta nefandae." But everything Mars says here is a notable attribute of the Virgin: the "humble chere," the "socour," the love for mortals, the "beaute, fredom, and manere," the honor, the "gentilesse." Once again it is important to see how Mars' own ignorance of this high application is functional. His emotional need, combined with his rhetorical appeal for justification (sympathy for Venus, as we have seen, will carry with it sympathy for Mars himself), has caused him to project a lady whose perfections are contradicted even by his own deepest sense of her, to say nothing of the "objective" truths of her mythical capriciousness and cruelty. We see arising from within the depths of a foolish lover's ignorance those very needs which can only be satisfied by the recognition, based on faith, that there is indeed a Lady who is so gentle, so humble, so honorable, and at the same time so powerful in doing "socour" to the distressed mortals. Chaucer's "ABC" reads almost like a commentary on this stanza when its description is referred to the Virgin. If the Christians in Chaucer's audience complain for Mary, it will be for reasons suggested in ll. 81–86 of this poem of devotion (Robinson ed., p. 525);

> Ladi, thi sorwe kan I not portreye
> Under the cros, ne his greevous penaunce.
> But for youre bothes peynes I yow preye,
> Lat not oure alder foo make his bobaunce
> That he hath in his lystes of mischaunce
> Convict that ye bothe have bought so deere.

Such a complaint would redound to the good of the complainer's soul, establishing his worship on a conviction as to the personal interest of Mary and her Son, the very sort of emotional conviction sought in innumerable devotional poems of the late Middle Ages. Thus as we laugh at Mars' flattering words about his lady, we are prepared to perceive how completely they fit that other Lady who is the "verrey lust of labour and distresse," the "Queen of comfort" ("ABC," ll. 106, 121).

Our reading of Mars' complaint must clearly draw on a continuing alertness to its various contexts, if we are to taste its pleasures and grasp its meanings to the full. The narrative setting helps us to perceive the subjectivity of Mars' sympathetic suffering for his lady. The full myth of the love of Mars and Venus, evoked especially in the reference to the Broche of Thebes and its "worcher," reminds us of the long-range consequences of this love, and qualifies our response to Mars' extravagant praise of his lady. The astrological machinery gives depth to some central aspects of the poem, expecially the theme of free choice. The Christian ideas about love, about the ultimate solace which Christ may bring, about the Virgin, help us to see all the questions in their brightest light, to resolve Mars' perplexities. The "personal allegory" probably furnished the original initiated readers with yet another dimension to the imaginative experience; the lovers in the poem "represent" persons of flesh and blood, whose experiences provide the "real-life" parallel and confirmation to the sorrows of Mars and Venus.

V. "THE COMPLAINT OF VENUS"

I have suggested above that in the very act of continuing *The Broche of Thebes* with an adaptation from another of "Venus' " admirers, Oton de Grandson, Chaucer may have established another sort of context, one which underlines the jealousies and cross-purposes of worldly love on the level of a literary game. This must remain a guess; but the really important issues do not depend on its accuracy at all. It is more certain that Grandson's *Cinq balades ensuivans* can be useful in helping us understand what Chaucer has done in the "Venus."[36] What is left out of the latter, or changed, may be as significant as what is retained or added, especially since we are as much as invited to make the comparison when Chaucer lays ironic claim to a "word by word" rendering of Grandson's "curiosite." To read the *Cinq balades ensuivans* with care is to be impressed with a psychological subtlety and an aesthetic rigor which utterly belie the poet's lamentable reputation. Chaucer could have found no better model for his own poem, and the reader should not assume that he has "improved" on his original. In the discussion which follows, I shall not be able to do justice to Grandson, but I can begin with a brief outline of his poem; and in the discussion of the "Venus" I shall attempt to give some suggestions about the import of Chaucer's changes.

The very title of *Les cinq balades ensuivans* exemplifies that medieval attitude toward serial unity which I have discussed above with respect to *The Broche of Thebes* and "The Complaint of Venus." The poem does indeed constitute a developing and essentially linked series whose overall meaning emerges only after a reading of the whole. Yet the full series is found in its proper order, and with this title, in only one manuscript, Bibliotheque Nationale f.fr. 2201. Other MSS betray that scribal freedom from notions of fixed texts which are apparent also (on a less destructive scale) in the late excerpting of Chaucer's poem in Ashmole 59 and Longleat 258. Chaucer almost certainly knew Grandson's poem in the

Paris version, which is the oldest and most authoritative of those listed by
the editor, Piaget. Thus we can assume that his major change, the omission
of the second and third balades, was quite deliberate, as was the change in
the speaker's sex. Grandson apparently presents himself as speaking in the
poem, but in reading it we must adopt as critical an attitude toward the
lover's complacencies and self-deceptions as we did with respect to Mars'
complaint. And as with both complaints in *The Broche of Thebes,* the life
of Grandson's poem resides in the details of the evolution of the lover's
self-presentation. Readers should therefore not take the following summary as an adequate indication of Grandson's "curiosite."

In the first balade the lover in effect declares his intention to think
about his beloved in order to gain comfort, and defends himself for doing
so. He then describes her with reference to her reputation, and this
attempt allows us to see the ambiguity of his attitude toward her—praise
gives rise to unspoken suspicions as well as to overt endorsement. In the
second balade, he continues to praise her beauty in yet more hyperbolical
terms, pointing out that this is his own opinion, with the one reservation
that her heart is too full of refusal. So good is she, he says, that the God of
Love himself could not find a better mistress; but his pleas also would fail
on account of her reluctance. This rather pale comfort felt by a rejected
lover does not suffice; in the third balade he sets out from the idea of her
refusal to talk about his own suffering, and this leads to appeals to all loyal
lovers to pray for him and to pray to his mistress for mercy. The final
stanza points in no uncertain terms to the heroism of his loyalty—a
considerable change from the uncomplicated "comfort" which, he had
declared, thinking of her afforded him. Thus the fourth balade can speak
of love almost exclusively in terms of suffering, and in fact it presents
unmistakable gestures of rebelliousness against the frustrations caused by
Jealousy and even by Love itself. Courtship is reduced to "le gieu," the
game. But in the last balade the lover reasserts his loyalty, again adopting
a heroic pose to do so. Here the various emotional complications are
orchestrated with great skill, especially in terms of syntax and grammar, as
the lover moves between his restlessness in the "amoureux las" and his
heroic loyalty: he is clearly doing all he can to convince his "Cuer" that it
ought to remain in submission, and he asserts that he will never be tired of
serving her—against the clear evidence of exhaustion in the last two
balades. The total effect is one of increasing spiritual discomfort, resulting
from the effort to hold many contradictory attitudes together in the mind,
and a movement from the seeming objectivity of thinking of his lady (to
obtain comfort) to an overriding concentration on his own emotions.

Chaucer's adaptation begins in the same way, with Venus stating that

she thinks of Mars in order to gain comfort. Succeeding changes have to
do partly with the speaker's sex and more generally with the context as a
whole. For we must be aware from the beginning of the "Venus" that it
shares in the contexts which inform and illuminate the "Mars." Christian
doctrine provides one of these; and the reader will catch some hints of a
"higher" interpretation of the complaint as we advance through it, noting
how Venus' praise of Mars resembles Mars' concluding extravagance
concerning Venus. But it seems best for our purposes to save this aspect of
the poem for the end, so that we may see how the complaint functions as
such, using the other contexts as a guide.

Whereas Grandson must demonstrate by the internal logic, or rather
illogic, of the first balade how hazardous and equivocal it is for a lover to
rely on the reputation of his beloved to justify his love, in the "Venus" we
are made to understand this by the contextual references:

> Ther nys so high comfort to my pleasaunce
> When that I am in any hevynesse,
> As for to have leyser of remembraunce
> Upon the manhod and the worthynesse,
> Upon the trouthe and on the stidfastnesse
> Of him whos I am al, while I may dure.
> Ther oghte blame me no creature,
> For every wight preiseth his gentilesse.

> (ll. 1-8)

The tameness and self-pity Mars has shown in his complaint do not
corroborate "manhod," while the refrain-line appears sheer self-deception
in view of ll. 66-67 of the narrative, "For hyt stod so that thilke tyme no
wight / Counseyled hym ther, ne seyde to hym welcome." Brusendorff
points out that these two lines are also apposite, in all likelihood, to the
situation of John Holande after he stabbed the Earl of Stafford's son; thus
the "real-life" context would sharpen the initiated reader's awareness of
Venus' infatuation. The mythic setting, moreover, suggests that "every
wight" would know Mars better for "cruelte, and bost, and tyrannye"
than for "gentilesse," and opinions might differ as to the "worthynesse"
and the "trouthe" of the cuckolder of Vulcan. Venus can hardly be very
secure in basing her claim to blamelessness on such doubtful praise. We
might recall that Mars' sense of Venus' excellence is "proved" by her
cruelty to the "wight" who shows his face at the wrong time.

By thinking about Mars, Venus gains "comfort to my pleasaunce,"
whereas Grandson's lover says, "Il n'est confort qui tant de biens me face
. . ." as to think about my lady. The nuance will prove significant: Venus

initially connects comfort with pleasure, not abstract "goods" (a shift
which is also characteristic of Chaucer's practical view of the love emotion). To justify her thoughts Venus invokes Mars' highly questionable
reputation for "gentilesse." As I have suggested, she seems to have no
well-defined audience in mind, but she wants to satisfy herself as to her
blamelessness by projecting standards which "every wight" accepts. In
other words, her private meditation is conditioned by an uneasy awareness
of a general code according to which she might be "blamed." The syntax
of this first stanza points out to us that there are two sides to her preoccu-
pation, just as there were with Mars. There is the love for Mars, and there
are the thoughts about that love and about Mars; and the possible
"blame" of l. 7 refers not only to l. 6, where Venus says that she is her
lover's "al, while I may dure," but also to the "remembraunce" of l. 3 and
to the general process of obtaining comfort. Thus the causal clause of the
refrain has complex reference to a state of mind. Her lover's reputation
justifies both her "remembraunce" and the very fact that she is his "al."

If we have smiled over Mars' putative "gentilesse," our smile becomes
broader as we read on:

> In him is bounte, wysdom, governaunce,
> Wel more then any mannes wit can gesse;
> For grace hath wold so ferforth hym avaunce
> That of knyghthod he is parfit richesse.
> Honour honoureth him for his noblesse;
> Therto so wel hath formed him Nature
> That I am his for ever, I him assure;
> For every wight preyseth his gentilesse.
>
> (ll. 9–16)

The opening lines are superbly ironic, in relation to Mars: If there is
"bounte, wysdom, governaunce" in him, it must indeed be inaccessible to
"mannes wit," since his obvious claims (as set forth, say, in *The Knight's
Tale*) are to destructiveness, madness, and ungovernable rage. Even in his
"tamed" state, his "wysdom" is less than exemplary. But this ironic
extravagance is of less value for itself than for what it shows about the
speaker's complex state of mind: Venus almost admits that she alone has
the key to such excellence—she who possesses a woman's wit, the sort
which is induced by sexual devotion. The fourth line carries Mars' self-
characterization as "patroun" of "hardy knyghtes of renoun" ("Mars," ll.
275, 272) yet further; but we have been compelled to agree instead with·
his self-deprecating "Al be I not worthy to so gret a name" (l. 274). In the
last three lines Venus gives two alternate reasons for being "his for ever,"

one in the protasis of a result construction, the other in the causal refrain. But from what we know of his reputation for "gentilesse," we must conclude that his natural form has the more effective influence on Venus' passionate affirmation. The reputation seems more than ever a projection of the lover's mind, justifying the passion which is aroused by immediate sensual experience—the natural form.

The third stanza continues this comedy of subjectivity:

> And notwithstondyng al his suffisaunce,
> His gentil herte is of so gret humblesse
> To me in word, in werk, in contenaunce,
> And me to serve is al his besynesse,
> That I am set in verrey sikernesse.
> Thus oghte I blesse wel myn aventure.
> Sith that him list me serven and honoure;
> For every wight preiseth his gentilesse.
>
> (ll. 17-24)

Once more context gives the lie to "suffisaunce," and Venus' other justifications appear in a strange light also. That he is tamed we need not dispute; indeed, his "besynesse" to serve was indirectly the impulse behind his own complaint, since he could do nothing at all to help her. Venus does not consider this negative side to his "besyness" but simply invokes it to justify her "sikernesse." But this stanza also reminds us strongly of the "subjeccioun" of Mars by Venus, together with Mars' equivocal attitude toward being "constrained" to love ("Mars," l. 220). He has reduced his own love to "unwit" (l. 271) and compared his desire to that of the "covetour." We cannot be so sure as Venus is that he "list" to "serven and honoure," though of course he would say so if asked. In such a situation this reason for Venus' self-congratulation is just about as questionable as the other she again gives, Mars' reputation for gentleness. And now this "gentilesse" reminds us far more of his self-pitying impotence than of the more substantial virtue it originally evoked. His helplessness, connected as it is with his current astrological status of feebleness (as he "dies" in conjunction with the sun) has very little to do with his own good will.

Chaucer has not used Grandson's second and third balades, except perhaps for some suggestions incorporated in the other three. For example, the reference to Mars' natural beauty in the first balade is like a condensation of Grandson's second balade, which subtly portrays the process of the sublimation of physical passion. In Grandson's third balade we see how the lover's response to his lady's refusal comes to support a

melodramatic posture of noble suffering, thus preparing for the mingled
self-pity and irritation of Balade IV. Chaucer's lover, of course, can make
no claim to such self-renunciation: the omission of these two balades is a
succinct but forceful reminder that the lady of Oton de Grandon (if Venus
does indeed represent his Isabel) is not the chaste and severe ideal which
Grandson's composition makes her out to be. She has already shown,
though to another lover, the "mercy" for which Grandson's lover pleads,
and she could hardly be allowed to dwell on the pains of frustration.

In spite of the very different circumstances of the respective lovers,
Venus' second balade is closer to Grandson's fourth than the first was to
its model. The complacency of Granson's lover is based on a sense of
noble self-sacrifice, whereas that of Venus, based on self-flattery with
regard to her lover's merit, is far from unqualified. She has just said she
"oghte" to "blesse wel myn aventure," and though the second balade
begins on a positive note, it picks up and expands the doubt which is
latent in a statement about what *should* be her feelings.

> Now certis, Love, hit is right covenable
> That men ful dere abye thy nobil thing,
> As wake abedde, and fasten at the table,
> Wepinge to laughe, and singe in compleynyng,
> And doun to caste visage and lokyng,
> Often to chaunge hewe and contenaunce,
> Pleye[37] in slepyng, and dremen at the daunce,
> Al the revers of any glad felyng.
>
> (ll. 25–32)

The "right covenable" of l. 25 seems affirmative enough; but Venus dwells
on the drawbacks, the reasons for "dere abye," instead of explaining the
"covenable." Such inconveniences are the stock-in-trade of love poems
since at least Ovid, but they are summed up here (following Grandson)
with admirable economy. Like Mars, Venus ascends to the level of gener-
alization; and though she seems unlike Mars to approve of such "costs,"
we can sense her own woeful experience speaking through the general
descriptions. This is even truer with the outburst which begins the second
stanza:

> Jelosie be hanged be a cable!
> She wolde al knowe thurgh her espying.
> Ther doth no wyght nothing so resonable,
> That al nys harm in her ymagenyng.
> Thus dere abought is Love in yevyng,

> Which ofte he yiveth withouten ordynaunce,
> As sorwe ynogh, and litil of plesaunce,
> Al the revers of any glad felyng.
>
> (ll. 33–40)

Again context is crucial for grasping the comedy of these lines. For "the sunne, the candel of jelosye" ("Mars," l. 7) has illuminated the "resonable" actions of Mars and Venus for an injured husband, Vulcan; while Venus emulates Mars in turning resolutely away from the concrete circumstances, even to the extent of making "Jelosie" a woman.[38] To her she imputes wild "ymagenyng" of "harm," as if to deny the import of the brutally explicit line in the narrative which consummates the lover's "grete joye": "Ther is no more, but unto bed thei go" (ll. 71, 73). Venus, like Mars, has made the transition from celebrating Love to blaming it. But since Venus herself is Goddess of Love, the situation seems yet more contradictory. Grandson's lover can personify and address love in quite a traditional way; when Venus does it, she points to the paradox which is the soul of the poem: the love which we feel is ultimately to be credited to (or blamed on) the first Mover and, by the Christian reader, to the God who is Love. In the first stanza of this balade Venus' personification seems merely a rhetorical convenience, allowing an apostrophe to the force which moves her as it moves her subjects; but later on we see that her irritation makes her refer to love as male ("he"). It is important to see the exact process: in l. 37, "Love in yevynge" really signifies an *emotion* which is "abought"; only in the next line does it become a *he*, as Venus projects a personal agent whom she can blame. By making "Jelosye" a woman, Venus can regard "her" as if "she" were a meddling rival or duenna (the exact relationship thus projected is neither clear nor important); by making Love a man she emphasizes his masterfulness and distinctness from her subjective self, thus freeing herself from responsibility for the woe she describes.

By the end of the second stanza, the refrain, which originally summed up all the woes which are the price of love, has come to express by implication the standard according to which the worth of love should be judged. Once more we see how Chaucer's adaptation deliberately emphasizes the emotional side of Venus' utterance: Grandson has as refrain "Tout à rebours de ce qu'on vuelt trouver," while Chaucer picks up the "pleasaunce" of l. 1 not only in l. 39 (where it also occurs in Grandson), but also in the refrain's "glad felyng." If "glad felyng" is the measure of a happy life, love is ill qualified to make us happy. Venus expands this implication in the third stanza, still referring to Love as masculine:

> A lytel tyme his yift ys agreable,
> But full encomberous is the usyng;
> For subtil Jelosie, the deceyvable,
> Ful often tyme causeth desturbyng.
> Thus be we ever in drede and sufferyng;
> In nouncerteyn we languisshe in penaunce,
> And han ful often many an hard mischaunce,
> Al the revers of any glad felyng.
>
> (ll. 41-48)

The "price" of love has come to appear more than love is worth; Venus seems to agree with Mars that "he that hath with love to done / Hath ofter wo then changed ys the mone" ("Mars," ll. 234-235). It is as if she were describing the effects of possessing the Broche of Thebes. Love's "yift" could almost be the Broche as Mars describes it, enticing in apprehension and painful in possession. The comparison with Grandson continues to emphasize Venus' experience: the French lover speaks of frustrations and of long-deferred hopes, while Venus has already found "ce qu'on vuelt trouver." The former says that lovers must "Sans nul certain languir en esperance," while the latter speaks of the "penaunce" of languishing in an uncertain love. "The revers of any glad felyng" now characterizes life itself as it is lived in subjeçtion to love, a particularly striking admission when we consider that Venus, the goddess both of earthly love and of earthly pleasure (*plaisance mondaine*, "glad felyng") is forced to make it.

In her third balade, Venus, like Grandson's lover, reaffirms her devotion to Love in spite of all the pains she has described. For both lovers, the "remembraunce" has clearly brought more "hevynesse" than "comfort to my pleasaunce." Venus also resembles the French lover in seeing her reaffirmation as a gesture of self-denial, almost heroic in its pretensions:

> But certes, Love, I sey not in such wise
> That for t'escape out of youre las I mente;
> For I so longe have ben in your servise
> That for to lete of wil I never assente;
> No fors thogh Jelosye me turmente!
> Sufficeth me to sen hym when I may;
> And therfore certes, to myn endyng day,
> To love hym best ne shal I never repente.
>
> (ll. 49-56)

But where Grandson's lover speaks of having borne "mon martire," my suffering, for such a long time that he will not be cured while he is alive, Venus speaks of her long "servise" to Love which she will not "lete of." Once more the context sets up ironic reverberations around Venus' re-the tortures of love. "Hevynesse" is far more evident now than it was at the beginning of the poem, and we know its sources, in jealousy, doubt, and a promiscuous heart.

The comic power and the meaning of "The Complaint of Venus" clearly depend largely on seeing how it fits into *The Broche of Thebes* as a whole. But we have yet to take into account the context which is most crucial of all, for the Christian, in defining what Venus' complaint really is. The reason for postponing this part of the discussion is that this poem can be read quite exactly as a complaint over earthly love and as a poem of religious devotion; and while the greatest energy of the literary experience emerges from the intersection of the two ways of reading, they are nevertheless independent of one another. All those emotional problems and intellectual contradictions which we see coming to the surface in Venus' attempt to comfort herself can be resolved only by raising our sights to consider Him who really is "the best that ever on erthe wente," Him whom a fathomless love caused to *go onto* earth to save His people, and who *walked upon* earth as a man among men, who is of a far higher "estat" than any "that man may represente"—and yet that a Man did indeed represent. These remarks will point to a remarkable feature of this literary achievement: not by interpreting the poem "figuratively," but by taking every hyperbole with the utmost seriousness, will we arrive at the transcendent meaning.[41]

What happens here raises to a higher level what was happening at the end of the "Mars." The sorrowful god of war was compelled by his emotional and persuasive purpose to project a lady in such extravagant terms that only the Virgin could fulfill them. Venus, trying to defend her love, to assuage her sorrows, to control her restless heart, both attributes an image to her lover which only Christ can justify, and on the basis of that projection utters a complaint of such intensity that it provides a model for Christian worship. In reading the poem from the point of view which Christian faith affords, we must keep in mind the exactness with which Chaucer has shown the connection between an idealizing and apologetic, though uncomfortable, sexual emotion on one side, and Christian devotion on the other. Like Mars, Venus is ignorant of the "fyn" to which her restless desires urge her. But for us who know that "fyn," her ignorance is a validation and a proof, as it were, of its power. That high Love operates in the deepest parts of the mind even when the creature is ignorant of its operations.

As the interpretation proceeds, it may be well to remember that its form is partly a matter of convenience. The medieval Christian reader, alert to hidden meanings and prepared more immediately by Mars' final stanza, would probably grasp both readings at once. Yet there is another reason for traversing the same ground twice, one which is intrinsic to the aesthetic experience: the poem offers us a sense of the simultaneity of two distinct experiences, of two distinct consciousnesses, and to savor this sense to the full we must grasp each side in its integrity. Moreover, one of these experiences is of the natural, human sort which we can grasp by means of ordinary literary alertness; the other has to do with religious faith, and its comprehension depends on that same faith, or at least an imaginative reconstruction of it. This distinction is as relevant to the medieval reader as it is to us: one need only recall the insistence of such men as Bonaventure and Thomas Aquinas that faith and philosophical reason, though ultimately in agreement, are two distinct ways of grasping the truth. Finally, the critical laughter at Venus' extravagance and self-deception, stimulated by one reading, is an almost necessary preparation for us to be able to see and accept the higher love in the second reading as a fulfillment and replacement of the "fol amour" in the first.

From the beginning we see how the Christian reference illuminates the import of every statement, once we see that the complaint is also a lay of devotion. We can take "manhod"—the first item of "remembraunce"—in its literal signification: not merely a vague "manliness" but the very fact that God became Man makes the contemplation possible and opens the way to comfort when one is in "hevynesse" about earthly woes. And "worthynesse" succeeds logically: no man is of more worth than the Man who was God. Christ defines "trouthe and . . . stidfastnesse" for all of mortal time: of him alone can they be said without qualification. Again, l. 6 has a literal accuracy: a mortal is completely Christ's, and all ability to endure is entirely dependent on this fact. The question of blame is totally transformed: no creature can blame a mortal for loving Christ, his Creator, or for thinking of him—for the two sides of the reference operate here as when the utterance is considered that of Venus; while his "gentilesse," praised by "every wight," does indeed obviate any possibility of blame.

The second stanza continues this loving contemplation of the excellence of Christ; and nothing could be truer than that his "bounte, wysdom, governaunce" surpasses any that "mannes wit can gesse"—Venus' unspoken sense of the absurdity of her claim for Mars turns into a recognition of Christ's ineffable virtue. In l. 11, "grace" is a technical term, while any reader of medieval romance must be aware of the high sense of l. 12, "of knyghthod he is parfit richesse"—again, "knyghthod" in its most ideal acceptation, the championship of oppressed mortality against its adversar-

devote himself to Christ. "Glad felyng" is a most inadequate criterion of those high goods which Love has promised.

Our interpretation here may profit from a reminder of the "spiritual dryness" which was a central theme of medieval religious writing. Sister Maria Madeleva has expounded the matter at length with relation to *Pearl*, and her remarks apply to the emotional progress of our poem. Speaking of the "spiritual athlete," she says,

He had thought that the religious life was a state of security and rest; he finds that it is a series of exercises, conflicts amounting at times to a very violent internal warfare. He has constantly to deny himself, to exercise himself, to hold himself in readiness. . . . [At times] God is almost a sensible Reality to him, and he literally feels the keenest delight in serving Him. . . . This condition is known in religious parlance as spiritual joy, sweetness, or consolation. . . . It is not to be relied or depended on, however, any more than is the physical athlete's own natural exuberance. It is his endurance which will count in the long run.[42]

We can be quite sure of Chaucer's acquaintance with these insights into the conditions of religious love: Sister Madeleva's citations are drawn from a wide range of religious thinkers, including Saint Teresa, Cassian, the *Ancren Riwle*, Juliana of Norwich, Richard Rolle of Hampole, Saint Bonaventure, Thomas à Kempis. All of these writers caution against relying on the "spiritual sweetness," the "comfort to my pleasaunce," which comes at times to the lover of Christ. The second balade evokes the tribulations in which he lives more often, as Richard Rolle suggests:

Þerfore if persecucion, wrechydnes, & oþer dises þou suffyr, þou has þat acordys to þe place in þe whilk þou dwellis. Is not þis þe vayle of teris & tribulacion in whilk þou art? hou wald þou þerfore be glad in presone, & lyfe in prosperite in all þine exile, or with-outen dyses go þi long pilgrimage? Haue mynde þat criste & his apostillis has suffyrd turmentry, & þou be blys sekis to com to ioy! bot þou sall not. . . . With tribulacion, seknes & dises behouys vs to be clensed.[43]

Thus there is a positive value to the sorrows which the lover must inevitably feel: they put love to the proof, strengthen it and renew its grounds. The "sorwe ynogh, and litil of plesaunce" really are gifts, in this sense. Ramon Lull's *Book of the Lover and the Beloved* may serve as a key to this way of thinking, for Lull is engaged in a task similar to Chaucer's— to make the love of a mortal for Christ comprehensible and beautiful in human terms. Lull often connects these "gifts" of sorrow to the Lover's love; three examples must stand for many:

Many persons were with the Lover, who was complaining of his Beloved that He increased not his love, and of Love, that it gave him so many trials and sorrows.

The Beloved made reply that the trials and sorrows for which he reproached Love were that very increase of Love.

The Lover cried aloud to all men, and said: "Love bids you ever love: in walking and sitting, in sleeping and waking, in buying and selling, in weeping and laughing, in speech and in silence, in gain and in loss—in short, in whatsoever you do, for this is Love's commandment."

The Beloved gave to His Lover the gift of tears, sighs, thoughts, weariness, and grief, with which gift the Lover served his Beloved.[44]

The first quotation illuminates one motive behind the entire second balade as a complaint; the second helps us understand the manifold "costs" of Love mentioned in the first stanza; and the third pertains to the "gifts" mentioned in the second and third stanzas.

The third stanza, moreover, enlarges the perspective according to which we see these sufferings. The difficulty of "usyng" the "yift" of love in a world where "subtil Jelosie, the deceyvable" dominates, comes to typify all life as it is lived with an awareness of the high demands of Love:

> Thus be we ever in drede and sufferyng;
> In nouncerteyn we languisshe in penaunce,
> And han ful often many an hard mischaunce,
> Al the revers of any glad felyng.

The instability of Fortune and the sinfulness of men (the pronoun is now "we") make "glad felyng" impossible to sustain. But this general recognition is still heavy with the resentful tone toward Love which rose in the second stanza. The concentration on "glad felyng" which was implicit in the original desire for comfort has put the Lover in some danger of breaking the "line" of love.

Whereas only Mars' complicated figures could suggest for us the resolution of his "wonder, that so juste a kyng / Doth such hardnesse to his creature," here the speaker shows it taking place. In the last balade we hear him reasserting his loyalty to Love, and his reaffirmation is clearly a matter of faith. We see that as Lull suggests the sorrows of love have for their purpose the increase of love. The lover would not escape out of Love's "las," would not break the fishing line. He repudiates the torments of "jelosye," and we see the rejection not as self-deception but as a reaction of the will to pains of the world, mastering them and passing beyond them. We know what he looks toward when he says, "Sufficeth me to sen hym when I may," and we know how the sufficiency of the promised reward can support him to his "endyng day."

In the second stanza, the speaker turns again to contemplate Christ.

"Any estat that man may represente" has a subtly apt significance in relation to the God whose Love made him become Man and "represente" mortality in atoning for its sins. The lines which for Venus suggested a confusion about necessity and free choice,

> Thus have ye maked me, thurgh your fraunchise,
> Chese the best that ever on erthe wente.
>
> (ll. 59-60)

take on precise meaning when addressed to the high Love. For Love is unquestionably operating through and upon man's choices. In the central cantos of the *Commedia*, Dante makes Marco Lambardo and Vergil expound the scholastic doctrine of love.[45] From his discussion it is clear that Love is the source of every action and every desire, and yet that this particular choice of the Best is dependent on the "fraunchise," the liberty, with which that Love endows the person who feels it: for he can consent to it or turn his will to a lower good. Thus these lines constitute the central resolution of the problem which has been with us from the beginning of *The Broche of Thebes,* the question of free choice in a universe which is apparently determined by Fortune or Fate. Man attains his highest freedom, and his only genuine one, in following the inner inclination of his nature toward "the best that ever on erthe wente," toward God, whose Providence governs even the slightest motions of the heart.

Thus when the speaker turns toward his heart and exhorts it to "love wel," we see how he has resolved on the higher path against all the distractions and hindrances which the world may interpose. We see, moreover, that he is now declaring his love on a higher level than was the case at the opening of the complaint. There he was looking for "comfort to my pleasaunce"; here he is recalling and transcending the discomforts to which, he now realizes, his love must subject him. We see in operation one of man's highest faculties, the "virtù che consiglia, / E dell' assenso de' tener la soglia," of which Vergil says,

> Quest' è il principio, là onde si piglia
> Ragion di meritare in voi, secondo
> Che buoni e rei amori accoglie e viglia.
> (*Purgatorio*, xviii, 62-66)

The paradigm is all the more complete in that, according to one reading, we see a major example of guilty love, "rei amori," while according to the other we are shown the operation of the best love of which man is capable. Moreover, in the very pretense that her decision to love is a matter of free choice, Venus shows that profound desire for freedom which is only realized by the Christian's decision to love God. Thus the two ways of reading the poem are dynamically related, not mutually exclusive.

The last stanza shows the resolved will disciplining the heart by pointing out to it the high grace of Love in enabling it to "chese the worthieste in alle wise / And most agreable unto myn entente." This grace is nothing less than the Incarnation, which made God's person available to the earthly emotions signified in "Herte." These in turn refer back to that desire for "glad felyng" which was expressed in the second balade; once more we are reminded how the passage through sorrow may strengthen the deepest love of the lover, which is based on an informed exercise of the will. Since the "entente" of the speaker is an ultimate solace, fruition which transcends all earthly possibilities, the speaker is simply stating a fact about his situation. Christ is the "wey" beyond which none other should be sought; he is "suffisaunce unto my pay" as Mars could never be. The last two lines constitute a gravely formal reassertion of love, a pattern for the will to follow continually:

> Thus wol I ende this compleynt or this lay:
> To love hym best ne shal I never repente.

The "compleynt" of the middle stanzas has been absorbed into a "lay" of devotion, giving the speaker the strength which comes from a clear-sighted recognition of the difficulties and sorrows of the high path he has chosen. Yet this alternate characterization of the poem also points to the larger alternatives in reading it: a "compleynt" about the pains of earthly love is also a "lay" of devotion.

I have suggested above that Venus' insecurity in her love is like a demonstration of the operations of the Broche of Thebes, which raises expectations of comfort and happiness only to render them impossible by the very fact of being possessed. Now it should be easy to see how the title pertains to the complaint in a yet deeper sense. For the final function of the Broche is to raise our attention to its "worcher." And on the mystic level that "worcher," like the fisherman, is God himself through his Word, Christ. In "The Complaint of Venus" the "Worcher" is held up for the contemplation of the initiate: we see as if by revelation that process which begins in desire and passes through disappointment to come to rest in "the best that ever on erthe wente," the Christ whose sublime "ordynaunce" pertains to the emotions of "his folk" as it does to the movements of the celestial spheres. Both the overall unity of the entire poem and the title by which it was known point to the profound and paradoxical ascent from the pains of the work to the comfort of the Worker. *The Broche of*

Thebes, like the Broche of Thebes, compels us to investigate the source and the end, the "fyn," of our desires.

But the Broche of Thebes as a historical object had a literal "worcher," the misshapen husband so carefully and conveniently forgotten by his wife and her lover. *The Broche of Thebes* has a "worcher," too, and he suddenly appears at the end to make a presentation to a "princesse." Statius does not describe in precise terms the occasion on which Vulcan gave the Broche to the other princess, Harmonia; but we can well imagine that he, like Chaucer here, might have sought to belittle the significance and power of his present. Chaucer invites us to think of his poem as the laborious and dull product of a painful old age, a mere exercise in translation. But if we are alert, we can catch in operation a magic which is as impressive in its way as the magic of Vulcan's Broche, reaching beyond the brilliance of sparkling forms and resplendent wit to a deeper understanding of psychological process and of the mysteries of faith. The Broche which seemed simply an ornament becomes the key to understanding, through its destruction of facile optimism and of the itch for premature fruition in the beauties of this world. These profound identities are the best justification which can be advanced for restoring the unity of the poem and for calling it by its original title.

Acknowledgements

I should like to thank those who have read and commented on this paper in its various stages, especially Janet Adelman, Charles Muscatine, Ronald Rebholz, and Larry Sklute, whose detailed criticisms and suggestions have been most helpful. My research was financed in part by a grant from the Leverhulme Foundation, to the Trustees of which I should like to express my appreciation.

MILTON AND THE SACRED FIRE:
SEX SYMBOLISM IN *PARADISE LOST*

Purvis E. Boyette

It is observable that in all other Poems Love is represented as a Vice, in *Milton* only 'tis a Virtue. The pictures he draws of it are naked as the Persons he speaks of, and as venerable. He removes with a chaste Hand the Veil which covers every where else the enjoyments of that Passion. There is Softness, Tenderness and Warmth without Lasciviousness; the Poet transports himself and us, into that State of Innocent Happiness in which *Adam* and *Eve* continued for a short Time: He soars not above human, but above corrupt Nature, and as there is no Instance of such Love, there is none of such Poetry.

Voltaire

A paper that advertises a study of Milton and sex is bound to invite suspicion. Most readers, except those who happen to be close students of Milton and seventeenth-century Puritanism,[1] are likely to think of Milton as indifferent, if not hostile, to the idea of human sexuality as we have come to understand it in our post-Freudian enlightenment. Ezra Pound, for example, could never reconcile himself to Milton's "beastly Hebraism," which, aside from what he imagined to be Milton's basic poverty of spirit, accounted for the poet's "Turkish contempt of females," as Dr. Johnson had peevishly put it two centuries before.

But inspired by the hymn to domestic love in Book IV, one may usefully study *Paradise Lost* as an epic of married love. In many traditional ways, Milton emerges as a celebrant of *eros*, who, like Dante, believed that romantic love was the human agency that could transform flesh into spirit.[2] This view, although suggested by a few students of the poem, has not found wide acceptance among readers of *Paradise Lost;* and to my

knowledge no one has considered in much detail the philosophical authority that lies behind the sexuality expressed in Milton's poetry.

Of those scholars who have addressed themselves to the subject of sex
in *Paradise Lost,* at least three have sensed the profound sexuality of the
poem. Denis Saurat was first to urge that Milton regarded sexual desire as
normal, necessary, and good, that "it is divine in its origin like matter
itself," that "there exists a sensuality which is good," and that "physical
love is legitimate when man and woman are united by the common
interests of reason, affection, religion, all the higher inclinations."[3]

Thirty years later, W. B. C. Watkins asserted that Milton's "view of sex
is one with his view of God, all facets of whose creation he finds good,"
and that the imagery of *Paradise Lost* shows "the untroubled, unembar-
rassed acceptance of sex without which Milton could convey neither his
imaginatively convincing picture of innocence between man and woman
nor vitality in Creation." He continues, "so full-blooded a poet as Milton,
so passionate a vitalist, could not help pouring enormous sexual energy
into *Paradise Lost,* both consciously and unconsciously."[4] To assert with
Watkins that there is unconscious sexual energy in Milton's epic is not to
say that poetry is sexual sublimation, but to recognize that poetry embodies the poet's full sense of experience, in which the physical and specifically the sexual are undeniable components. The Christian poet's own
sexuality will lend urgency (often unconscious urgency?) to his effort to
discover the body's place on the road to Heaven.

Joseph H. Summers persuasively defends Milton against charges of
sexual immunity: "Those readers who have complained that Milton's
Paradise is dull, that it lacks scope for action, must either have failed to
respond to Milton's evocations of sensuous and sexual fulfillment or else
have considered it unrespectable." The concept of male and female "is
central to the entire poem." And although he warns against barbarous
overreading, Summers believes that a recognition of the role of the "two
great Sexes" (*PL.*VIII.151) "provides one of the most immediately accessible ways into the meaning and method of *Paradise Lost.*"[5] This study seeks
to explain that meaning and method in greater depth.

If the principle of male and female is important for a fuller understanding of *Paradise Lost,* just how does that principle illuminate Milton's
poetry? Specifically, I hope to show that the male-female principle is a
category of epistemology applicable to the poetic of *Paradise Lost.* Poetry
is a way of knowledge that makes words the defining vehicle of what men
can understand. As Milton said, metaphors are the "similitudes" that
enable Spenser to be a better teacher than Aquinas. Finding implicit
comparisons, according to Milton, is a process of reasoning by which one

discovers "proportion" and "*analogia*," arguments for making ideas plain rather than for proving them.[6] As a way of poetry, the imagery of male and female is often the "similitude contracted to a word"[7] by which we conceptualize patterns and relationships that explain such diverse problems as Milton's cosmogony, the Christology of erotic love, the biological and ethical basis of human relationships, and the perversions of Satan. Much of the power of *Paradise Lost* comes from the recognition that Milton's poetry is an adventurous way of thinking that seeks to eliminate apparent differences, paradoxically *without* eliminating them, by forging unity out of opposites: *ex uno plura*. More than the arrangement of scenes and dialogue, this unity establishes a quality of mind and a process of thinking that freely accommodates man to a conception of God as both center and circumference of all things, a divine *coincidentia oppositorum*. My contention is that a part of Milton's accommodation is best understood in terms of human sexuality. This study, then, is about one way of finding knowledge, and it seeks to show how Milton's poetry brings us into that uneasy encounter.

I

Traveling all levels of medieval correspondence, human sexuality is the hieroglyph of divine fertility. Raphael tells Adam that

> . . . other Suns perhaps
> With thir attendant Moons thou wilt descry
> Communicating Male and Female Light,
> Which two great Sexes animate the World.
> (vⅢ,148–151)[8]

Striking because of the parallelism between cosmogonic and human generation, this figure is charged with the kind of erotic power Milton frankly celebrated in his fifth Latin elegy:

> Exuit invisam Tellus rediviva senectam,
>   Et cupit amplexus, Phoebe, subire tuos.
> Et cupit, et digna est; quid enim formosius illa,
>   Pandit ut omniferos luxuriosa sinus,
> Atque Arabum spirat messes, et ab ore venusto
>   Mitia cum Paphiis fundit amoma rosis?[9]

Having learned early the poetic force of erotic metaphor, Milton develops a sexual symbolism in *Paradise Lost* that works in two directions: images of human fertility move outward into the universe and images of cosmic fertility, in turn, express man as the image of divine generation. Thus, ordinary masculine and feminine roles join symbolically in the procreative effluence of God. A reflex, in consequence, exists between earthly and heavenly sexuality.

Milton's specific authority for transforming the cosmic forces of generation into human metaphors is Calvin's doctrine of accommodation, but both Milton and Calvin could have learned the system of correspondences between all orders of existence from the classical philosophers and the medieval exegetes. Raphael states the principle clearly:

> . . . how last unfold
> The secrets of another world, perhaps
> Not lawful to reveal? yet for thy good
> This is dispens't, and what surmounts the reach
> Of human sense, I shall delineate so,
> By lik'ning spiritual to corporal forms,
> As may express them best, though what if Earth
> Be but the shadow of Heav'n, and things therein
> Each to other like, more than on Earth is thought?
> (v.568–576)

Metaphor thus has an epistemological function, making human sexuality both fact and figure. The principle enables Milton to humanize the universe while at the same time spiritualizing the biological basis of life.[10]

Raphael's words to Adam formulate the epistemological question exactly: How can finite man, given the limited resources of language, express the unsayable and transcendental nature of the universe? His answer turns on the principle that words are actions, which can travel up and down a scale of thought. Words have more than assigned value; and when words do more than signify things they become metaphors, generating, in turn, ideas that play on, elicit, and act out the intelligence of men capable of thought. One category of word-as-action is the drama of symbolic sexuality, working as a "corporal" form that tells us what "spiritual" reality is like. If we are to talk of sexual metaphors in Milton, we must understand that this is the kind of epistemological authority Milton assumed as basic to his poetic.

Milton learned much about the technique of representing the abstract in terms of the sexual concrete from Plato, who had himself learned from the Ionian physicists that the cosmic principle of alterity could be described as the opposites of male and female.[11] Analogy functioned to illustrate a correspondence in the various levels of being, necessary, as Benjamin Jowett said of the Timaean myth, because "the abstract is a vacant form to us until brought into relation with man and nature."[12] Thus, the phenomenal world is a copy of the transcendental Idea. Language, moreover, is of this world, in which words, as Plato says, "need only be likely and analogous to the real world. . . ."[13] It is enough if "we adduce probabilities . . ." and assume that the "words are akin to the matter which they describe . . ." (*Timaeus*, 290).

The tenuous relationship between language and reality explains Raphael's equivocal, as well as rhetorical, question, ". . . though what if Earth / Be but the shadow of Heav'n . . .?" Words are inadequate and imperfect vessels for a wholly self-sufficient representation of the real (nonphenomenal) world, but they are essentially accurate insofar as they represent what is ultimately beyond language. Like the medieval and Renaissance exegetes, Milton believed that the truth of Scripture, plain as it was, lay in some nonlinguistic Form that could only be approached by words.[14] The means were partial but nonetheless sufficient. In theory, words were never more than a means to an end, and the final truth language sought, as in the empirical investigation of nature, never depended on the terms of inquiry. While "there can be much use of reason without speech," Milton wrote in his *Logic*, there can be "no use of speech without reason."[15] Language and metaphor therefore predicate thought, which in Milton's view was either intuitive or discursive. The converse, however, is not necessarily true because the further implication is that the highest form of nonverbal reasoning is mystical instead of symbolic, intuitional instead of linguistic. But Milton, too much the poet, never goes the whole way to contemplative retirement and inevitable silence. He hedges and admits that reason is not wholly independent of language or linguistic forms because poetry, as one of the "general arts," can be employed to perfect reason "for the sake of proper thinking,"[16] which leads in the end toward vatic recognition. Once he allowed that possibility, he opened the doors through which rushed the poetry of *Paradise Lost*.

Raphael's words to Adam in Book v suggest that Milton, while profoundly aware of the limitations of language, believed in the unity of knowledge and in the instrumentality of metaphor for making that unity relevant and understandable. Thus metaphor, as in all good poetry, is grounded in familiar experience, but at the same time is capable of meaning more than that experience alone. Let us, then, be clear at the outset about the degree to which sexual imagery is to be taken literally and symbolically. An image is literal insofar as it is derived from observable human experience and thus pictures phenomenal reality. It is symbolic when it signifies an idea (itself a generalized metaphor) that is *analogous* to human experience vested in the concrete and particular. Words therefore are images and act as "things" analogous to Platonic corporality. As "shadows" they signify Ideas. Language is thus the means of our moving between the phenomenal and nonphenomenal worlds; and sexual imagery, as metaphoric "action," bridges the gap between biology and metaphysics.

Origen's commentary on the Song of Songs affords us some insight into the thinking of the early Christian writers regarding the use of sexual symbolism.[17] Saint Jerome's encomium attests to the influence of Origen's work on patristic thought,[18] and Milton himself approves it in the *Reason of Church Government* (*Prose,* I, 815). Milton's approval, however, does not extend to Origen's scarcely disguised embarrassment at expressions of physical love, a discomfort that goes a long way toward explaining why allegorical interpretations of the frankly erotic Song of Songs flourished during the Middle Ages and early Renaissance. What Milton would have embraced is the proposition that sexual metaphor leads to an understanding of divinely instituted truths of this world and the other. "The Holy Spirit has veiled the form and shape of the mysteries of Holy Writ," according to Origen, "and . . . He did not wish them to be accessible to the grasp of all." Because these hidden meanings were assumed to be part of God's revelation, the Church Fathers devoted long hours and countless sermons and tracts to the discovery of the "interior" or symbolic meaning of Scripture. In the third book of his commentary, Origen cites Saint Paul as his authority, who, he says, teaches "that the invisible things of God are understood by means of things that are visible, and that the things that are not seen are beheld through their relationship and likeness to things [seen]." This is an explicit statement of the image-likeness relationship between phenomenal and nonphenomenal worlds. As one of Origen's preeminent themes, the relationship between terrestrial and celestial things shows that "this visible world teaches us about that which is invisible, and that this earthly scene contains certain patterns of things heavenly." Perhaps foreshadowing the Renaissance emphasis on a Platonized ladder of love, Origen concludes that it is possible "for us to mount up from things below to things above, and to perceive and understand from the things we see on earth the things that belong to heaven."[19] This is precisely the effect of Milton's spiritual discipline, in which we, as the Attendant Spirit explains in *Comus,* learn "how to climb / Higher than the Sphery chime."

The key to Origen's exegetical technique is thus a figurative reading of the visible-invisible, and like Milton, he derives his authority in part from Hebrews 9:23-24, in which the patterns of the things in heaven, when symbolized by man, become "figures of the true." To justify the privilege of the *perfecti* or initiates, Origen could also have turned to the apocryphal Book of Wisdom, which says that God directs and guides those whom He chooses to teach "all that was secret or manifest" (7:21). Origen applies this exegetical principle to the Song of Songs and identifies three senses in which it may be regarded: as a wedding song, as a hymn of the mystical nuptial of Christ and the Church, and as a symbolic account of the bridal union of the Logos and the human soul. Thus, the principle of looking for the multiple senses of Scripture was established early in the history of biblical commentary, and it adumbrates Saint Augustine's *figurata locutio* (*De doctrina Christiana,* xi.15) as well as the popular explanation in Hugh of Saint Victor's *De Sacramentis Christianae* that there are three ways of understanding Holy Scripture, that is, historically, allegorically, and tropologically. Saint Thomas Aquinas gave the principle final authority when he distinguished the *sensus historicus* from the *sensus spiritualis* (*Summa Theologica,* i. art. 10). That one of the chief preoccupations of the medieval exegetes—thinkers like Saint Bernard of Clairvaux and Saint Methodius of Olympus—was the inquiry into the religious meaning of sexual metaphor helps to explain the pertinence and utility of an examination of the male-female principle in *Paradise Lost.*

It was evidently an easy step for medieval and early Renaissance writers to transform the principles of biblical exegesis into a theory of literary criticism. The step was easy because the Church Fathers had made both the Bible and the world into a metaphor that acted as an essential, if not indispensable, epistemology. Dante is the classic, if obvious, example, though one could point to other writers like Sir John Harington, whose preface to his translation of Ariosto's *Orlando Furioso* (1591) makes Dante's same point, that image and metaphor are symbols of truth.

Sir Henry Vane, to whom Milton addressed his seventeenth sonnet, was at some pains to remind the readers of his *The Retired Mans Meditations* (1655) of the inadequacies of human expression, of the "earthliness of the vessel." He adjured them, moreover, to "be ready and willing . . . to supply what is deficient" in his design to show "the knowledge of things." His aim is to explain the "inward and spiritual meaning" of the Scriptures and hence of the world; but know, he says, that the discovery of the hidden meaning of God's words "is not to exclude thereby their literal and historical sense, but to show how well both may stand together."[20]

Working within the kind of epistemological context I have been discussing, Milton made the image of the human body a natural symbol of the universe and thus exploited the philosophical (and hence literary) appeal of the Renaissance analogy drawn between the microcosm and macrocosm. If the commonplace seems too easy, it is so only because we have failed to discriminate the complexities of reading the Book of Nature

aright. Sophisticated intelligence during the Middle Ages was often preoccupied with the idea, as Bernard of Tours's *De mundi universitate libri
duo sive megacosmus et microcosmus* (c. 1156) shows. Ficino develops
most of his Neoplatonism from a strong belief in analogy,[21] and Sir Henry
Vane expresses an orthodox Puritan view, that "the truth which is spoken
in Gods word, hath also its testimony from human principles. . . ."[22] Translating this correspondence into an artistic vocabulary for metaphysical
statement, Milton made Adam and Eve the microcosmic focus of *Paradise
Lost:* to pursue their relationships was also to pursue the knowledge of the
universe. It was another way, perhaps the only way, of learning the ways
of God; and in the creative process Milton, in effect, sexualized the
universe as he sought to make a poem that rendered divine truth as human
truth.

Adam and Eve, the two great sexes, are the dominant images of *Paradise Lost.* As the male-female principle that animates the world, Adam
and Eve embody an essential principle of reality. Human sexuality becomes, moreover, the metaphor or conceit by which we understand the
sustaining force of the universe—love, the sacred fire that is, as Dante put
it, *una fiamma di caritade,* the fire of love and symbol of God. Because
First Man and First Woman are the emblematic power and sum of nature,
our understanding of Milton's treatment of this symbolism is considerably
enhanced when we are fully aware of the philosophical assumptions on
which his metaphors rest.

I take it as self-evident that the imagery of male and female is a primary
means of conceptualizing all forms of reality. As noted before, the idea is
of great antiquity, going back at least to Hesiod's *Theogony* (eighth
century B.C.) where we find male and female imagery used extensively to
describe the generation of many personified types of phenomena. Two
centuries later, if Aristotle can be counted a reliable guide, the Pythagore-
ans formulated ten pairs of opposites which represented the fundamental
principles that underlie all reality. Among them was the polarity of male
and female, along with two others that figure prominently in the conception and structure of *Paradise Lost,* those of good and evil, and light and
dark. From this Pythagorean table of opposites, Empedocles (fifth century
B.C.) probably developed his theory of the two cosmic principles of Love
and Strife, or the forces of attraction and repulsion, operating to attract
like to like and to assimilate unlikes to one another so that a new, homoge-
neous compound would be formed (*Fr.* 22). Aside from the pre-Socratics,
Plato, Aristotle, and Proclus (to name only three) contributed basic insights to the understanding of human sexuality as it was perceived in the
Renaissance. These writers (along with the subterranean course of the

Cabala, Hermetica, and alchemical tradition) and those they influenced—
Plotinus and Ficino especially—invested sexual polarity with a metaphysical significance that enabled poets and philosophers alike to bridge the
gap between the seen world and the unseen, between the mundane and
the supermundane.[23]

Milton, in spite of Christ's caveat in Paradise Regained, was thoroughly
steeped in Platonic philosophy, and the fact is well illustrated in Milton's
accommodation of Plato's dual principle of Idea and Space to his own
cosmogony. By analogy and augmented by the concept of the Same and
the Other, Plato's principle expressed on a cosmic level the biological
opposites of male and female, while the contraries associated with this
opposition—active and passive, form and matter, to dominate and to
yield, giving and taking—suggest the psychological force implicit in the
principle.

Plato explains in the Timaeus that feminine Space is the universal
nature that receives all bodies and all things, that it is the recipient of all
impressions which are the informing likenesses of real existences (50E).
While receiving the images of masculine Ideas, Space never assumes a
form like that of any of the things which enter into her. She is formless
and must be free of any of the shapes she is to receive from without. In
short, "that which is to receive all forms should have no form . . ." (50E).
And again: Space is "the mother and receptacle of all created and visible
and in any way sensible things . . ." (51A). In the Timaeus then, form,
image, and Idea are synonyms for the seminal force, the father, in the
generation of the world. Space is that which receives these impressions
and is described as a "receptacle," "shapeless," "the receiving principle,"
and "mother." That Plato chose to use such images to describe the
procreative powers existing before the heavens is evidence that sexual
metaphor is a ready, perhaps inescapable, means of conceiving primordial
acts. It illuminates and justifies Milton's own practice.

By way of amplification, one turns to Aristotle who, with a lucidity that
Plato might well have envied, asserted that "the male and female principles may be put down first and foremost as origins of generation, the
former as containing the efficient cause of generation, the latter the
material of it."[24] Aristotle is here talking specifically about the generation
of animals and not about the forces existing before the heavens, but he is
quite clear about their application to other orders of reality: "Men apply
these terms [male and female] to the macrocosm also naming Earth
mother as being female, but addressing Heaven and the Sun and other like
entities as fathers, as causing generation" (716a20). His understanding of
the male animal and thus, by extension, of the male principle is "that

which generates in another," and of the female animal and the female principle "that which generates in itself" (716a15). The Sun and Earth were metaphors of procreation old by the time of Aristotle, and he sustains the tradition when he says that the Sun and other heavenly bodies were supposed to cause the generation of plants and animals in the Earth. His gloss is, therefore, apposite: the Sun generates in another, the Earth in herself. In consequence, what Aristotle thought to be an observable reality in nature and among animals, he supposed accounted for poetic designations of the Sun and Earth as father and mother (716a20).[25]

It is of major importance in the philosophical understanding of sexuality that Aristotle plainly says that male and female differ in their essence. This is to say that the sexes differ in definition, in their final cause, and in the law of their being. "The distinction of sex," he declares, "is a first principle"; and "when that which distinguishes male and female suffers change, many other changes accompany it, as would be the case if a first principle is changed" (716b10).[26]

We know, on the other hand, that Plato denied a natural inferiority of women and in the *Republic* prescribed that they be given equal training and equal responsibilities. But Aristotle insisted on the inferiority of women, declaring expressly that "the relation of husband to wife is one of superior to inferior . . ." because the female is biologically a sort of "imperfect male," an "arrested development" (728a17). While his gynecology may appear primitive, Aristotle is on firm philosophical ground when he allows his imagination to play on the materials of his prescientific observations. Touching on a basic ontological distinction, Aristotle says that "while the body is from the female it is the soul that is from the male, for the soul is the reality of a particular body" (738b25).[27] For precursors of this ontology, he could have cited the authority of Empedocles, Parmenides, Hesiod, and to some extent Plato, who had himself cited two of these authorities in the *Symposium*.[28]

Because he makes a sharp distinction between soul and body and identifies them explicitly with male and female, Aristotle implies that a corresponding difference exists in all levels of being: if male and female are of different essences, then sexual differentiation defines their different ontologies. Plato, I think, did not go so far; in fact, one cannot be sure that Plato believed there was any ontological difference in human sexuality, especially in the light of his view expressed in the *Republic* and the *Laws* that the procreative function does not indicate basically different natures. What mattered for Plato was the union of equal souls, and sexual difference had very little to do with it. Because he maintains a sharp, almost hermetic, distinction between body and soul, his argument was essentially that since soul is more elemental and significant than body, similarities of soul are more important than differences of body. On the other hand, the tidiness of Plato's distinction between body and soul is blurred when one recalls those parts of the *Phaedrus* and the *Symposium* in which Plato advances a telic view of the growth of love through stages that begin in an honest sexuality. In spite of arguments in the *Republic* and the *Laws* for a spiritual (or intellectual) love that is independent of the bodily senses (physical and erotic), Plato does imply in the *Symposium* that physical love, which necessarily expresses sexual impulses, is a means by which some men could climb toward the good. The first step toward an ultimate union with God, he says, is to respond to the attraction of a beautiful body:

And the true order of going, or being led by another, to the things of love, is to begin from the beauties of earth and mount upwards for the sake of that other [spiritual and intellectual] beauty, using these as steps only, and from one going on to two, and from two to all fair forms. . . . (*Symposium* 210)

The lover, therefore, rises consciously through a series of stages or levels. Ultimately, his will becomes one with the Divine, making the operations of love, in consequence, our means of converse with God.

However much the idea of Plato's ladder of love may be vexed by modern scholarship, Renaissance Neoplatonists freely subscribed to what they believed to be Plato's account of the divine love by which man could ascend to beatitude. The influence of Ficino's commentary on the *Symposium* cannot be overemphasized. Castiglione owed an obvious debt to it, and Thomas Stanley's *A Platonick Discourse upon Love* (1651) kept the tradition vigorous throughout the seventeenth century. Stanley's work was, in turn, a translation of Pico della Mirandola's commentary on Benivieni's *Canzona dello Amore Celeste et Divino* (1487), and is largely of Ficinian derivation. According to Stanley's translation, "From Material Beauty we ascend to the first Fountain by six Degrees," in which the seventh stage of the ascent, not included by Pico, is that of divine union. Michelangelo's lines bear testimony to just how commonplace the idea was: "It was I, Love, who in your youth, turned your feeble sight to Beauty; and that will lead you, living from earth to heaven."[29]

Milton, in his characteristically eclectic way, sought to blend what he had learned from Plato and Aristotle with the Neoplatonic prejudices of his day, and in the mixture to produce something marked by the independence of his own thought. Aristotle's Form and Matter thus became equivalent, if not interchangeable, terms for Plato's Ideas and Space; and insofar as the terms described a cosmic duality, they established the ontological importance of the two sexes. The Neoplatonic concept of soul and body as male and female reflects this development. Space receives Idea and Matter desires Form as the female desires and receives the male. Soul (or essence) defines the body and like Eros in search of Anteros seeks its likeness-companion. The human symbol of that quest is the emblematic love between Adam and Eve, an attraction that reconciles them in creative union. Restored they become the new androgyne, male and female being the distinct though intimate parts of the mystical marriage.

Following the principle in Aristotle of identifying the Sun as the cause of generation in the Earth, Milton repeatedly associates Adam with the sun and Eve with both the moon and the earth. The Eve-moon / Adam-sun parallelism was obviously Milton's strategy for showing female subordination to male authority and for making the harmony of the heavens a paradign of human order. Raphael's account of the formation of the celestial bodies describes the relationship between Adam and Eve exactly: as Eve followed Adam in the order of creation, so God created the sun first and then the moon (VII.354-357). Again Raphael's words describing the heavenly bodies are apposite to Adam and Eve:

> . . . less bright the Moon,
> But opposite in levell'd West was set
> His mirror, with full face borrowing her Light
> From him, for other light she needed none.
>   (VII.375-378)

Working within the enveloping imagery of sun and moon, two other images in this passage (the mirror and light) mediate the analogous relationship between male and female. Both evoke traditional philosophical and literary meanings, the more so in *Paradise Lost* because of the mirror-reflection configuration that dominates much of the poem. As Eve contemplates her own perfection in a pool of water, so Adam sees himself reflected in Eve. Light, of course, is the symbol for the creative power emanating from God. In this context, Eve's fertility subsists in the generative potency of Adam; and "With borrow'd light her countenance triform / Hence fills and empties to enlighten the Earth" (III.730-731). The science of the universe is thus the biology of human life: impregnated wombs grow and issue in the continuing promise of life, spiritual as well as physical.

Once one has recognized that human sexuality is the hieroglyph of divine fertility, he understands how Milton humanizes the universe and at the same time spiritualizes the first facts of life. Milton's account of creation gains thereby because it corresponds organically with human generation and because it is a cosmic enactment of man's dependence on God. In the person of Christ, God *said,* and

> . . . The Earth obey'd, and straight
> Op'ning her fetile Womb teem'd at a Birth
> Innumerous living Creatures, perfet forms,
> Limb'd and full grown: out of the ground up rose. . . .
> (vII.453-456)

Christ, then, through a process of symbolic linking, is both the sun and light. Through these natural agencies he calls forth the creatures of the world. Just as man has his being in God, so the moon has its being in the reflected light of the sun. So also Eve has hers in Adam. The symbolic equivalence is such that Christ, the sun, light, and Adam (a masculine configuration) are interchangeable ciphers in a divine equation that balances a feminine configuration made up of the Womb, earth, moon, and Eve, which two image clusters combine in turn to yield Milton's monistic God.

This kind of symbolic linking, which Milton could have learned from the mythological patterns of Neoplatonists like Philo, Iamblicus, and Proclus, enables the poet to fuse many levels of meaning—ontological, cosmological, psychological, and ethical—into a dynamic whole:

> . . . the Earth
> Though, in comparison of Heav'n, so small,
> Nor glistering, may of solid good contain
> More plenty than the Sun that barren shines,
> Whose virtue on itself works no effect,
> But in the fruitful Earth; there first receiv'd
> His beams, unactive else, thir vigor find.
> (vIII.91-97)

It is obvious here that Milton conceives of the Earth as matter, the female principle of the universe, and the Sun as form, the male principle. Each is necessary to the other if either is to be fruitful. Nature's law is such that all causes act according "to the reception of thir matter" and "not to th' extent of thir own Sphere" (x.805-808). Newton explained *reception* by quoting the axiom: "Every efficient (i.e., everything which acts) acts according to the powers of what receives its action, not according to its own powers."[30] Aristotle expressed the same idea when he said that potentiality existed in matter and not in form. Put another way, that which creates is limited by that on which and in which it works. Applying this principle to human generation both physical and spiritual, Eve as the receiving principle limits the efficient powers of Adam. As such she is not only his "other self" but the very boundaries of his existence. In another context, she is the Moon, a "moist Continent" exhaling "nourishment" to "higher Orbs": "The Sun that light imparts to all, receives / From all his alimental recompense" (v.423-424). The physics of the Heavens is such, therefore, that the mechanical becomes organic. Thus, the Sun's "fervid Rays" warm "Earth's inmost womb" (v.301-302) to bring forth new forms of life, while the stars prepare the Earth "to receive / Perfection from the Sun's more potent Ray" (IV.672-673).

Walter Clyde Curry has shown us the significance of Proclus' influence on Milton's cosmogony, and it is instructive to note the use Proclus makes of sexual myth as a means of "unfolding divine natures."[31] Proclus' contribution to the evolution of the male-female principle is a system of sexual analogies and symbols. This system, in turn, supplies authority for arguing that part of the structuring symbolism of *Paradise Lost* is the principle of the two great sexes.

According to Proclus, all the divinities proceed analogous to Heaven and Earth.[32] Because the modes of existence are "adorned and distributed from analogous principles," the two principles of Heaven and Earth (father and mother, male and female) must be admitted "in each of the elements of the world" (II.193). If a man is said to be a microcosm, each of the elements should contain in itself appropriately all that the world contains totally (II.193-194). Heaven, therefore, is in Earth, and Earth in Heaven (II.194). And "we may survey the same things everywhere, according to the analogous . . ." (II.195).

Grounded in this doctrine of analogies, Proclus developed an elaborate philosophy of emanations beginning in what he called paternal and maternal causes. "We may suppose," he says, "that the cause of a more excellent and uniform nature is paternal; but we may say that the cause of a more subordinate and partial nature preexists in the order of a mother" (I.88). In this connection, Proclus uses a highly technical and specialized vocabulary. He identifies the male principle with the "monad" and designates it the cause of "bound." The female principle is called the "duad" and expresses the "infinite power which is generative of beings" and the cause of "infinity" (I.88).

By *monad* Proclus means something very much like *wholeness,* that is, the unity that comprehends multiplicity. Each order of emanation is a monad. In the divine order, it contains "distinct" but at the same time "profoundly united" multitude. In the sensible universe, the created world is a monad which comprehends in itself all the multitude of which it is the cause. For example, each sphere of the Ptolemaic universe is a monad, comprehending each in turn an appropriate multitude. Likewise, the spheres of the elements are monads.

Bound is identified with the principle of form, which is measure and boundary. *Infinity* is identified with the principle of matter, which has the capacity to generate all things in infinite multitude. All beings are made from bound and infinity, that is, analogous male and female, which two principles derive their subsistence from God (I.169). The combination of these two principles results in what Proclus calls *mixture*, receiving stability from bound and occult power from infinity.

Harking back to the *Timaeus*, Proclus reminds us that Plato calls being the father and matter the mother and nurse of generation. All natures, he says, subsist from these twofold preexisting principles. Some are assimilated to the paternal cause whose function it is "to produce, to contain, and to defend" (I.89). Others are assimilated to the maternal cause, which is "prolific," "vivific," and supplies "motion, . . . the multiplication of powers, . . . variety and progressions" (I.89). These two principles are, in consequence, subsumed under the occult rubrics bound and infinity.

Turning to classical mythology, Proclus appropriates symbols for the male and female divinities and uses them to give a quasi-religious authority to the abstractions of his philosophical system. Saturn is the first intellect and reigns over all the intellectual gods (I.317). He is the father of Jupiter, who is called the father of all things. Thus Saturn is the father of the father of all things (I.318). Jupiter is distinguished from Saturn in that Jupiter is the instrumental cause of life.

Rhea is the mother of Jupiter but subordinate to Saturn. She is the cause of the whole of life, that is, the mother of the demiurgus, which is the cause of generation. She generates some things together with Saturn but others in conjunction with Jupiter (I.318–319). As the receiving bosom of the generative power which is in Saturn, Rhea calls forth those causes which abide in him and becomes the maternal order within the paternal (I.335). She is filled, Proclus says, "from the father [that is, Saturn] prior to her with intelligible and prolific power, but filling the demiurgus and father [that is, Jupiter] subsisting from her, with vivific abundance (I.335). Thus uniform and multiform, she is at once total energy—the primogenial goddess (I.336–337).

Within these polarities of male and female, however intricate the relationships, Proclus elaborates a series of analogous correspondences. Masculine Phanes is the father of feminine Night, as Saturn is the father of Rhea, thus paternal and generative (II.191). The sun and moon refer to the same analogy because they are opposed to each other among the planets: "The sun indeed through his light preserves a similitude to Phanes, but the moon to night" (II.191–192). And as we have seen before, Heaven has the relation of father and Earth of mother, repeating the same male-female analogy (II.193).

Whereas there is an implied sexual union between these figures, Proclus explicitly states that there is no marriage between Phanes and Night because they are "intelligibly" united to each other and are by implication androgynous (II.198). Generation in this order, as in that of Heaven and Earth, is not effected by copulation, because in the occult conjunction of their powers they are one and indivisible. However, in lower orders of emanation—that, for example, emanating from Heaven and Earth and designated Ocean and Tethys—generative unions are properly called marriages (II.198); and to the degree the productive principles are in "sensibles" (that is, in the material world), their unions are copulative (II.201). In short, all spermatic productive principles are under the order of nature, the world of organism (II.209). Moreover, Proclus adapts sexual love imagery to the purposes of holy longing and calls the fire of divine love copular because it binds natures to each other and to itself according to the order of reality in which love is manifested (II.256).

In the history of ideas, Proclus helps to define what the Renaissance writer understood of the philosophical basis for the male-female polarity, especially if he were of a Platonic turn of mind. The *Hermetica*, however, added a good deal of authority to Proclus, since the religious and philosophic teachings ascribed to Hermes Trismegistus were thought in the late fifteenth and sixteenth centuries, as Ficino believed, to be the work of a man contemporary with Moses. But in 1614 Isaac Casaubon concluded that the whole book, that is, the *Poemandres,* was the work of second-century Christians, probably of the Alexandrian school, although Ralph Cudworth attempted to refute Casaubon's opinions in *The True Intellectual System of the Universe* (1678). Like Proclus, the *Hermetica* relies heavily on the metaphorical relationship between male and female.[33] As the father of all, the first Mind (*Nous*) is bisexual, as is his image and offspring, Man. When Nature beholds Man, she feels insatiate love for his beauty, which is the image or form of God, and with this archetypal Man she engenders and gives birth to seven Men: "And Nature, when she had got him with whom she was in love, wrapped him in her clasp, and they were mingled in one; for they were in love with one another" (14). These seven Men are also bisexual—Nature having supplied their bodies, earth the female element and water the male element—and correspond to the seven planetary Administrators or Destiny (17). After a "period" had ended, God "parted asunder" all the bisexual living creatures, "and man with the rest; and so there came to be males on the one part, and likewise females on the other part. And thereon God spoke thus in bold speech: 'Increase and multiply abundantly, all ye that have been created and made' " (18). Nature, then, inspired by the love of God, generates out of the sexual elements of her own being. She is both male and female, though she is referred to primarily in her female aspect. This symbolism is important because it anticipates the symbolic ambiguity of Milton's own treatment of Chaos and Old Night.

As two of the chief allegorical representations in *Paradise Lost,* Chaos is described as a male figure and Night his female consort. His throne borders on light.

> . . . and his dark Pavilion spread
> Wide on the wasteful Deep; with him Enthron'd
> Sat Sable-vested *Night,* eldest of things,
> The consort of his Reign. . . .
>
> (ii.960–963)

Milton consistently identifies Night and Chaos with the womb of nature, with uncreated matter, with the "unreal, vast, unbounded deep" (x.471), and with the "immeasurable Abyss" (vii.211). Here the male-female exchange between form and matter collapses. Although the "womb / Of unoriginal *Night*" (x.476–477) parallels the feminine principle of the universe, Chaos can hardly be identified with the masculine principle of order manifested in Christ, the sun, and Adam. What the reader must recognize is that Night and Chaos are at the farthest extreme from the Light and Order they may become through divine agency. The symbolic bivalence between Light and Night is explicit when we recall that Milton designates Night "eldest of things" in Book ii (962) and identifies "light ethereal" as "first of things, quintessence pure / Sprung from the Deep" in Book vii (243–245). Light becomes therefore the highest possible refinement of what Night supplies potentially. Metaphorically, the symbol for male form (Light) acts as an exponent of female matter (Night). In this configuration Old Night appears to be transexual, female in its basic property as matter, male in its refinement as "quintessence pure." Grounded in a philosophical monism, Milton makes Light partake of and expresses a materiality that has been transmuted into essentiality. Matter has become form, as body may become spirit. Milton's use of the word *quintessence* helps us to eliminate the confusion some readers have felt. Philemon Holland's translation of *Plutarch's Morals* (1603) points to Aristotle's fifth element: "Aristoteles . . . hath put down . . . for elements, foure; and for a fifth, quintessence, the heavenly body which is immutable" (p. 662). And Randle Cotgrave's *A French and English Dictionary* (London, 1660) defines *quintessence* as "the vertue, force, or spirit of a thing extracted." Thus, Light is "extracted" from Night and is the created agency through which God creates,[34] and the sexual polarity in the natural world comes down to a question of ontological distance, with matter (or Night) at one extreme and form (or Light) at the other. In this manner, Milton is able to assert that all differentiation in being distinguishes not differences in kind but differences in degree.

Chaos, on the other hand, is a parody of the generative potency of male form. Though he is the male consort of female Night, he is unable to create anything, since it is God who "build[s] / In *Chaos*" (VII.92–93). The effect of this detail is to make Chaos a metaphor for the materiality of matter and thus an aspect of the female principle in whom God creates, for it is never the union of Chaos and Old Night that creates but rather the agency of God operating on them both. Chaos is, in a word, impotent, and has no phallic power over the womb and abyss he is said to rule, for to "hold / Eternal Anarchy" (II.895–896) is not to reign at all. Chaos, then, along with Old Night, creates only under the agency of God's command and only in this way fulfills his relationship to Night as male to female. Worth repeating is that Milton did not conceive of matter as evil or as antithetical to spirit but as the material with which God created the world, itself an attribute of his own nature and such a world as may change all to spirit. The metaphorical inversions in Milton's scheme are, in turn, poetic renderings of his monism, with the further poetic function of showing that the basic principles of the natural order are under the governance of Providence, whose power gives them all life.

Looking again at Proclus' system, we find that bound and infinity are analogous to form and matter in the "intelligible triad," mixture being the third hypostasis in a monad that is masculine and paternal. The "intelligible and at the same time intellectual triad" subsists according to infinity. It is the receptacle of paternal causes, feminine, and maternal. In this way, as Curry says, "Proclus provides for a union of masculine and feminine principles through which original essences are nurtured and transmitted into all posterior being."[35] The female principle subsists in the primary masculine order of emanation because it expresses God's dual nature, signifying thereby the generative or creative power of God, the One, an androgynous self-sufficiency. Thus, Milton had authority for presenting Chaos as a male god in its feminine attribute as "the infinite" or the Many-in-One, while at the same time establishing Night, the nurse and receptacle of generation, as the goddess and consort of Chaos. According to Curry, the principle of each in all and all in each explains both Milton's and Proclus' symbolism for representing male and female as subsisting in all orders of emanation from the most nearly perfect down to matter itself. But Curry fails to observe that Milton altered Proclus' idea radically to show that Chaos is a negation of the masculine principle and thus does not in Milton's scheme communicate phallic power.

Unlike Spenser in the Garden of Adonis section of *The Faerie Queene* (III.vi.36), Milton does not hold that the world is created out of an eternal first matter, a *prima materia* existing apart from God. But neither does God create *ex nihilo;* rather he creates from his own divine nature, *ex deo,* or, more exactly, *ex chaos,* since chaos in an aspect of his divine nature, all things being of God (*CD*.xv.21). But while it is clear that Chaos is ontologically feminine in Milton's account of creation, there is no denying that Milton's use of masculine pronouns to describe Chaos allows him to have it both ways, since the implication is that within the feminine potentiality of Chaos is the masculine element that emerges at God's will and generates in posterior forms of being. If Milton had read the cabalistic teaching collected in the thirteenth-century *Zohar* (published in Mantua, 1588), he would have had recourse to another tradition of sexual symbolism more ambiguous even than that of Proclus, although the *Cabala* tends to standardize the idea "that every figure [scriptural image] which does not comprise male and female elements is not a true and proper figure."[36] Whatever his reading, Milton is making his way, however timorously, toward a position that not only holds matter to be basically good but one that asserts chaos to be a necessary constituent of the divine mind and by extension a functional part of man's nature.[37] In this regard, he has moved away from the early Neoplatonic distrust of the body and taken a stand like that of Pico della Mirandola in the *Heptaplus* (1489), in which matter and flesh are viewed as an expression of divine goodness.

Because "shape" or being is an infused principle, matter requires form as the female demands the male:

> Matter unform'd and void: Darkness profound
> Cover'd th' Abyss: but on the wat'ry calm
> His brooding wings the Spirit of God outspread. . . .
> (vii.233–235)

As the male principle which gives form, Christ is both the Word and the Spirit (vii.208–209) and

> . . . from the first
> Wast present, and with mighty wings outspread
> Dove-like satst brooding on the vast Abyss
> And mad'st it pregnant. . . .
> (i.19–22)

In this context, Milton makes the dove, a traditional image of the Holy Spirit, the sexual symbol of God in His creating powers. Popular accounts held that the Virgin Mary conceived when the Holy Ghost descended in the figure of a dove and whispered in her ear, and John Swan's *Speculum Mundi* (1635) identified the dove as one of the animals whose life was a perfect pattern of "chaste, mutual, and matromoniall love."[38] Iconographically, the dove symbolized the rapture inspired by Venus Urania, the highest exponent of God's creative powers. In Archille Bocchi's *Symbolicae quaestiones* (1574), for example, one of the images (defined as *divinus amator*) shows a youthful Mercury contemplating a dove descending on beams of celestial light, thus linking light, the bird, and God's grace in a symbolic unit.[39] As an image of love, Milton's dove is altogether appropriate as a symbol of what is truly creative, of a divine *spiritus* empowered to join "like things to like" (VII. 241), to shape a birth from "Nature's Womb" (v.181), to command the Earth to put forth her seed (VII.309–312), and to make the unreal real (X.471).

But like Milton's Chaos, much of this imagery is sexually ambiguous, neither clearly male nor clearly female. The Spirit's "brooding wings" spread "dove-like" suggest a mothering hen; this same Spirit, however, impregnates the womblike "vast Abyss." As we have come to expect, the ambiguity is functional. It allows Milton to build into his poetic Godhead the generative principles of male and female and to show the divine unity anterior to the sexual duality of subsequent creation. God, in short, may be either male or female or androgynous; and if Milton needed philosophical authority, he could have turned, as we have seen, to Proclus and the *Hermetica*.

When Milton brings the womb into symbolic dominance as an auxiliary to phallic Godhead, he embraces a body of thought that has traditionally linked man with God; and the image gains immeasurably when one remembers that the womb is one of the controlling figures of potentiality in matter and that by a symbolic inversion (in the allegorical figure of Sin) it becomes the image of oblivion and extinguished life. Impregnated by the "Power of the most High" (XII.369), the human womb shall yield the Perfect Man, a second Adam; and Adam salutes the Virgin Mother:

> . . . Hail,
> High in the love of Heav'n, yet from my Loins
> Thou shalt proceed, and from thy Womb the Son
> Of God most High; So God with man unites.
>   (XII.379–382)

Thus, the atonement for mankind is the paradigm of mutual love between man and woman, the at-onement of all nature lost with the "sin original." The womb, therefore, mediates separation and relieves the unbearable disjunction of sexual opposites as well as the spiritual sterility of man without God.

Augmenting the womb motif, one of Adam's responses to the growing understanding of his fallen condition is a desire to "be Earth / Insensible" (x.776-777), and more: "how glad would lay me down / As in my Mother's lap ..." (x.777-778). The psychology here is that Adam wants to return to uncreated innocence—in modern terms, to return to the womb where love is unconditional and requires no responsibilities. Adam has failed to earn his father's love (that is, God's), which was conditional in its demanded obedience ("wilt thou enjoy the good, / Then cavil the conditions? ..." [x.758-759]). In consequence of his failure, Adam desires to escape from all knowledge of his act of separation and, like Satan, to lose himself in "the womb / Of unoriginal *Night* and *Chaos* wild" (x.476-477). The significance of Adam's desire to return to Night and Chaos is that he wants to begin his life anew. Chaos, as we have seen, is undifferentiated power or potentiality. A wish to return to that primal state is a ritual impulse to reclaim the energy lost through failure.

By placing sexuality within a cosmic (and by implication Christological) context, I have tried to show thus far that it is one of Milton's chief metaphors for the mystery of Creation and its preservation. Necessarily, Adam and Eve become Milton's symbols for the two great sexes that animate the world. They are Heaven and Earth (the little world) in whom all mankind acts. As part of the controlling symbolism of Milton's epic, male and female represent the power and sum of nature; experience of that figurative sexuality is one way to knowledge.

Our first vision of Milton's perfect man and perfect woman occurs in Book IV of *Paradise Lost:*

> Two of far nobler shape erect and tall,
> Godlike erect, with native Honor clad
> In naked Majesty seem'd Lords of all
> And worthy seem'd, for in thir looks Divine
> The image of thir glorious Maker shone,
> Truth, Wisdom, Sanctitude severe and pure,
> Severe, but in true filial freedom plac't;
> Whence true autority in men; though both
> Not equal, as thir sex not equal seem'd;
> For contemplation hee and valor form'd,

For softness shee and sweet attractive Grace,
Hee for God only, shee for God in him:
His fair large Front and Eye sublime declar'd
Absolute rule; and Hyacinthine Locks
Round from his parted forelock manly hung
Clust'ring, but not beneath his shoulders broad:
Shee as a veil down to the slender waist
Her unadorned golden tresses wore
Dishevell'd, but in wanton ringlets wav'd
As the Vine curls her tendrils, which impli'd
Subjection, but requir'd with gentle sway,
And by her yielded, by him best receiv'd,
Yielded with coy submission, modest pride,
And sweet reluctant amorous delay.
Nor those mysterious parts were then conceal'd,
Then was not guilty shame: dishonest shame
Of Nature's works, honor dishonorable,
Sin-bred, how have ye troubl'd all mankind
With shows instead, mere shows of seeming pure,
And banisht from man's life his happiest life,
Simplicity and spotless innocence.

                                        (IV.288-318)

An essential reality of human life is the fact of male and female, displayed in naked "honor" as the image of God. Like Albrecht Dürer in his "Adam und Eva" (1504), Milton asks us to contemplate the image of God and the world in the figure of two sexes and to see in their relationship the prefiguring of two of the major themes of *Paradise Lost:* that in knowing man one sees into the nature of God, and that the condition of our being is the recognition of order.

In representing the sexual alterity of nature, Milton celebrates the beauty of man and woman as the epitome and final glory of God's creation. The Garden, symbolic of the unfallen world, is completely dominated by the two human figures. The meaning is clear: man and woman are the center and most important constituents of the world. As the fundamental principles of biology and metaphysics, they embody the given facts of the cosmos. The descriptions of Adam and Eve draw an immediate contrast and imply a *concordia discors* of opposites in union.

Milton emphasizes Adam's manliness, with his dark Hyancinthine locks clustering above his shoulders, and Eve's feminacy, with blonde tresses hanging veillike to her waist. These details are more than decorative. Saint Paul wrote to the Church in Corinth: "If a man have long hair, it is a shame unto him. But if a woman have long hair, it is a glory unto her; for her hair is given unto her for a covering" (1 Cor. 11:14-15). Milton, like Paul, uses—iconographically, one might say—the length of a man's and woman's hair as a symbol of the sexual differentiation which must be preserved in a rightly ordered relationship. This should not be seen as Milton's androcentricity, nor as a simple reflection of the prevailing thought of Milton's times, in which women were relegated to positions of secondary importance. Rather, the subordination of woman is a condition of society because it is the condition of biology. In an image of perfect man and perfect woman, there has to be a naked reflection of sexual reality and a suggestion that the roles of male and female are rigidly prescribed by natural law, which Boethius, for one, had taught was also the law of God.

Milton particularizes the sexual distinction by calling attention to "those mysterious parts" that were displayed with no hint of shame. This detail gains significance when one notices that it is self-evident from the beginning, especially after the redundancy of "with native Honor clad / In naked Majesty." Part of this emphasis is nothing more than Milton's assertion that prelapsarian man was free of shame; but beyond that it affirms Milton's strong belief in the beauty and holiness of what is natural, a Christian celebration of the goodness of God's creation.

Eve's hair, dishevelled and hanging in "wanton ringlets" like a veil down to her waist is more profoundly symbolic than one would at first suppose. The key to Milton's treatment is in his comparing Eve's golden tresses to a veil. An ancient custom, the veiling of women signifies maidenhood, purity, and fidelity, each an appropriate description of Eve; and its connection with marriage is explicit in Genesis 24:65, where Rebekah wears a veil as she approaches Isaac. But more important is the implication that Eve's long hair protects and guards something mysterious and holy. It becomes symbolic of the hidden mystery of her body, the ground from which new life issues.

Milton describes Eve's hair in such a way as to suggest not only her fertility but her relationship to Adam. The curls of her locks are like the tendrils of a vine, which depends for its growth and support on the strength of a more stable plant. Milton makes the comparison exact: male strength must necessarily dominate, the female yielding for the sake of their mutual well-being. Milton sustains this vegetative symbolism throughout, implying that the right order of nature reflects the harmony of man and woman. Eve "half imbracing lean'd / On our first Father" (IV.494-495) is the first instance. Milton repeats the figure even more specifically when he describes the daily work of Adam and Eve in the Garden:

> . . . or they led the Vine
> To wed her Elm; she spous'd about him twines
> Her marriageable arms, and with her brings
> Her dow'r th' adopted Clusters, to adorn
> His barren leaves. . . .
>
> (v.215-219)

And again the vine associates with Eve and the shaping hand with Adam when Eve suggests that they divide their labor:

> . . . thou where choice
> Leads thee, or where most needs, whether to wind
> The Woodbine round this Arbor, or direct
> The clasping Ivy where to climb, while I
> In yonder Spring of Roses intermixt
> With Myrtle, find what to redress till Noon. . . .
>
> (ix.214-219)

The parallelism is obvious: Eve is organically related to Adam as the vine is to the tree. The homology is almost perfect. But beyond this superficial correspondence, Milton's representation introduces a theme of natural fertility that identifies Eve with the prolific powers. In this it suggests a paradigm for cosmic fecundity: the natural processes of generation are sustained in order; the life giving power of God is sustained in obedience.

The identification of Eve with vine, Adam with elm links naturally with the imagery of husbandry in Books IV and V:

> With first approach of light, we must be ris'n,
> And at our pleasant labor, to reform
> Yon flow'ry Arbors, yonder Alleys green,
> Our walk at noon, with branches overgrown,
> That mock our scant manuring, and require
> More hands than ours to lop thir wanton growth:
> Those Blossoms also, and those dropping Gums,
> That lie bestrown unsightly and unsmooth,
> Ask riddance, if we mean to tread with ease. . . .
>
> (iv.624-632)

> On to thir morning's rural work they haste
> Among sweet dews and flow'rs; where any row
> Of Fruit-trees overwoody reach'd too far
> Thir pamper'd boughs, and needed hands to check
> Fruitless imbraces. . . .
>
> (v.211-215)

The significance of these images is at the very core of Milton's vision of order, both natural and social. To bring the superfluity of natural energy into productive channels, one must shape with intelligent care its endemic drive toward disorder. Stylistically—which is to say, artistically—the achieved shape in both life and art is characteristically baroque, an accumulation of detail so as to generate a sense of enormous energy barely contained by the pattern of composition.[40] The world requires husbandry, and Shakespeare expressed the basic idea in both *Romeo and Juliet* and *Richard II.* Friar Lawrence's monologue (II.iii.1–29) draws the analogy between husbandry and virtue, for "Virtue itself turns vice, being misapplied, / And vice sometime's by action dignified." The two kings, "grace and rude will," are encamped in "man as well as herbs"; "And where the worse is predominant, / Full soon the canker death eats up that plant." In *Richard II* (III.iv)—where the Duke of York's garden becomes the symbol of the state—the poor husbandry of the King has brought the kingdom to misrule: "O, what pity is it," laments the Gardener, "That he had not so trimm'd and dress'd his land / As we this garden!"

In Milton, Nature is the principle of potentiality, infinitely capable of receiving the forms and shapes of an informing "intelligence." Without this shaping intelligence its energies are never defined and eventually become chaotic. Just so, then, does the vegetation in the Garden of Eden (particularized in the vine and tree) require the husbandry of our first parents. In a still finer adjustment, that same husbandry requires that "wanton" Eve yield to "manly" Adam. As a metaphysical formulation, it demands that female materiality receive male ideation.

If we invoke a mythology going back at least as far as Plato, we can identify Eve as the symbol of Earth and Adam as the symbol of Heaven. Milton's imagery supports this identification. Eve is "dishevell'd," "wanton" (in the sense of rambling profusion), and submissive to him who is to rule her. Adam's countenance is upwardlooking: his "Eye sublime declar'd / Absolute rule." His manly strength and broad shoulders make him superhumanly handsome, recalling the athletic figures in Renaissance art of Apollo, the Sun god, and suggesting a story from the *Odyssey* in which Athena makes Ulysses taller and mightier than ordinary men and gives him locks like the hyacinth flower.[41] Significantly, Eve looks earthward on her first efforts to discover who she is, while Adam looks skyward in the contemplation of God. We appreciate this identification when we realize that Milton followed a Neoplatonic tradition which associated Earth with matter and chaos (though he displays an Aristotelian bias in not regarding matter as evil) and which associated Heaven with Neoplatonic "Intellectuals." Earth, then, is archetypal Mother and Heaven archetypal Father, Adam and Eve being the images or ectypes of these primordial forms. To add Ficino as authority: the Sun is male and furnishes light to all; whereas the Earth is female, receiving from everything and giving to nothing except in the sense that generation results from the union of the two principles.[42]

The sexual principle, grounded in Classical and Renaissance philosophy, thus illuminates several of the controlling metaphors of *Paradise Lost*. Adam and Eve are symbolic of the male-female principle that travels all levels of correspondence because the figure is basic to human perception and analogous to the creative potency of God. God's generative power, in turn, has meaning only insofar as we conceive it in terms of our own limited (because human) understanding. Man is made in God's image; and although God reveals much of his purpose indirectly in the order of nature and directly through Raphael and Michael, Adam's—and thus our—chief access to the knowledge of God is the right understanding of man. Part of that knowledge is the discovery that the order of this world does not exist apart from God, that all true knowledge is unitive, and that our bodies rightly understood are the indices to Heaven. Acted upon by Milton's poetic, images of human sexuality elaborate a mode of knowing that travels outward from primary perceptions of sexual reality—the male, the female, wombs, and births—to embrace themes that describe the metaphysical significance of human activity. It is Milton's way of translating nature into revelation and revelation into relevance.

II

When not perverted by Satan, the erotic motive in *Paradise Lost* in an invocation of beatitude. The idea is clearly evident in Milton's first portrait of Adam and Eve (IV.288-318). She gives herself to Adam "with coy submission, modest pride, / And sweet reluctant amorous delay." In their love making, they lack neither "gentle purpose, nor endearing smiles," nor want "youthful dalliance as beseems / Fair couple, linkt in happy nuptial League, / Alone as they . . ." (IV.337-340). Against the theologically orthodox "Male he created thee, but thy consort / Female for Race" (VII.529-530), we may oppose a characteristically Miltonic asseveration "Hee for God only, shee for God in him" (IV.299), which, when added to "Our Maker bids increase" (IV, 748), establishes the purity of physical union and celebrates a sexual love antipathetic to the self-destroying perversions of Satan: "Who bids abstain / But our Destroyer, foe to God and Man?" (IV.748-749).

A few critics of romantic persuasion have condemned Milton's subordination of erotic love to Reason,[43] believing apparently that the sum of the poet's appreciation of physical union is represented in Raphael's words to Adam:

> But if the sense of touch whereby mankind
> Is propagated seem such dear delight
> Beyond all other, think the same voutsaf't
> To Cattle and each Beast. . . .
>
> (VIII.579–582)

But against the biological mechanism of orgasm, the common denominator of animal life, Milton would juxtapose what is exclusively human and therefore rightly called love. Retiring to their nuptial bower, Adam and Eve lie down side by side; and Milton imagines that Adam did not turn from

> . . . his fair Spouse, nor *Eve* the Rites
> Mysterious of connubial Love refus'd:
> Whatever Hypocrites austerely talk
> Of purity and place and innocence,
> Defaming as impure what God declares
> Pure. . . .
>
> (IV.742–747)

This is a frank celebration of *eros,* and it is considerably augmented when one recalls perhaps the most strikingly sensual passage in the poem:

> . . . [Eve] with eyes
> Of conjugal attraction unreprov'd,
> And meek surrender, half imbracing lean'd
> On our first Father, half her swelling Breast
> Naked met his under the flowing Gold
> Of her loose tresses hid. . . .
>
> (IV.492–497)

Physical love, therefore, is very much a part of the marriage union. It is sanctified, however, not by the "impetuous nerve" Milton condemns in his divorce tracts but by that divine spark, the Reason, which enables love to be itself.

The philosophical context is the Platonic, or more specifically, the Neoplatonic ascent from earthly to heavenly love, moderated by as Aristotelian naturalism. Raphael sets forth the doctrine:

> In loving thou dost well, in passion not,
> Wherein true Love consists not; Love refines
> The thoughts, and heart enlarges, hath his seat
> In Reason, and is judicious, is the scale

> By which to heav'nly Love thou may'st ascend. . . .
>   (VIII.588–592)

Love, beginning in *eros* (distinct from mere animal conjunction), "Leads
up to Heav'n, is both the way and guide" (VIII.613). Body (the sphere of
eros) may, however, "at last turn all to spirit" (v.497) as does the root,
Raphael explains, from which

> Springs lighter the green stalk, from thence the leaves
> More aery, last the bright consummate flow'r
> Spirits odorous breathes. . . .
>   (v.480–482)

Two metaphors dominate in these lines: the Platonic ladder of love and
the organicism of a growing plant. Implicit in both is the idea of upward
movement from darkness to light, from grosser elements to purer, of the
transformation of flesh to spirit. The way of progress is such that "in
contemplation of created things / By steps we may ascend to God"
(v.511–512).

Milton's disposition of these traditional motifs requires notice. In the
first place, love's growth—if we are to take Raphael's analogy seriously—
proceeds toward God, the first begetter, and metaphorically the sun,
whose rays have mythologically generated in the earth. The desire for
union with the divine (the growth of love) is therefore the natural condition of man and builds in organic stages as his spiritual capacity enlarges.
But unlike the growth of Raphael's plant, man's ascent to beatitude is not
through the ineluctable attraction of God as sun but is achieved through
an action of the will, through the "contemplation of created things." Love
is contemplation. It is an activity, which implies that it will flourish best
when practiced and disciplined. Like Plotinus, Milton identifies contemplation with the active pursuit of ideal forms; but unlike Plotinus, he
accepts each part of the created world as perfect in kind.[44] To contemplate "created things" is to contemplate the perfect ordering of God's
sudden word in all its particulars.[45]

Because of the Platonic cast of Milton's thought, it is important to
understand that Plotinus, though a philosophical dualist, is able to make
human love a way of contemplating spiritual reality. Lovers can break
away from the flesh and rise into spirit. The divisions of body and soul
learned from Plato are not nearly so hermetic as one might suppose.
Aristotle thought that they were at best logical abstractions, and the idea
that there could be any ascent from body into spirit suggests a reciprocity
that appears more compatible with monism than dualism, with (from
another point of view) a materialism that enables matter to be refined into

spirit. The logic of the dualist's bridge between body and soul may seem distressingly fuzzy to close students of philosophy, but the Neoplatonists ignored the problem, if in fact they were even aware of it. On the one hand, for Christian Neoplatonists like Ficino, who had learned much from Plotinus, matter was evil whereas spirit and pure soul were good. But the soul, on the other hand, could remain inviolable when lodged in the body (matter) and could even participate with the body in the love for and striving toward ideal Forms. Milton, of course, followed this idea only insofar as he understood soul to be purer than body, matter itself being good because it was a part of God's creation. Thus, as in Plotinus, because generation is a species of contemplation, lovers "must be counted among those who contemplate and pursue forms" (En. III.viii.7). Generation "results from the longing of pregnancy to produce a multitude of forms and objects of contemplation" (En. III.viii.7). What the so-called father of Neoplatonism means, in part, is that there is no reality except in the forms created by the Intelligence, that is, the first Plotinian emanation and father of all things, including the soul which proceeds as a second emanation (En. III.viii.9; VI.ix.9; V.ix.6).[46] The "longing of pregnancy" to produce forms is obviously a symbolic phrase, used to show the powerful urging the human psyche or soul feels to perpetuate itself in the bearing of children.[47] This desire is the drive of the soul toward Being, a Neoplatonic version of an Aristotelian entelechy in which potentiality develops into actuality, in which matter yields to the defining forms that give it actual existence (En.II.v.2 and 5).

According to Plotinus, the power of generation derives from the soul and not from the body, a belief of special usefulness for the Neoplatonist who wants to render love an act of contemplation. The soul directs the organism from above and is the superior part of the animal organism (En. I.i.7). And though there may be a higher nature in us, human beings do not exist apart from the living organism. We exist as a composite of form and matter. Soul, as the exponent of active form, furnishes the power or capacity of sensation. What the soul perceives in sense or sensibles is the image of an archetype divorced from the body and the external world. In such manner is the soul "truer and more real and consists in the unperturbed contemplation of form" (En. I.i.7). The "real man" is free from animality (En. I.i.10), because the soul is really the human self (En. I.i.7). Sexual love can, in consequence of this logic, be transmuted into transcendental contemplation. Put another way, the desire to know God inspires man to love His divine creation. As one of the "created things," man contemplates his own being in the act of loving, which, though it may issue in offspring, is a different order of experience from animal propagation. The procreative act (that is, the "genial Bed"), though common to all, is "higher . . . by far" in men than in beasts (viii.597–598). Erotic love, therefore, is a uniquely human experience; for it is a way of knowing oneself and, in consequence, of experiencing God. There is, of course, the possibility that erotic love may become lust; insofar as it does, it ceases to be love as an act of contemplation and leads away from God and the true knowledge of self.

In the context of Milton's thought ("In loving thou dost well, in passion not"), passion is precisely identified with lust and not with *eros*. Erotic love and lust are not, obviously, equivalent terms; and the distinction between the two, in the way I suggest above, should be carefully maintained. Following Ficino and his Neoplatonic successors, Spenser makes much the same point first in the *Fowre Hymnes*, in *The Faerie Queene*, and most richly in the conclusion of the *Epithalamion*. His argument is that the ascent through the various stages of earthly and spiritual love expresses differences in the degree of human and divine love and not differences in kind. Physical love, therefore, may properly be a stage in the progress toward union with God. If it is transcended in divine rapture, it nevertheless points the way to beatitude. It is the sign and promise of what spiritual discipline can bring and makes *amor humanus* capable of being ideal because it leads to divine love.

Although there have been demurrers, most scholars agree that Spenser drew substantially from the Neoplatonism transmitted under the tuition of the Florentine Academy. In small compass, the *Fowre Hymnes* (1596) illustrate how Christian Neoplatonic concepts of love and sexuality could be translated into poetic statement. And it is doubtless because of Spenser's *poetic* rendering of ideas that Milton announced him a better teacher than Aquinas and Scotus. The thematic content of the *Hymnes* describes the ascent from earthly love to heavenly beauty; and though ultimately traceable to the *Phaedrus* and the *Symposium*, Spenser derives the stages of this ascent from Ficino. I know of no evidence that proves beyond all doubt that Spenser read the Ficinian commentaries on Plato's *Dialogues*, but that Spenser was under the spell of Florentine Neoplatonism, however transmitted, can scarcely be questioned. Spenser might well have known Benivieni's *Canzona dello Amore Celeste et Divino* (1487), along with Pico's *Commentary*, which was chiefly of Ficinian derivation.[48] He even more likely knew Castiglione's fourth book of *Il Courtegiano*, in which the master of Renaissance courtesy identifies the six stages of love described by the Florentines: one progresses from love of (1) the beauty of a particular woman; to (2) the idealized image of the woman; to (3) the universal beauty of woman; to (4) beauty as an inherent part of the human spirit; to (5) universal beauty, which is identical with divine love, wisdom, and goodness; and finally to (6) identity of universal beauty with God.[49] Precisely to what extent these stages in the Platonic ascent were prefigured in Spenser's four poems can be argued, but that he understood the implication of the ladder of love seems clear enough. After all, Spenser was concerned not so much to write a coherent philosophy of love as to express in a traditional framework his belief that human and divine love differ in degree and not in kind. In addition to this structured progression, but a close corollary of it, one should recall Ficino's classification of the ascending orders of love ranging from *amor bestialis* to its highest degree in Theocentric union. Spenser's first two hymns may be profitably read to speak the wisdom of Ficino's *amor humanus* and *amicitia*, the third of Christocentric love, and the last of Theocentric love. These Neoplatonic patterns suggest the philosophical context in which the *Fowre Humnes* were generated and, in consequence, sharpen our understanding of how amatory and erotic imagery functions in highly philosophical poetry.

As in Milton's *Paradise Lost,* the sexual symbolism in Spenser's *Hymnes* is so thoroughly woven into the imaginative texture of the poetry that its independent philosophical life hardly matters to us. That is as it should be: poetry answers to its own imperatives. But this is not to say that the symbolism is unphilosophical or, worse yet, irrelevant. The symbolic image is essential metaphor (that is, a recognized similitude), and insofar as such imagery has already been made for him, Spenser's task as poet is to persuade us of its authenticity.

Infused with the fire of Love, all living things desire "to multiply the likeness of their kynd,"[50] and "to quence the flame, which they in burning fynd" (I.198). This fire of Love, Spenser carefully says, is erotic love of the noble kind. It seeks in man to engender his progeny "not for lusts sake, but for eternitie" (I.104): "Therefore in choice of love, he doth desyre / That seemes on earth most heavenly, to embrace" (I.110–111). These lines approve the honest sexuality of Socrates' climactic speech on love in the *Symposium,* although the attraction of a beautiful body is something more than the kind of apparent beauty that strikes the eye: "For love is not so light / As streight to burne at first beholders sight" (II.209–210). Indeed, the "fleshes frayle infection" mars the "first perfection" of true beauty; but we are not to take these hesitations about the love of physical beauty as a condemnation of erotic love. When true lovers find each other, "Then wrong it were that any other twaine / Should in loves gentle band combyned bee / But those whom heaven did at first ordaine" (II.204–206). Spenser thus seeks to persuade us to a belief that in true earthly love there is an image of divine love, the source and preserver of all that we are.

In Spenser's third and fourth hymns, on heavenly love and beauty, the love between man and woman has given place to the divine "extasy" that consumes and ravishes all earthly desire. As in the fourth stage of Pico's and Castiglione's ladder of love, woman has dropped out of Spenser's scheme; the perception of physical beauty, in other words, has led the soul out of the body by means of the mind's idealization of the love object. As one moves toward mystical union with God, all previous experience of love is unsatisfying. Because human love is imperfect, "that faire lampe, which useth to enflame / The hearts of men with selfe consuming fyre, / Thenceforth seemes fowle, and full of sinfull blame" (IV.274-276). And it is significant that Spenser says that earthly love *seemes* "fowle," for it is so only when one rises to a view from divine perspective. For the Christian Neoplatonist, as for Milton in *L'Allegro* and *Il Penseroso,* the contemplative life is superior and preferable to the practical and voluptuous life, but it is not to say that the active way has no place in the growth of a man in the religious life.

Ficino provides the kind of norm that enables us to measure both Spenser's and Milton's treatment of love themes more exactly. The Florentine master never overcame an essentially medieval view that sexual love was basically evil. Like the Church Fathers who were committed to a defense of clerical celibacy, Ficino distrusted the desire for sexual union because it arose from the irrational appetites grounded in the vegetable and sensitive souls and was thus opposed to the contemplative life of Reason: "We can never indulge too much, or even enough, the proper, pure, and divine passions" of a true love, honorable and virtuous, but this love is not to be confused with physical desire, which because of its turbulent passions attracts men to ugliness and seduces them to wantonness.[51]

The body, when it is an instrument of simple carnality, cannot satisfy: "The passion of a lover is not quenced by the mere touch or sight of a body, for it does not desire this or that body, but desires the splendor of the divine light shining through bodies . . ." (p. 140). When lovers do stand in awe and amazement before a beautiful body, it is because they are looking upon an image of God (p. 141). Love thus becomes the desire for divine beauty, the perfect harmony of all forms as they originate in the mind of God. The opposite of such love is the "mad lasciviousness" that drags a man down to intemperance and disharmony (p. 130).

Ficinian thought is not without inconsistencies. Whereas Ficino generally associates physical love with carnality (*amor bestialis*), he occasionally admits that coition is proper in marriage, when its end, as in Saint Augustine, is the begetting of children. A man who respects love, he says, must praise the beauty of body as "a kind of track" of the beauty of soul. The two kinds of beauty, however, do not always go hand in hand (p. 132); for the beauty of body is "nothing but splendor in the ornament of colors and lines," whereas the beauty of soul is "a harmony of knowledge and morals" (p. 146). Carnality "is not a part of love, nor is it the desire of the lover, but rather a kind of wantonness and the derangement of a servile man" (pp. 146–147), who has surrendered his freedom of choice to the tyranny of ungoverned sensuality. One's praise of physical beauty, in other words, should take the form of contemplation. A man abuses the dignity of love if he is "too eager for procreation" or immoderately desires copulation (p. 143). Temperance, in such passages as these, seems to be the key to Ficino's understanding of the use of physical love. If the lover truly loves, he performs the functions of generation and coition within the bounds prescribed by natural and civil law (p. 143). The instinct for procreation, Ficino concludes (after giving the devil his due), is a kind of love, for it is "the desire of a thing for the propagation of its own perfection" (p. 149). It is therefore a natural desire and because natural, tends to the good (p. 153). Moreover, because "generation renders mortal things like divine, it is certainly a divine gift" (p. 203). In that which is beautiful, procreation is a divine function seeking beautiful things and shunning ugly and carried out "exactly and easily." The impulse to sexual love is to the end that "everlasting life may be preserved in mortal things." And in a sentence that recalls Shakespeare's sonnets (3, 7, and 10 especially), "love . . . arouses the pleasure of producing offspring so that what is unable to live forever in itself may live forever in offspring like itself" (pp. 203–204).

Thus, however obscured by his insistence on the soul's contemplation of divine beauty, Ficino distinguishes between the love unions of husband and wife and lustful unions that express an unqualified and anonymous carnality. Love and not animal appetite is the source of sexual desire because true lovers really seek not each other's body but the image of God expressed in their bodies. On these assumptions, Ficino is able to make sexual love an attribute of the soul: both soul and body are "aroused to procreation by the stimuli of love," although the soul itself does not experience physical sensation (p. 207). One pursues heavenly love and the other earthly.

Ficino knows that procreation is a biological fact of life and that the urgencies of human sexuality have to be accommodated to his scheme of divine and human love. He thus admits sexual generation as a kind of love or contemplation (*amor humanus*) and distinguishes this form of love from the "mad lasciviousness" of lust (*amor bestialis*). His guiding principle is that love organizes and sustains the world, preserving its unity as well as motivating each of its parts. With this as his basic premise, he develops a logic of love that progresses through four other stages, each progressively higher than animal love and human love. The love between men or *amicitia* (as seen in the true friendship between Valentine and Proteus in Shakespeare's *Two Gentlemen of Verona* or that between Pyrocles and Musidorus in Sidney's *Arcadia*) is a more perfect form of human love than *amor humanus* because it does not involve the physical appetite, however much the visceral impulse may (when very rigorously governed) participate in the divine. The important point here is that Ficino is the first significant philosopher and teacher in the Renaissance to make *amor humanus* capable of being idealized. No one before Ficino saw marriage as the goal of romantic love. The love of a beautiful woman was for Dante and Petrarch a way of starting a man on his ascent to the love of God. But the idealization of love in marriage is implicit in Ficino's account of the desire of earthly love "for generating divine beauty in earthly matter." The beauty of a beautiful woman stimulates in the lover a desire to embody that beauty in a "worldly creation." Earthly love, deriving its power from the Earthly Venus that is in the World Soul, "tries to prepare in earthly matter the beauty divinely conceived in itself" (p. 192).

Like most Renaissance mythographers, Ficino was fascinated with the idea of two Venuses, one heavenly and the other earthly. The thrust of his interpretation of the two pagen love goddesses is to show how human and divine love are related, and he explains the relationship in terms of his system of divine emanation. There are three forms of emanation from God: the *Mens angelica*, the *Anima mundi*, and *Natura*. *Natura*, in turns, sows seeds (the *rationes seminales* derived form Saint Augustine, Plotinus, and the *logos spermatikos* of the Stoics) in the World, from which springs the plenitude of sensible nature. With this mythology as a frame of reference, Ficino says that the Heavenly Venus is in the *Mens angelica,* the first order of emanation from God, and participates in the means of begetting lower forms as an inspirational power. The Idea of Heavenly Love attracts to itself; its very existence elicits love. The Heavenly Venus is an extension of God, born of Heaven of no mother "because for the natural philosopher, *mother* means *matter* [a false etymology], and the Angelic Mind is completely foreign to any relationship with corporeal matter" (p. 142). The second and lower Venus is in the World Soul and has the special faculty that moves the heavens. She has both mother and father because she is related to matter and is the power of generation with which the World Soul is endowed.

The meaning of Ficino's mythology, when transmuted into a metaphysic of Christian love, is that the Heavenly Venus is a metaphor for innate love that is stimulated to know the beauty of God. The Earthly Venus is stimulated by love to procreate the same beauty in bodies. Thus, the soul has two powers, derived from each of the two Venuses. One is the desire to contemplate beauty, the other to propagate it (p. 143). Both, because they are concerned with the divine image, are sacred.[52]

Against the background of Ficino's Christian Neoplatonism, Spenser's story of Amoret and Sir Scudamour in Books III and IV of the *Faerie Queene* develops strong philosophical themes. The narrative illustrates the necessity of purging married love of lust and establishing a nuptial union in true chastity. After Sir Scudamour has won Amoret from the Temple of Venus, they fall into lust on their wedding night and she is carried off to the castle of the enchanter Busirane. The flames at the castle gate (symbolic of lust) prevent Sir Scudamour from rescuing the beleaguered Amoret until Britomart (symbolic of chastity in earthly love) teaches him the rule of temperance and the chaste love in marriage that leads beyond physical love to its active and contemplative planes. The Masque of Cupid, which Britomart watches at Busirane's castle, is a perverted version of the true Cupid we encounter in the Garden of Adonis (III.vi) and in the Temple of Venus (IV.x). Each of the maskers represents one of the many faces of lust, which distorts the psyche and renders true love vicious. In a savage image of diseased love, Spenser shows Amoret chained to a "brasen pillour" with Busirane, "the vile enchaunter," sitting before her and trying to make her love him by

> Figuring straunge characters of his art:
> With living blood he those characters wrate,
> Dreadfully dropping from her dying hart,
> Seeming transfixed with a cruell dart.[53]

Britomart's rescue of Amoret symbolizes the triumph of chastity over lust; and when Amoret is restored to Sir Scudamour, they both have learned through their trials to live in married chastity. Britomart herself represents the kind of married chastity that embraces physical love as a part of earthly love. Clearly, as the knight of Chastity, she embodies Spenser's idea of true love, which (as C. S. Lewis remarked) is "constant, fertile, monogamous, felicific love."[54] And although she is a virgin throughout the action of the poem, she will be the mother of kings and heroes:

> For from thy wombe a famous Progenie
> Shall spring, out of the auncient *Trojan* blood.
> (III.iii.22)

In her love of Artegall she testifies to what love between man and woman truly means.

Much the same idea is developed in Milton's *Comus*. As the offspring of the two voluptuaries Circe and Bacchus, Comus is the image and figure of all the sins of *luxuria*. His attempt to seduce the Lady, like Busirane's, argues a perversion of nature and hence a distortion of the true love (or chastity) the Lady defends and preserves. But chastity means virginity for Milton only when the Lady is unmarried; in marriage the bride remains chaste though not virginal because her life signifies the true love that is grounded in temperance. Married chastity embraces erotic love as a right response to natural law: it is Milton's way of seeing God in the world.

To say, therefore, with Edwin Greenlaw, that Raphael's words to Adam (VIII.521–643) are an attack on Venus Pandemos is, in my view, not quite accurate,[55] because Venus Pandemos denominates not lust (though she may degenerate to that) but erotic love. Earthly love, according to Milton, has its seat in Reason as much so as does the heavenly love to which it may ascend. "Love refines the thought," which I take to mean that in the act of exchanging mutual prerogatives one achieves ever finer adjustments of self-understanding and self-realization. The lover is process. He is in the act of becoming the image of the God to whom his Reason testifies. Coordinately, love also enlarges the heart (VIII.590); that is, it increases one's capacity to love the Not-Me, the Other, that which exists outside one's own ego. Paradoxically, to love another well is to love oneself best: "He that loveth his own wife loveth himself" (Ephesians 5:28). Ficino corroborates the idea: one kills himself when he rejects the heart of proffered love.[56]

The wide popularity of Denis de Rougemont's *Love in the Western World*, Nelson Nygren's *Eros and Agape*, Martin D'Arcy's *The Mind and Heart of Love*, and, most recently, Rollo May's *Love and Will* makes almost mandatory the addition of two other terms to the concept of *eros* I have been discussing: *philia* and *agape*. The distinctions that these three terms make in regard to physical and spiritual love help to clarify the loosely abstract thought that underpins much of what we see in Milton. De Rougemont conceives of *eros* as the dark passion of physical love flying upward from the earth only to crash into the realities of spiritual love and thus working its own destruction. Nygren, on the other hand, identifies *eros* as the self-centered or egocentric love represented in Greek culture and distinguishes it from *agape* or theocentric love, which has nothing of man, however ideal, in it. Father D'Arcy's work suggests that *eros* and *agape* are not antithetical loves, that they complement each other, and that they are mediated by *philia*—all of which relationships have been pursued by Father D'Arcy's disciple D. S. Bailey in *The Mystery of Love and Marriage.*

When we appropriate these terms to describe Milton's thought, one sees *eros* (still bearing the marks of Neoplatonism) as an expression of love directed to the whole person as a physical being and therefore more than sexual desire. *Philia* is the common exchange of mutual friendship, wherein the operative effect is *exchange,* a giving and receiving that makes possible the full achievement of *eros.* As a term to describe a human capacity of love, *agape* represents a free act of the will, is not evoked in any way nor affected by any value outside itself. It is, to use one of C. S. Lewis' terms, "gift-love," usually described as that expression of love one sees exemplified in the New Testament, in God's gift of himself as Christ to the world. In the human sphere, it does not supersede—that is, displace or cancel—*eros* and *philia* but controls and enriches those expressions of love. These three forms of love may be said to describe the same progression as that in the Neoplatonic ladder of love but with this difference: *eros* and *philia* describe the preparation of the human soul to receive *agape,* the free gift of God's love and mercy which, strictly speaking, comes down to man rather than requiring the impossibility of man's ascending to it. Man does not earn Grace but accepts it. In that we imitate *agape* in our human relationships, we offer unconditional love, which is indifferent to its reception.

Milton never loses sight of the human being with whom man participates in love. The center of Milton's marriage union, however, is not *eros* but *philia:*

> . . . happy in our mutual help
> And mutual love, the Crown of all our bliss
> Ordain'd by thee. . . .
>
> (iv.727-729)

And the point should be emphasized. *Philia,* in turn, comprehends *eros* and makes erotic love an activity of the soul. Together, these two expressions of love point the way to God.

The implication of this categorizing of the modes of love applies particularly to love expressions in a postlapsarian world, but the radical implication is that *eros, philia,* and *agape* are identical in prelapsarian Eden, where love had neither logical nor spiritual division. Before the Fall there would have been no sin to separate God from man or man from woman. Love was total communion and required neither sign nor symbol to teach that in love's ecstasy the human and divine were one. For fallen man, unable to look directly into the face of God, the truth is hidden in dark conceits: vision is an act of grace, needful to complete the insufficiency of fallen nature and necessary to draw man out of his own imperfection. Milton, however, takes a middle way. The ideal love between Adam and Eve in Paradise, while perfect, is not in that perfection irrelevant to the condition of fallen man. It is not, that is, inhuman. The love relationship between our First Parents shows us the pattern of true love, achievable when we are perfected in grace. Milton's lovers, unlike Donne's in *The Canonization*, require no admonition to beg meaning from Heaven.

Milton's hymn to marriage is, in fact, one of the great celebrations of domestic love in English literature:

> Hail wedded Love, mysterious Law, true source
> Of human offspring, sole propriety
> In Paradise of all things common else.
> By thee adulterous lust was driv'n from men
> Among the bestial herds to range, by thee
> Founded in Reason, Loyal, Just, and Pure,
> Relations dear, and all the Charities
> Of Father, Son, and Brother first were known.
> Far be it, that I should write thee sin or blame,
> Or think thee unbefitting holiest place,
> Perpetual Fountain of Domestic sweets,
> Whose bed is undefil'd and chaste pronounc't,
> Present, or past, as Saints and Patriarchs us'd.
> Here Love his golden shafts imploys, here lights
> His constant Lamp, and waves his purple wings,
> Reigns here and revels; not in the bought smile
> Of Harlots, loveless, joyless, unindear'd,
> Casual fruition, nor in Court Amours,
> Mixt Dance, or wanton Mask, or Midnight Ball,
> Or Serenate, which the starv'd Lover sings
> To his proud fair, best quitted with disdain.
> These lull'd by Nightingales imbracing slept,
> And on thir naked limbs the flow'ry roof
> Show'r'd Roses, which the Morn repair'd. Sleep on,
> Blest pair; and O yet happiest if ye seek
> No happier state, and know to know no more.
>
> (IV.750–775)

It bears emphasizing that these lines are a flat rejection of any conception of *eros* that subsists in the frustration of active desire. Marriage is an act of fulfillment; its frustration is a perversion of divine purpose.

The hymn may be usefully studied as an excursus on the difference between love and lust. In the first place, love is a "mysterious Law" which, in the act of generation, subsists only between man and woman. It is not vouchsafed to animals, because true love is grounded in the Reason, a capacity uniquely man's. Its attributes are paternal, filial, and brotherly. The law of love, moreover, restrains sexual love from "sin or blame" and preserves the marriage bed "undefil'd and chaste." Against the mystery of love, Milton opposes lustful unions with harlots. There is nothing in these venereal excitements of love, joy, or endearment. Because there is no mutual exchange either of bodies or soul, they are the meaningless purchase of an "impetuous nerve."

The law of love, moreover, is mysterious because it partakes of revelation: it is the human equation of divinity in motion. Erotic rapture is possible only when it engages the whole man, when the body works in concert with the soul. Otherwise it is lust, and instead of union there is fractured sensation. Following the dictates of his philosophical monism as well as his reading of Aguinas, Milton believed that body and soul could not be separated. If he could not share Tasso's youthful opinion of the vanity of loving virtue alone to the exclusion of the body, he could certainly join in the later opinion of the Italian that bodily intercourse could be desired as a sign of the union of souls.[57] Whereas lust results in flight from the other, love embraces the Other and in union finds rest. The emblem of that spiritual and bodily peace is perfectly expressed in the naked figures of Adam and Eve, linked in an embrace, asleep in their bower and showered with rose petals. It is Milton's poetic rendering of Aquinas' doctrine (learned from Albertus Magnus) that in Paradise physical love, because spiritual, was more exquisite than anything we can know in our fallen condition. And more, it is Milton's personal testimony, as Professor Summers said, that "there could be no original paradise for man without sexual love. . . ."[58]

Raphael's condemnation of Adam's passion for Eve's beauty (VIII.561 ff.) is not a rejection of sexual love but a warning that Passion can undermine the Reason. The transport of emotion which the first sight of Eve evokes in Adam (VIII.528-530) is through no fault either in Adam or in Nature, but rather an indication of erotic potential, which—if it is to flower—must be subordinated to the Reason as Adam is to subordinate Eve. Passion is censured because it disorders, and the sum of Raphael's words to Adam is to assert the primacy of Reason over the Desires and Passions. It is true that Adam thinks Eve possessed of powers which transcend authority and logical reason, that she has some special vision denied him. And as an isolated man, denied a helpmeet, he is right indeed to believe that she possesses secrets he cannot know without her; what Raphael teaches him is that the secret of true love is infinitely more ennobling than the "sense of touch whereby mankind / Is propagated" (VIII.579-580).

Adam's reply to Raphael (VIII.595-617) amplifies the angel's words by distinguishing between generation in animals and nuptial love between man and woman. After the "procreation common to all kinds" is granted, there yet remains the "mysterious reverence" that attends the human act of generation. This reverence comes not from any "higher" sense of touch but from the "unfeign'd / Union of Mind" that antecedes it. Likeness of soul assures harmony between the first lovers. A true love union is possible for Adam because his Reason has approved what his sense has represented to him. If his will is free to love, then he is free to follow what his Reason directs; and he assures the angel that though his love for Eve is physical, nothing delights him more than "those thousand decencies that daily flow / From all her words and actions" (VIII.601-602).

Now, part of the explanation for Adam's insistent celebration of Eve is that she is the vehicle through which he first experienced his sexual identity or, put another way, the reality of his manhood. The first moments of Adam's consciousness (VIII.253 ff.), after a quick survey of his physical surroundings, turn directly to an examination of his body and a trying of its athletic powers. Once he is aware of it as a physical instrument responding to his will, he is immediately concerned to know what the fact of his existence means. He wants to know who he is, whence he came, and why (VIII.270). The ontological question is thus posed at the outset. God's answer is not forthcoming in a whirlwind. The answer may be read, instead, in the surrounding world. Adam's first step in taking possession of his being is to claim the earth as his own by speaking the name of whatever he saw. Naming the things of the world is a profoundly metaphysical act; it testifies to an understanding that instantly perceives the true nature of the world about him; and in the act of naming its features and denizens, he possesses them for what they are. By experiencing the quiddity of things outside the self, he delimits the question of what the self is.

Transported during his sleep to the Garden of Eden by a "Heav'nly vision," Adam discovers that the order of the animals proceeds "two and two"; it is his first intuition that he cannot be fully man without his sexual complement. The crux of this proleptic intuition is simply that without Eve he cannot love God:

> . . . how may I
> Adore thee, Author of this Universe,
> And all this good to man, for whose well being

> So amply, and with hands so liberal
> Thou hast provided all things: but with mee
> I see not who partakes. In solitude
> What happiness, who can enjoy alone
> Or all enjoying, what contentment find?
> (VIII.359–366)

Adam cannot love God because he does not know himself. Eve is necessary. It is she alone who can bring him to the fullness of his manhood.
Nothing in the "brute" world can answer to Adam's need because "among
unequals what society / Can sort, what harmony or true delight?"
(VIII.383–384). It is clear too that merely another human being, of indifferent sex, is not what Adam lacks. He has correctly inferred that "each with
thir kind, Lion with Lioness" consort, and that God has fittingly combined
them in pairs of sexual opposites. The disjunction built into our bodies is
therefore necessary for human love.

From another point of view, Adam's inference that Eve is necessary has
some rather shocking implications. Did Milton mean to say that a man has
to love a woman before he can know, love, and adore God? Milton's
intention, of course, is no such blasphemy as that, and our way out of this
apparent heterodoxy is to see Adam and Eve as differentiations of symbolic mankind. As a Proclean monad, microcosmic man expresses the idea
of a wholeness and unity in which opposites are reconciled. Hierarchy
within the monad (for example, Eve's subordination to Adam) thus works
as an *hypostasis* that, while subordinate or "inferior," is contained by and
in the One. This idea is comparable to Milton's views on the Trinity and
makes the two persons (*hypostaseis*) of mankind indivisible (one *substan-
tia*).[59] Adam's primacy over Eve acts poetically as Milton's graduated
metaphor for the sexual principle that necessarily exists in the world if it is
to have life. Because she is a part of Perfect Man, she is essential and
indispensable metaphor: the proposition asserts a paradigm answerable to
cosmic similitude. As a part of Milton's poetic formula, she is the mundane
counterpart of feminine and generative Godhead.

At its fully abstract level of meaning, the idea that Adam cannot love
God without Eve is Milton's way of saying that the knowledge of God
attends on the right use of divinely instituted vehicles of revelation.
Understandably, everything in original nature expresses the good, but
even with the liabilities of sin and death, nature tends toward the good.
Eve, therefore, represents for Milton the highest office of nature. Beyond
what the Book of Nature teaches about God is the vatic revelation of the
Divine Voice itself; but Milton is not concerned to explain how we can
hear the voice of God *in propria persona*. In the event of such utterance,

we will hear clearly enough. Instead, the poet's part is to guide us through more difficult paths, to lead us to understand what the shadow of Heaven means.

God tells Adam, in fact, that there can be no pleasure without a companion, however otherwise pleasurable the world around him may be. This confirms Adam's intuition. It also shows that Milton's strategy here is to represent in a dialogue between God and Adam the evolution of man's consciousness through intellection. We see the mind searching and in the end finding what it is to be human. In order to prepare him to understand the difference between God and man, the Almighty confronts Adam with divine potency and sufficiency. Adam replies:

> Thou in thyself art perfet, and in thee
> Is no deficience found; not so is Man,
>
> .   .   .
>
> ... No need that thou
> Shouldst propagate, already infinite;
> And through all numbers absolute, though One;
> But Man by number is to manifest
> His single imperfection, and beget
> Like of his like, his Image multipli'd,
> In unity defective, which requires
> Collateral love, and dearest amity.
>
> (viii.415–426)

God, then, is the inclusive sexual monad, metaphysically both male and female, the symbolic configuration of solidarity and pure being. Adam, as the context makes clear, wants a female partner in "kind," the requisite half of the sexuality he has observed in nature. In the union of male and female, he approaches the sufficiency of God and repairs the "unity defective" of man alone without woman. Propagation is, quite literally, the image of infinitude. The impulse to generation—which is to say, the impulse to erotic love—is the desire for transcendence. Procreation, in turn, is the mercy of God. It enables man to escape his finitude, and in the postlapsarian world to gainsay death. Thus, the symbolic value of "collateral love" turns on procreative union: it is the means of transcending one's own isolation through creativity.

Plotinus gives authority to Milton's idea. The desire to procreate is an expression of a lack: "The subject [that is, lover] is conscious of insufficiency and, wishing to produce beauty, feels that the way is to beget in a beautiful form." It is this insufficiency which keeps human love craving, seeking for more of what it knows. When sexual love is lawless or "against the purposes of nature," we have failed to understand "whither Love sought to lead" and the "instinct to production," which is to beget beauty. We have not, that is, "mastered the right use of the images of beauty. . . ." Copulative love, according to Plotinus (and later Saint Augustine), is justified when the motive is self-perpetuation, in which sexual love rightly practiced refines and becomes a "last outgrowth" of the love of beauty for beauty's sake (*En.* III.v.1).

Adam's importuning, epistemologically a necessary preparative for loving Eve, moves God to say:

> What next I bring shall please thee, be assur'd,
> Thy likeness, thy fit help, thy other self,
> Thy wish, exactly to thy heart's desire.
> (VIII.449–451)

Eve, of course, is the creation. As woman she is the creator of nothing less than human love and the inspiration for erotic love not only in man but in all nature:

> And in her looks, which from that time infus'd
> Sweetness into my heart, unfelt before,
> And into all things from her Air inspir'd
> The spirit of love and amorous delight.
> (VIII.474–477)

The love which Eve commands from man and Nature is simply the inspiration to sanctity. To love her is to desire order and being and to elevate romantic love itself into an image of God.

Eve comes to Adam not "uninform'd / Of nuptial Sanctity and marriage Rites" (VIII.486–487). Led by the powerful nature within her, she offers him the experience of manhood. In winning her by "pleaded reason," Adam wins himself:

> . . . I now see
> Bone of my Bone, Flesh of my Flesh, my Self
> Before me; Woman is her Name, of Man
> Extracted; for this cause he shall forgo
> Father and Mother, and to his Wife adhere;
> And they shall be one Flesh, one Heart, one Soul.
> (VIII.494–499)

Woman is the mirror image of man, without whom he cannot contemplate his own being. She is the existential reality of flesh and spirit. To claim her is to claim himself and God.

In themselves, the relevant biblical texts are only superficially adequate to gloss these lines;[60] for Milton goes beyond the scriptural account to emphasize that in the one-flesh union there is union of mind (heart and soul) as well. The *henosis* in coition is a cognate function of body and mind. They are categories of one identity: the *whole* person is involved in the reconciliation of opposites. Seen through the lenses of a Christian humanist, the Eros-Anteros myth comes to the fore, symbolizing both the completion of man and a *concordia discors* between male and female. That woman was "extracted" from Adam's side is one cause of Adam's love for Eve: flesh has an affinity for its own likeness. She is a part of Adam with which he desires to be reunited. In that man "adheres" to his wife, his love is distinguished from and supersedes his love of father and mother. Filial love is therefore differentiated from erotic love because only in the latter expression of love is the physical body joined to spirit. Filial love is imperfect because it offers not transcendence but dependence. Only in the freedom of the flesh to make itself whole can the self become itself.

When Adam brings Eve to the nuptial bower "blushing like the Morn," there to consummate their marriage, "all Heav'n / And happy Constellations on that hour / Shed thir selectest influence" (VIII.510–513). Thus does Milton's God approve the erotic motive in nuptial union, where the conjugation of flesh in true love symbolizes the creative potency of God to bring order out of chaos: at the creation of the universe the stars also "danc'd / Shedding sweet influence" (VII.374–375). Although the parallelism is traditional, the linking imagery reinforces the profundity of a union that creates the consciousness of one's own being.

Eve's awakening, to borrow Cleanth Brooks's phrase, focuses on the relationship between the sexes from a different point of view. Milton thinks of the female as ontologically derived from the male and thus "inferior" in the scale of nature: "Hee for God only, shee for God in him" (IV.299). Eve invokes her subordinate role, with its full complement of psychological prescriptions, as a part of divine institution:

> . . . O thou [Adam] for whom
> And from whom I was form'd flesh of thy flesh,
> And without whom am to no end, my Guide
> and Head. . . .
> (IV.440–443)

And again to Adam she says:

> My Author and Disposer, what thou bidd'st
> Unargu'd I obey; so God ordains,
> God is thy Law, thou mine; to know no more
> Is woman's happiest knowledge and her praise.
> (IV.635–638)

Here, Aristotle and Saint Paul are the authorities. Eve exists solely for

Adam; she has no character, *ethos,* except as she bears the impress of his shaping mind. She is the fertile body and spirit in whom Adam generates for them both the love of God. As Adam she is herself, she is woman. Separated, she—like Adam—has no sexual identity and therefore denies them both the power of being either fully man or fully woman.

Professor Brooks, it seems to me, sees clearly into Eve's character, especially in the first moments of her consciousness, and understands thoroughly Milton's conception of woman:

The psychology of Eve is sound and convincing. To the student of Freud it may seem even preternaturally so; for Milton has made Eve recapitulate the whole process of the child's growing up and transferring the affections to the other sex. According to Freud, the child must transcend the mother image with which it has first associated warmth, nourishment, and affection, and center its affections elsewhere. In the case of a female child the task is more difficult, for it must transcend an image of its own sex.[61]

But whereas Professor Brooks says there is something "preternaturally" Freudian in Milton's treatment of Eve, he might also have said that there is something unequivocally Aristotelian—certainly by extension—in the psychological insights Milton brings to bear on the first woman. In other words, the pattern of development into an adult is first to discover that one exists as object; second, to recognize sexual differentiation; third, to exchange one's will with his sexual opposite in order to reconcile the opposition; and fourth, to understand that love (the sign of beatitude) is the only knowledge we require. This sequence of self-discovery, though not as obvious, is equally true of Adam.

When Eve awakens at her nativity, her first thoughts are to wonder "where / And what I was, whence thither brought, and how" (IV.451-452). These are almost precisely the questions Adam considers in the first moments of his consciousness. Eve quickly discovers a pool of water, and "with unexperienc'd thought" looks down to discover her reflected image. Ovid's account in the *Metamorphoses* of Narcissus' fascination with his own reflected image is, of course, the apposite classical source. But unlike Narcissus, Eve learns that what she sees is nothing more than a reflection, sterile in that the image is not real. It flatters with the appearance of sympathy and love but, as God warns, can create neither. The fertility theme is emphatic: Eve is born to create; to "bear / Multitudes"; longing for union with her own image is barren. But she has learned, however imperfectly, to appreciate her own beauty, the meaning of which will fully emerge as she comes to love Adam.

When she first sees Adam, Eve recoils because she thinks he is "less fair, / Less winning soft, less amiably mild" than her own image, and if not frightened she is certainly disquited and runs from him. The psychology behind these lines conforms with Aristotle's, where the tension between male and female is a tension between order and disorder, a *coincidentia oppositorum*. Eve prefers the soft enchantment of her "smooth wat'ry image," an irresponsive beauty that appeals to her vanity. She resists Adam because it is her nature to resist order and the wisdom "which alone is truly fair" (IV.491). But once she yields, she responds to his "manly grace": "hee / Whose image thou art, him thou shalt enjoy / Inseparably thine" (IV.471–473). In short, she does not know herself until she discovers that she is not her own mirror image but the "interinanimate" (as Donne uses it) image of man.

The mirror symbolism explicit in Eve's account of her awakening is one of the major configurations of the poem. It illustrates the necessity of seeing oneself in nature as object, but implies that if that seeing goes no further it is deceptive. By extension into a human relationship, however, the reflection becomes real—"him thou art, / His flesh, his bone" (IV.482–483)—instead of illusionary. The symbolism thus illustrates the experiential difference between internalization and externalization of the will, between love for oneself and love for another, between constriction and expansion. The mirror symbol also posits a system of order: Eve is the image of Adam and Adam is the image of God. The relationship of object to image, if we reduce the metaphor to its mechanical operation, is exact; neither exists without the other. The relationship of Eve to Adam is therefore different from his relationship to her. In one sense, the relationships operate in two different directions. He looks at God in order that he can love her; she looks at him in order that she can love God. The mirror images, however, are reversible. In that Eve is the image of Adam, she reflects what he is. In turn, what he is she is. Together, they are the glory of God.

Eve's love poem is a fine *epanados* in which identical words and phrases mirror each other for rhetorical effect:

> With thee conversing I forget all time,
> All seasons and thir change, all please alike.
> Sweet is the breath of morn, her rising sweet,
> With charm of earliest Birds; pleasant the Sun
> When first on this delightful Land he spreads
> His orient Beams, on herb, tree, fruit, and flow'r,
> Glist'ring with dew; fragrant the fertile earth
> After soft showers; and sweet the coming on

> Of grateful Ev'ning mild, then silent Night
> With this her solemn Bird and this fair Moon,
> And these the Gems of Heav'n, her starry train:
> But neither breath of Morn when she ascends
> With charm of earliest Birds, nor rising Sun
> On this delightful land, nor herb, fruit, flow'r,
> Glist'ring with dew, nor frangrance after showers,
> Nor grateful Ev'ning mild, nor silent Night
> With this solemn Bird, nor walk by Moon,
> Or glittering Star-light without thee is sweet.
>   (iv.639–656)

All that Eve experiences is possible only because Adam exists. Lines 650–656 repeat lines 641–648 almost exactly but for the addition of negative correlatives. Milton's purpose is to render with a distinct poem the poetic shape of Eve's life in Adam; and the impact of these lines, I think significantly, depends on the mirroring effect of word played against word and phrase against phrase. The rhetorical effect is an extension of one of the dominant symbol-images associated with Eve.

If it is true, then, that the condition—divinely instituted—of Eve's being is her subordination to Adam, it is also true that subordination for her means integrity and not flaccidity. She knows her own worth and virtue, however preeminent Adam may be. That knowledge, an intuition of her sex, requires that Adam woo her:

> She heard me thus, and though divinely brought,
> Yet Innocençe and Virgin Modesty,
> Her virtue and the conscience of her worth,
> That would be woo'd, and not unsought be won,
> Not obvious, not obtrusive, but retir'd,
> The more desirable, or to say all,
> Nature herself, though pure of sinful thought,
> Wrought in her so, that seeing me, she turn'd;
> I follow'd her, she what was Honor knew,
> And with obsequious Majesty approv'd
> My pleaded reason.
>   (viii.500–510)

Now, we know from Eve's own account in Book iv that she turns from Adam because she thinks he is "less fair" than she. Adam, on the other hand, imputes to her motives a good deal more complex. It is obvious, in the light of what Adam says, that Eve has not told all. The reason is that she imperfectly understands her own motives. She responds only to the current of nature in her. This is not to say that her "innocence" is childish naivete but that her "Honor" is unmeditated: it is a given constant of her character as woman.

Milton's use of the word *honor* seems especially significant when one recalls another description of Adam and Eve: "O when meet now / Such pairs, in Love and mutual Honor join'd?" (VIII.57-58). The phrase "mutual Honor" can be adequately paraphrased "mutual respect and dignity." But I suspect that Milton's meaning goes deeper. Here the sense is akin to the Renaissance commonplace of magnanimity, an idea which held that a right love of oneself is the spur to all good action.[62] It testifies to the constancy of one's commitment to the highest ideal of personal conduct. For Milton, Eve's sense of her own honor and the mutual honor of her union with Adam are celebrations of personal integrity founded both in the law of Nature and the law of God. Honor, therefore, is the expositor of self-knowledge or self-love in the service of God. As a factor in marriage, it expresses nobility of soul, the common denominator that reduces difference to likeness and ends in a *concordia discors,* a union in one flesh.

Eve's subordination, in which her "honor" is part, is thus not so much a denial of her own will as an exchange with Adam's. In submission she fulfills the order of nature. To love is an act of the will (v.539). In giving her own will to Adam she accepts the condition that frees her to become fully woman. Obedience is freedom to be what one is by nature. Disobedience separates from the ordering principle; it disables the will and denies the capacity to love. It ends in sterility and isolation. Raphael, in fact, tells Adam that there is no happiness without love (VIII.621). To love God is to obey him (VIII.634), for love is Reason. Eve, in turn, loves Adam by obeying him, which is the way to her own happiness. The love between our first parents is therefore the image of divine order—"Where faith and realty / Remain" (VI.115)—and the prescription whereby man and woman claim each other in one unity as the two great sexes in creative harmony.

The union of Adam and Eve, as I have already noted, promises the issue of "multitudes." Love, divinely sanctioned, expresses fecundity, and fecundity in turn asserts grace. Striking corroboration of this theme may be found in Milton's classical allusions to describe the operations of love. Adam addresses Eve after their night in the nuptial bower with a "voice / Mild, as when *Zephyrus* on *Flora* breathes" (v.15-16). The comparison is thoroughly conventional: one remembers Chaucer's

> . . . Zepherus and Flora gentilly
> Yaf to the floures, softe and tenderly,
> Hire swoote breth, and made him for to sprede,
> As god and goddesse of the floury mede;
> (*The Legend of Good Women,* F.171-174)

or thinks of Jonson's masque *The Vision of Delight,* where

> In curious knots and mazes so,
> The Spring at first was taught to go;
> And *Zephire*, when he came to wooe
> His *Flora*, had their motions too . . .

and knows that the classical cource is Ovid's *Fasti*. Milton's allusion, however, takes on special meaning when one notes that he links Eve not only with Flora but with the Graces, who for the Neoplatonists were a symbol of love:

> With Goddess-like demeanor forth she went;
> Not unattended, for on her as Queen
> A pomp of winning Graces waited still. . . .
>   (VIII.59-61)

Ficino is apposite in that he regarded Venus, the symbol of love, as the mediatrix between God and man: "love is the perpetual knot and link of the universe: *amor nodus perpetuus, et copula mundi*" (p. 56). Following the precedent in Spenser of linking the Graces with flowers, the symbol of fruition,[63] Milton identified the three Graces in *L'Allegro* (11-16) as the daughters of Venus. The Graces, therefore, are the symbolic attributes of Eve's power as a love goddess. In this configuration, Eve is the link between Adam and beatitude: the love she inspires is an invitation to learn what man can know of God.

In their triadic relationship of *pulchritudo-amor-voluptas*, the Graces were for the Neoplatonists the inclusive symbol of love, and their relationship as the phases of divine love shows how Love starts from Beauty and ends in Joy.[64] The characteristic grouping of the Graces displays iconographically the sequence or pattern of the love relationship: Love is in the center, looking toward Joy (often on her right), with Beauty, which Love holds by the hand as if for support, to her back and left. The Neoplatonic interpretation of this image is twofold. When Beauty descends from God to the world, Love turns her back on common things and looks toward Joy in the beyond. A second interpretation, which would have been more amenable to Milton, held that Love unites Beauty and Joy. The idea goes back to Plato, who in the *Symposium* said that "Love is Desire aroused by Beauty." Without Beauty as the innervating principle, Desire is never more than animal passion; it is never true Love. At the same time, passion is a necessary element in love if it is to be other than an abstraction. *Amor*, therefore, mediates between the contraries *Pulchritudo* and *Voluptas*. Love is the middle term of an equation that turns Beauty into Joy. Or said another way: romantic love, sanctified by Divine Reason, points the way to beatitude.

Since Milton identifies Eve with Venus, we have good authority for regarding the three Graces as descriptive of the power of love in woman. The Neoplatonic sequence seems implicit in Satan's envious praise of Eve as

> . . . fair, divinely fair, fit Love for Gods,
> Not terrible, though terror be in Love
> And beauty. . . .

Mitlon's adaptation of *voluptas* as imbued with a kind of divine terror seems peculiarly his own,[65] although there is something like it in Virgil, but entirely fitting for a poet who responded to the memory of Saul on his knees in fear and rapture. The Graces may be interpreted, therefore, as an iconographic gloss on the love Eve gives to Adam, inspired by the beauty of God in her, so that together in the joy of "nuptial league" they may return to the one source of being. Expressing the qualities of both the earthly and heavenly Venuses, Eve's love is the power that transforms Beauty into Joy and enables man to ascend to God.

Adam's devotion to Eve, whether uxorious or idolatrous, or both,[66] becomes a good deal more profound when we understand what she offers him: that is, quite simply, the experience not only of himself as a man but the experience of God, for romantic love is the sign of divine love. The love Eve offers Adam is literally the invocation of life, the inspiration to a creative union that will issue in "multitudes" (IV.474). Divinely sanctioned, their union is the symbol of fecundity, sustaining unity in number and making fertility (one of the pervasive metaphors of the epic) the embodying logic of human sexuality.

When Adam, as the god of fertility, speaks to Eve like Zephyr breathing on Flora (v.15–16), Eve is recreated under the agency of Milton's imagery as Flora, the Italian goddess of flowers, spring, and love. The relevance of the image is obvious when one remembers that Flora is the nymph Chloris transformed by the touch of Zephyr into a fruitful woman, and Botticelli's *Primavera* testifies to the idea as a Renaissance commonplace. Love, therefore, manifests itself in some pattern of fecundity that conforms roughly with the Zephyr-Chloris-Flora progression, as indeed when Adam on Eve

> . . . in delight
> Both of her Beauty and submissive Charms
> Smil'd with superior Love, as *Jupiter*

> On *Juno* smiles, when he impregns the Clouds
> That shed *May* Flowers.
>
> (IV.497–501)

The themes of love and fertility are thus linked through Milton's allusions to the Graces and to the Zephyr-Flora configuration, which together function as an expositor of a Neoplatonic metaphysic of love. When raised to its highest symbolic level, the promise of "multitudes" is the assurance of grace. In the experience of human love, Adam discovers the way to beatitude and, in the desire to procreate, the impulse to transcendence. Adam follows Eve into disobedience because he is reluctant to turn away from what God has given him as a vehicle of revelation, though he errs in confusing the vehicle with the revelation itself.

III

True potency is spiritually productive. It creates life, harmony, and love. Characteristically, Milton works a symbolic equation between the natural world and the spiritual, whereby he shows that degenerate sexuality, unlike the holy relationship between Adam and Eve, signifies the corruption of mind and soul. Spiritual degeneration, for a Christian writer, is worse of course than corporeal deterioration because only in mind lies the true essence of a human life. That is, the core of one's being—his spiritual identity—transcends its bodily manifestation. But such transcendence, however independent of time and place the Idea of a person is, does not controvert the possibilities of making physical sexuality a metaphor for spiritual realities. Thus, Satan's disruption of heavenly order graduates down into perversions of natural fertility and acts as a dramatic foil to the pure love between Adam and Eve.

When Satan and the fallen third of heaven's host deny God, they reject in that choice the creative power which derives from the one source of life. Their act of separation begins a process of spiritual deterioration that ends in illusion and impotency. Milton records that movement away from divine essence and spiritual power in images of degenerated generation. They are, in consequence, Milton's controlling metaphors for describing the reductive agency of evil.

As the chief image of evil in *Paradise Lost,* perverted sexuality explains why Milton characteristically transformed the womb of life into the womb of death and made evil the process of creation reversed.[67] Milton makes the terms of the contrast between Hell and Heaven unmistakable. The infernal regions are

> A Universe of Death, which God by curse
> Created evil, for evil only good,
> Where all life dies, death lives, and Nature breeds,
> Perverse, all monstrous, all prodigious things,
> Abominable, inutterable, and worse
> Than Fables yet have feing'd or fear conceiv'd,
> *Gorgons* and *Hydras,* and *Chimeras* dire.
>   (ii.622–628)

Separated from God all births are monstrous, and the universe of the fallen angels is a metaphor for their own spiritual deformity. Birth ceases to be a celebration of joyful union and becomes instead the testament of evil recoiling on itself, constricting body and soul into "inutterable" nightmare.

Milton's account of the fall of man and the consequences of that first sin focuses sharply on the illusory properties of evil. As the climactic action of *Paradise Lost,* it levies heavily on sexual motifs and draws a contrasting parallel to the true eroticism and love that exist between Adam and Eve in unfallen Eden. Satan's performance before Eve suggests an obvious phallicism:

> So spake the Enemy of Mankind, enclos'd
> In Serpent, Inmate bad, and toward *Eve*
> Address'd his way, not with indented wave,
> Prone on the ground, as since, but on his rear,
> Circular base of rising folds, that tow'r'd
> Fold above fold a surging Maze, his Head
> Crested aloft, and Carbuncle his Eyes;
> With burnisht Neck of verdant Gold, erect
> Amidst his circling Spires, that on the grass
> Floated redundant: pleasing was his shape,
> And lovely, never since of Serpent kind
> Lovelier, not those that in *Illyria* chang'd
> *Hermione* and *Cadmus,* or the God
> In *Epidaurus;* nor to which transform'd
> *Ammonian Jove,* or *Capitoline* was seen,
> Hee with *Olympias,* this with her who bore
> *Scipio* the highth of *Rome.* With tract oblique
> At first, as one who sought access, but fear'd
> To interrupt, side-long he works his way.
> As when a Ship by skilful Steersman wrought
> Nigh River's mouth or Foreland, where the Wind

Veers oft, as oft so steers, and shifts her Sail;
So varied hee, and of his tortuous Train
Curl'd many a wanton wreath in sight of *Eve*,
To lure her Eye; shee busied heard the sound
Of rustling Leaves, but minded not, as us'd
To such desport before her through the Field,
From every Beast, more duteous at her call,
Than at *Circean* call the Herd disguis'd.
Hee bolder now, uncall'd before her stood;
But as in gaze admiring: Oft he bow'd
His turret Crest, and sleek enamell'd Neck,
Fawning, and lick'd the ground whereon she trod.
                                        (IX.494–526)

The dance is lascivious, and Milton's imagery commands what amounts almost to prurient inspection. We are, after all, watching the seduction of mankind.

The phallic implications of the serpent image require no Freudian prejudices. Merritt Hughes notes that Edward Topsell's *Historie of Serpents* (1608) cites four sources for the story that Olympias was beloved by Jupiter Ammon in the form of a serpent and that Scipio's mother was similarly loved by the Capitoline Jupiter.[68] Kester Svendsen also finds that Camerarius' encyclopedic *The Living Librarie* (1595) provides in a single work most of Milton's allusions and supplies the inference of sexual sin.[69] It seems unlikely, then, that Milton could have been ignorant of the phallic suggestions of the serpent figure. If his own poetry does not convince us, the force of allusion and contemporary natural history certainly ends all doubt.

While it is true, as Professor Cope says, that "when sexuality enters the poem, it enters as Sin," it is misleading to say that the chief image of evil is "the choice of sexuality."[70] Sexuality is evil not of itself but when it is made so by wrong use. God Himself is the ultimate symbol of creative sexuality, Reason is the image of true fertility, and human love is the copy of divine love. Phallicism is therefore not an ugly concupiscence but the figure of generative power, grounded in Natural Law and sanctified by the Divine Will. It is a fact of biological life and metaphysically the symbol of creating power. Conversely, Satan is the perversion of true phallicism. He denies the source of all good and rejects the power that sustains life. In the image of a serpent, he is ironically the figure of precisely what he is not.

It is true that the serpent has often been a symbol of evil, especially in the Hebraic tradition. But Milton could have learned that the serpent was a symbol of life and therefore of good from Plutarch's essay "Isis and Osiris," one of the books of the *Moralia*.[71] Spenser, too, used the myth in the Isis Church episode of *The Faerie Queene* (v.viii).[72] Plutarch, in fact, regards the Egyptian use of symbols as a means of "guiding the intelligence toward things divine" (p. 157); and all that was required of Milton's imagination was to make the obvious association of serpent with phallus.[73] According to one of the traditions Plutarch traces, the jealous Typhon killed Osiris (born of the Sun and consort of Isis), cut his body into fourteen pieces, and scattered them throughout Egypt. When Isis learned of Osiris' dismemberment, she sought out the fragments of his body and held a funeral for each part when she found it. The only part Isis did not find was the male member and, in consequence, "made a replica of the member to take its place, and consecrated the phallus, in honour of which the Egyptians even at the present day celebrate a festival" (p. 47). When they celebrate the festival, Plutarch continues, the Egyptians "expose and carry about a statue of which the male member is triple; for the god is the Source, and every source, by its fecundity, multiplies what proceeds from it" (p. 89). The phallus is triple because of "the nature of moisture, [which] being the source and origin of all things, created out of itself three primal material substances, Earth, Air, and Fire" (p. 89). The significance of this legend, Plutarch says, "plainly comes round to this doctrine, that the creative and germinal power of the god, at the very first, acquired moisture as its substance, and through moisture combined with whatever was by nature capable of participating in generation" (p. 89). Plutarch adds that Osiris is symbolically represented by the rush that grows on the banks of the Nile. He interprets it "to mean the watering and fructifying of all things, and in its nature it seems to bear some resemblance to the generative member" (p. 87). Thus, the Egyptians regularly identified Osiris with phallic images and clothed his statues "in a flame-coloured garment, since they regard the body of the Sun as a visible manifestation of the perceptible substance of the power for good" (p. 125).

Plutarch's account, which is a good deal more elaborate than my summary, establishes symbolic valences that extend phallic imagery into numerous categories other than simple fertility, into, that is, the areas of cosmology, ontology, and ethics. For example, Osiris, when opposed to Typhon, is the principle of good. Typhon, as the symbol of evil, emasculates. He destroys life and perverts phallic power.

Osiris, as a male god, polarizes Isis, whom Plutarch names exactly "the female principle of Nature" (p. 129). Osiris stands in the same relationship to Isis as the Sun to the Moon: "for this reason it is said that the statues of Isis that bear horns are imitations of the crescent moon, and in her dark garments are shown the concealments and the obscurations in which she in her yearning pursues the Sun" (p. 129). Isis receives every form of generation, "because of the force of Reason [that is, Osiris]" and innately yearns for and pursues "the first and most dominant of all things, which is identical with the good" (p. 129). She rejoices in pregnancy fostered by Osiris and takes pleasure in the teeming "effluxes and likenesses" within her (p. 131). The meaning of these symbolic equations is that the creative property of Nature moves toward Osiris, "toward existence while the annihilating and destructive moves away from him towards non-existence" (p. 143). In short, the wisdom of this mythology—worthy of our reverence and honor, says Plutarch—is that Isis is the symbol of "what is orderly and good and beneficial" because she is "the image and reflection and reason of Osiris" (p. 151). One could hardly find a better statement of Milton's understanding of true phallicism.

Against this background, Satan's imbrutement takes on both philosophical and iconographic meaning. The serpent, red, gold, and green, is erect, rising from a base of circular folds. He approaches with "tract oblique . . . as one who sought access." He is like a ship coming into the mouth of a river, and one remembers with a difference Cassio's lines to Montano in *Othello:*

> . . . Great Jove, Othello guard,
> And swell his sail with thine own pow'rful breath,
> That he may bless this bay with his tall ship,
> Make love's quick pants in Desdemona's arms,
> Give renew'd fire to our extincted spirits,
> And bring all Cyprus comfort!
>
> (II.i.77–82)

Curling in "a wanton wreath," the serpent finally attracts Eve's attention by what is plainly a display of his physical beauty. He is doubtless a splendid creature holding his tail in his mouth and turning loops. The symbolism of the Ouroboros serpent clearly shows the uterine and phallic aspects of sexual union and implies very strongly the subliminal working of Eve's seduction.[74] As ithyphallic serpent, Satan seeks to evoke in Eve a response that is natural to her sex.[75]

Satan, of course, is metaphysically impotent, a hideous imposture. However dazzling, he is no more than a simulacrum of what is truly phallic, of what is biologically and spiritually creative. He violates the sanctity of love, perverts reason and order, and works his own annihilation. Like Comus' invitation to *luxuria,* Satan's "fradulent temptation"—dressed in the garb of Reason—is quite simply an invitation to insanity.

The imagery of sterility and decay dominates, in turn, the description of the infernal angels. They lie on the Stygian Lake "thick as Autumnal Leaves" (I.302), the issue of "frozen loins" (I.352), unnatural and destructive. Love gives way to lust and hate (I.412-417), and the procession of fallen angels is a virtual catalogue of sexual perversions. Baalim and Ashtaroth, symbols of male and female turned to enmity, prefigure the eternal discord of men and women unfulfilled by "works of love" (I.431). Astarte, whom Milton would have known from scriptural references,[76] represents a false goddess of love with powers to betray even Solomon into idolatry.

> . . . With these in troop
> Came *Astoreth*, whom the *Phoenicians* call'd
> *Astarte*, Queen of Heav'n, with crescent Horns;
> To whose bright Image nightly by the Moon
> *Sidonian* Virgins paid thir Vows and Songs,
> In *Sion* also not unsung, where stood
> Her Temple on th' offensive Mountain, built
> By that uxorious King, whose heart though large,
> Beguil'd by fair Idolatresses, fell
> To Idols foul.
>
> (I.437-446)

This passage adumbrates Adam's own erring worship of Eve and implies that every woman is potentially a love goddess whose power over man makes her dangerous in the extreme. She can usurp the authority of Reason vested in man, which once displaced by Passion can lead both man and woman away from each other as well as away from God.

Denied the control of Reason, the "wanton passion" of women may also transform a "love-tale" into heat and idolatrous infection. Like the women on the plain whose amorous ditties pleased Adam, Thammuz's

> . . . annual wound in *Lebanon* allur'd
> The *Syrian* Damsels to lament his fate
> In amorous ditties all a Summer's day,
> (I.447-449)

and as the "smooth *Adonis*," whom Saint Jerome identified with Thammus,[77] he inspires the women of "alienated Judah" to weep in "dark Idolatries."

Last in the procession of rebel angels is Belial: "Than whom a Spirit more lewd / Fell not from Heaven, or more gross to love / Vice for itself" (I.490-491). Though there are no pagan temples erected in his honor, the Sons of Belial are more numerous than all the others and fill "with lust and violence the house of God" (I.496). Recalling the sin of sodomy, Milton makes the Sons of Belial a symbol of radical evil. They stand for an extreme distortion of natural sexuality and for the conclusive reduction of self. As sexual metaphor, they invert the natural order of generation, deny its impulse to transcendence, and become the cipher that works the disintegration of true potency.

The procession of fallen angels is thus dominated by images of perverted sex. Professor J. B. Broadbent even sees the sexual element in Dagon's lopping off his head and hands (1.457-462) as a "perverted form of brutal sadism. . . ." Some readers may think that he goes too far when he identifies "the potent Rod" of Moses (1.338) and the banner of Azazel (1.535-536) as obvious "phallic emblems."[78] But his idea is suggestive, especially when one remembers the magical power of Comus' wand, glossed by such conventional configurations (learned from Ovid's *Fasti*) as Chaucer uses in *The Parliament of Fowles* to describe Priapus holding his scepter. Moreover, against Azazel's standard "unfurl'd" and "full high advanc't," one could see the "millions of flaming swords, drawn from the thighs / Of mighty Cherubim" (1.664-665) as a phallic parody and ironic salute to impotence. Our good sense, however, tends to boggle at such subtleties, and it is certainly enough to be aware that the controlling metaphor is a distortion of the sexuality Milton accepts as good and symbolizes in the creative love between Adam and Eve.

The allegorical figures of Sin and Death guarding the Gates of Hell are hideous travesties of divine fertility. As the monstrous issue of incestuous intercourse between Satan and his own daughter, they symbolize the final horror of man alienated from God:

> Before the Gates there sat
> On either side a formidable shape;
> The one seem'd Woman to the waist, and fair,
> But ended foul in many a scaly fold
> Voluminous and vast, a Serpent arm'd
> With mortal sting: about her middle round
> A cry of Hell Hounds never ceasing bark'd
> With wide *Cerberean* mouths full loud, and rung
> A hideous Peal: yet, when they list, would creep,
> If aught disturb'd thir noise, into her womb,
> And kennel there, yet there still bark'd and howl'd
> Within unseen. . . .
>
> . . . The other shape,
> If shape it might be call'd that shape had none
> Distinguishable in member, joint, or limb

> Or substance might be call'd that shadow seem'd,
> For each seem'd either; black it stood as Night,
> Fierce as ten Furies, terrible as Hell,
> And shook a dreadful Dart; what seem'd his head
> The likeness of a Kingly Crown had on.
>   (II.648-659; 666-673)

Satan, Sin, and Death are, of course, a parody of the Holy Trinity; but, more than that, Satan and Sin are parallel figures to Adam and Eve. Our vision of evil (Book II) gives point and drama to the vision of good to follow (Book IV), and for this reason we see the image of lust and its issue displayed before we encounter the harmonious love of our first parents in Eden. The epic formula makes it possible for Milton to engineer an ironic tension between the symbols of love denied, worse than anything in ordinary experience, and the symbols of love fulfilled, more exquisitely good than anything in human experience. Thus, when we see Adam and Eve a loving pair together, we know that they are at the polar extreme from what they may become through disobedience, making, in consequence, the threat of Satan's seduction all the more frightening.

The progression of images in Milton's description of Sin reveals a deep psychological insight into the nature of evil. Whereas Sin at the outset is "fair," symbolically a beautiful woman inducing us to pleasure, it ends in a "foul" treachery: within the scaly folds of the lower half of Sin's body, there lies a "mortal sting." And the metaphor for accomplished evil is the howling desperation of cowardly dogs, fathered by her incestuous union with Death.

The symbolism of sexual insantiy is crucial to Milton's conception of the infernal trinity. Though Satan is first repulsed by the image of his own evil—the first issue of alienation—he is pleased when he grows more familiar. Inflamed with lust, he takes her in secret with "such joy" that her "womb conceiv'd / A growing burden . . ." (II.761-767). The distortion of Sin's "nether" parts is, in fact, the result of having given birth to Death:

> . . . Pensive here I sat
> Alone, but long I sat not, till my womb
> Pregnant by thee, and now excessive grown
> Prodigious motion felt and rueful throes.
> At last this odious offspring whom thou seest
> Thine own begotten, breaking violent way
> Tore through my entrails, that with fear and pain
> Distorted, all my nether shape thus grew
> Transform'd. . . .
>   (II.777-785)

This transformation and imbrutement are the signs of incarnate evil, the outward manifestations of inner and spiritual deformity.

The symbolic technique operating here is basic to Milton's poetic, and he explained it early in his career. Thyrsis, the Attendant Spirit in *Comus*, leads his audience into the action of the mask by telling how the enchanter's potion works to change the "human count'nance, / Th' express resemblance of the gods, . . . Into some brutish form . . ." (68–70). The effect of evil is to create illusion, whereby the transformed men do "Not once perceive their foul disfigurement" (74). The act of sin, as the Elder Brother says,

> Lets in defilement to the inward parts,
> The soul grows clotted by contagion,
> Imbodies and imbrutes, till she quite lose
> The divine property of her first being.
> (466–469)

The meaning of Milton's "grotesques" is unmistakable in the light of these lines: his antic rout symbolizes a degenerate condition of the soul and shows men deceived into a confusion of the senses whereby they are unable to distinguish between appearance and reality. Using the same technique, Milton builds into the allegorical figure of Sin a prolepsis that anticipates Satan's final emasculation in the ironic figure of a hissing serpent.

The chaos of sexual riot and excess that dominates the last third of Book II can hardly be overlooked. Generation goes mad, and its progeny, Death, pursues his mother "more, it seems, / Inflam'd with lust than rage" (II.790–791). Incest on incest, the rape issues in "yelling Monsters" that are "hourly conceiv'd / And hourly born," hell hounds who feed howling and gnawing on the bowels from whence they sprang (II.796–801). Analogous (but with a polar difference) to the human spirit ravaged by the love of God, Sin initiates an agonizing rape of its own evil genius which fosters its own anguish, evil compounding evil.

The pleasure God takes in his creation contrasts diametrically with Satan's pleasure in Sin. God works through love instead of lust and initiates life instead of death. One celebrates union, the other alienation. Sexual lust as the operative metaphor of evil emphasizes the self-defeating nature of diseased Passion overriding Reason: the act of coition (that is, symbolic oneness) recoils on itself, fractures the sensibility, and degenerates into radical denial.

The pattern of Satan's sin parallels almost exactly Eve's disobedience. Conceived in pride, the lust for power generates the capacity for all sins.

Superficially, Satan is like Eve in his narcisistic love of his own image: as Sin reports, "full oft / Thyself in me thy perfect image viewing / Becam'st enamor'd . . ." (II.763-765). But his is the parodic worship of an evil that fosters only greater evil and leads away from God, whereas Eve's is the contemplation—at first narcissistic—of the perfection of her sex, which teaches her to know her own worth and in that virtue to receive best the love of God in Adam. Eve as symbolic Earth opens to receive the impregnating rays of the Sun. Like God, Adam initiates; like Christ, Eve receives and creates, in the promise of birth giving in return the love she has accepted. Satan, on the other hand, denies the gift of being symbolized in procreative love and generates nothing but his own dissolution. The words of Saint James (1:15) are Milton's authority: "When lust hath conceived, it bringeth forth sin: and sin, when it is finished bringeth forth death."

The feeding of the Cerberean mouths on the entrails of Sin has a signification that links with other images of evil in *Paradise Lost*. Emblematically, gluttonous eating is typically identified with the persons of the infernal trinity and thus contrasts with the temperate eating in the paradisal garden. Satan assures Sin and Death that once he has seduced mankind from the "dear pledge of their obedience" the progeny of evil "shall be fed and fill'd / Immeasurably, all things shall be your prey" (II.843-844). The insatiable appetite of Sin and Death contrasts, of course, with the temperate banquet Eve spreads before the convivial angel Raphael.[79] But the identification of eating with evil is implied in the euphoric drunkenness which assaults Adam and Eve after eating the forbidden apple. Its extension leads to lust as inordinate desire made concrete in the image of a lascivious sensuality. The eating-lust-evil configuration is therefore a symbolic paradigm of ungoverned appetite and represents the progressive stages of vain empires hatched in darkness (II.377-378).

This symbolic context also makes the coordinate image of Satan as a bird of prey the more appropriate. Walking on the outer orb of the world, Satan is likened to a vulture (III.431) ready "To stoop with wearied wings, and willing feet / On the bare outside of this World" (III.72-73). As Professor Hughes has noted, the word *stoop* in this passage means "to pounce like a hawk."[80] It marks again Satan's opposition to what is creative in God, who

> . . . with mighty wings outspread
> Dove-like satst brooding on the vast Abyss
> And mad'st it pregnant.
>
> (I.20-22)

Dove contrasts with Vulture; the descent of fertile love, with the attack of destructive hate: "*Satan,* now first inflam'd with rage, came down" (IV.9).

The thought of human love, grounded in obedience to God, is intolerable to Satan. Adam's words to Eve summarize his motives precisely: the arch fiend designs to withdraw their "fealty from God, or to disturb / Conjugal Love," a bliss than which nothing else "excites his envy more" (IX.261–264). Only in destroying does he find ease from his "relentless thoughts" (IX.129–130). As a self-abased voyeur, Satan retreats from the sight of Adam and Eve making love in the Garden of Eden. Though stricken with remorse, he, like Judas, cannot bend to contrition and acceptance. His resolution "to do what else though damn'd I should abhor" (IV.392) confirms him in ultimate paralysis.

That paralysis comes in the form of physical and psychological imbrutement. Having recounted to the infernal host his seduction of mankind and having boasted "A world who would not purchase with a bruise" (x.500), Satan stands and expects to hear

> Thir universal shout and high applause
> To fill his ear, when contrary he hears
> On all sides, from innumerable tongues
> A dismal universal hiss, the sound
> Of public scorn; he wonder'd, but not long
> Had leisure, wond'ring at himself now more;
> His Visage drawn he felt to sharp and spare,
> His Arms clung to his Ribs, his Leg entwining
> Each other, till supplanted down he fell
> A monstrous Serpent on his Belly prone. . . .
> (x.505–514)

The climax of Satan's defeat turns, therefore, on the ironic inversion of a phallacism emblematic of life. He and his accessories roll in serpentine "heaps"

> . . . and up the Trees
> Climbing, sat thicker than the snaky locks
> That curl'd *Megaera:* greedily they pluck'd
> The Fruitage fair to sight, like that which grew
> Near that bituminous Lake where *Sodom* flam'd;
> This more delusive, not the touch, but taste
> Deceiv'd; they fondly thinking to allay
> Thir appetite with gust, instead of Fruit
> Chew'd bitter Ashes, which th' offended taste
> With spattering noise rejected. . . .
> (x.558–567)

The symbolic "bitter Ashes" signify death and are corroborated by two allusions (to Megaera and Sodom) which enforce the motif of perverted sexuality.

Of the first, Milton could have drawn his image of Megaera from the avenging goddess in the chorus of Aeschylus' *Eumenides*. That Milton chose to mention Megaera rather than either of the other two Furies is significant because the name means "envious anger." All three, according to the *Choephori* of Aeschylus, were bitches, like Hecate, who sounded their approach by barking; and in the Greek drama, they appear most often in pursuit of one who has flouted blood-kinship and filial duty. As usual, when one looks closely at Milton's classical allusions, the reference turns out to be more than learned display because it shows Milton's poetic rendering of an existential situation. The fallen angels are appropriately trapped in the image of their own persecutor, whereby they are at once both the tormentor and the tormented, caught in inescapable anger and ingratitude. But there is a characteristic Christian meaning, for instead of learning from their humiliation the remorse that could lead to repentence, the infernal legions suffer the paralysis of spirit and sense that cannot distinguish fruit from ash. Milton's adding to the figure of Megaera the detail of her "snaky locks," like Medusa's, works a variation on the parodic phallicism that distinguishes the fallen angels. Unlike the serpent that Moses lifted up in the wilderness to signify his recognition of the generative mode of the Holy Spirit, Megaera's "snaky locks" show us the devils entwined in confusion, deprived of the Life Principle, emasculated, and reduced to impotency.

Milton's second allusion (to Sodom) adds to the pattern of sexual symbolism built into the allusion to Megaera's "snaky locks." As I have already observed in Milton's description of Belial, Sodom and the men of Sodom are among Milton's major images of sterility and radical evil. Why the basic image suggested itself to Milton may be seen in Josephus' story of Sodom, once a blessed region but destroyed by fire for impiety.[81] There one sees "ashes reproduced in the fruits, which from their outward appearance would be thought edible, but on being plucked by the hand dissolve into smoke and ashes" (*Jewish War*,IV.484). Milton makes good, moreover, Christ's warning that those who reject the truth of God will suffer a fate worse than that of Sodom and Gomorrha.[82] A sexual meaning develops when we remember Milton's association of Sodom with the place of "worse rape" (I.505), and his opposing chastity to "all kinds of impurity; effeminacy, sodomy, bestiality, &c. which are offences against ourselves in the first instance, and tending to our own especial injury" (*CD*,XVII.219). Milton's emphasis on perverted sex in *Paradise Lost*, for poetic reasons, is

significant because the word *sodomy* was generally applied in Elizabethan
English to intercourse between unmarried men and women as well as to
that between members of the same sex or with beasts.[83] The strategy of
this imagery in *Paradise Lost* is to compound the figure of sexual absurdity, whereby lust disfigures both body and soul. Milton doubtless understood the irony of associating the debased angels with the men of Sodom:
the Hebrew word for *sodomite* (from *kadash*) means literally *sacred*. But
Milton did not have to invent the irony of contrasting holy things with
unholy, since the incongruity was already made for him in Old Testament
history. As religious prostitutes, sodomites (the term does not have any
necessary relation to the city of Sodom) represented a Hebrew fertility
cult which practiced a debased form of phallic worship under the guise of
celebrating the generative power of God.[84] Against this background, one
detects Milton's characteristic parody of infernal sexuality, and senses in
the leitmotif a distortion of God's life-giving power into unholy perversion.
The suggestiveness of Milton's allusion, coupled with that to Megaera,
illustrates in fine how thoroughly alive Milton was to symbolic statement.

The purchase of evil for Milton is thus the denial of manhood, theologically the rejection of being. Its metaphor is the illusion of potency. Nor
could it have been otherwise if perverted sexuality was to be, as Professor
Cope says, "the only possible symbol for the jealousy of the Creator which
hurtled Satan downward."[85]

IV

Whereas Adam's failure during the temptation is discretional, Eve's is
wholly physical, tied by nature to the female imperatives of her body. She
is less guilty than Adam because the sins of the flesh are less culpable than
those of the spirit. The complex of Milton's sexual symbolism is at work
here. As microcosmic man, Adam and Eve are bifurcations of a corporate
whole and in consequence differentiate the three operations of a human
soul.[86] Each of the three parts—vegetable, sensitive, and rational—has a
sexual valence. Adam stands in analogous relation to the rational soul,
while Eve expresses the lower relationships of the sensitive and vegetable.
Eve is hungry and she thinks the apple pretty; she is deceived because she
does not "understand" (that is, intuit the higher wisdom of) the divine
injunction and is incapable of detecting logical fallacies. But working
within this context, the idea of Man, with a single, symbolic soul, allows
Milton, however Adam and Eve are distinguished as personalities, to
integrate the psychology of masculine and feminine souls into a philosoph-

ical unity. The method does not work against the human interest we have
in our first parents but allows instead for the possibilities of complex
metaphor. Milton, of course, does not think that women are incapable of
reason any more so than Donne does when he distinguishes between
man's love and woman's love in *Aire and Angells.* The point is simply that
there is a difference, however subtle, in the way men and women love
each other and in the way they think. Both poets transcend the platitudi-
nous and redeem the commonplace by making it relevant to the psychology of their lovers. Unlike Donne, Milton is less direct and does not
announce his *topos* but assumes it as a referent his "fit" readers will use as
a matter of course. Eve is deceived by the Serpent because she does not
fully understand the injunction not to take of the forbidden fruit. She has
been told, to be sure, not to eat of the Tree of Knowledge and thus
"knows" what she is and is not to do, but true knowledge in the Miltonic
scheme implies moral understanding that sees conduct in terms of consequences. Eve's female nature evidently mitigates against her "knowing" if
Adam's special charge to "guide" her is to have any significant meaning.
Like the Reason which is to govern the Desires and Passions, Adam is the
sovereign power that is to direct Eve's winsome vagaries. Together, they
are an unbeatable couple, and Satan says so. Separated, the "lif and feling
and nat resoun" (as Trevisa would put it) that is Eve's portion may be
successfully attacked. Once corrupted, the "lif and feling" that underpins
the strength of Adam's "resoun" weakens the crown of his soul, and thus
made vulnerable, he completes the original sin.

Sir Kenelm Digby's *Observations of the 22. "Stanza" in the 9th Canto
of the 2D. Book of Spencers Faery Queene* (probably written in 1628;
revised and published in 1643) lends authority to Milton's technique of
making abstract ideas concrete. Spenser's intention in the second canto,
Digby says, "is to describe the bodie of a man inform'd with a rational
soul . . ." and in stanza 22 to show how body and soul are "joyned together
to frame a compleat Man . . ." and thus make "one perfect compound. . . ." The stanza is particularly interesting for its use of sexual
symbolism in lines four and five:

> The Frame thereof seem'd partly Circular,
> And part Triangular: O work divine!
> Those two the first and last proportions are;
> The one, imperfect, mortall, feminine;
> Th' other immortal, perfect, masculine.
> And twixt them both a Quadrate was the Base
> Proportion'd equally by seven and nine;
> Nine was the Circle set in Heavens place,

           All which compacted made a goodly Diapase.

Taken "all together, Man is a little world, an exact type of the great world, and of God himself."

Commenting on the feminine and masculine properties of the body and soul, Digby says that the body "of it self alone . . . can do nothing." The body, moreover, if it is ever "deprived of the form which actuates it . . ." is "liable to corruption and dissolution. . . ." Conforming to a long literary tradition, the soul and body act as analogous male and female principles. Milton, who had easy access to this equation, simply extended the logic of the metaphor and assigned to Adam and Eve the respective qualities of a masculine and feminine symbolism. According to Digby, "as the feminine Sex is imperfect, and receives perfection from the masculine: so doth the Body from the Soul, which to it is in lieu of a male." "Corprall generations" (that is, propagation) correspond to "spiritual generation" (that is, the operations of the mind). Therein is the "mutuall appetence between the Male and the Female, between matter and forme" and likewise between "the bodie and soul of Man. . . ."

Like Spenser (but more successfully), Milton creates characters that engage our imagination at a primary level, but that kind of sentience on our part is only a necessary beginning. It allows our minds the further pleasure and insight of working out all the analogies built into the metaphor, of seeing how the images of Adam and Eve explain the psychology of human difference and the possibility of harmony.

After Eve has plucked and eaten the forbidden fruit, she expects to add to herself through its agency "what wants / In Female Sex" (IX.821–822), never realizing that in that "want" lies the condition of her being. Whereas she had earlier thought herself happier than Adam because of her subordination, she now thinks that to be less than equal is servitude, "for inferior who is free?" (IX.825). Her ambition and failure to understand the nature of her female sex threatens the order of her being. Tilting at the preserving hierarchy of male and female, she soon feels instead of love the first stirring of lust. Returning to Adam, she says:

> Thee I have misst, and thought it long, depriv'd
> Thy presence, agony of love till now
> Not felt, nor shall be twice, for never more
> Mean I to try, what rash untri'd I sought,
> The pain of absence from thy sight.
>
> (IX.857–861)

Eve's thoughts are reminiscent of Donne's "dull sublunary lovers" whose love "cannot admit / Absence" because its "soul is sense" and absence "doth remove / Those things which elemented it."[87] The violence of Eve's passion ends, as C. S. Lewis said,[88] in nothing less than a resolve to murder Adam rather than suffer her own death alone and see "*Adam* wedded to another Eve" (IX.828). Thus, love has become lust and issues not in the promise of life but in the threat of death.

Adam thoroughly understands what has happened to Eve: she has been "defac't, deflow'r'd, and now to Death devote" (IX.901), the sad victim of an insidious rape. She is like one of the faded roses in the garland he has let slip from his hand. Weakened by fear, he wilfully accepts ruin:

> . . . with thee
> Certain my resolution is to Die;
> How can I live without thee, how forgo
> Thy sweet Converse and Love so dearly join'd,
> To live again in these wild Woods forlorn?
> Should God create another *Eve*, and I
> Another Rib afford, yet loss of thee
> Would never from my heart; no no, I feel
> The Link of Nature draw me: Flesh of Flesh,
> Bone of my Bone thou art, and from thy State
> Mine never shall be parted, bliss or woe.
>   (IX.906–916)

Again he rationalizes his disobedience of God's single edict:

> So forcible within my heart I feel
> The Bond of Nature draw me to my own,
> My own in thee, for what thou art is mine;
> Our State cannot be sever'd, we are one,
> One Flesh; to lose thee were to lose myself.
>   (IX.955–59)

On the face of it, Adam's sin is uxoriousness, a version of idolatry. Edwin Greenlaw identified many years ago Spenser's Bower of Bliss episode in Book II of *The Faerie Queene* as an analogue to Adam's fall. Eve is the enchantress Acrasia. Adam, like Guyon, must stand the test of temperance and assert the primacy of Reason; but unlike Guyon, he fails "because the irrational principle in his soul, inflamed by a provoking object, triumphed over temperance. . . ."[89] However one interprets Adam's fall, there are can be little doubt that Adam is in theological error, that he has deliberately chosen to follow Eve to "bliss or woe" over the commandment of God. What makes Milton's account of Adam's decision more than a rehearsal of old orthodoxy is its psychological credibility. Though obedience to God should transcend every other consideration, Adam did what most men would have done; and it is an arrogant and legalistic piety to condemn him for being less human. Milton obviously did not do so since he allows us to see what makes Adam's soul vulnerable. Eve, of course, is the instrument of his undoing, but she weakens Adam not because she is a woman but because she has been dispossessed, when she comes to tempt him, of what God had needfully given him. By acquiescing in Eve's wishes to work alone, Adam surrendered part of his authority to his helpmeet and thus opened the way to possible sin. When she returns, she is less than what she was when he sent her forth, and that corruption strikes at his own superior strength. His fall, with all its sexual overtones, is thus like the fall in every man's experience; and that quality of universality enables *Paradise Lost* to transcend its own theology.

Adam's reasons for following Eve into disobedience are, moreover, closely allied with the theology of love I have already outlined. Eve is his "other self" and insofar as he is part of Eve, Adam has already sinned. It remains for that part of himself distinct from Eve to complete the action: Nature wept at his "completing the mortal Sin / Original . . ." (IX.1003–1004). Adam's overriding passion is his fear of being left alone, without recourse to the fulfillment he has found in nuptial love: "to lose thee were to lose myself." To his mind and heart, there can be no substitute; "another *Eve*" could not repair the damage. In one sense, Adam's fall is not only a failure of right reason but a lapse of faith. He has mistaken the image of God's love for the thing itself. Raphael, of course, had already told Adam (VIII.579 ff.) that physical love was no more than that "vouch-saf'd" to animals unless it were embraced by an encompassing and higher love between like souls. But Adam, "fondly overcome with Female charm" (IX.999), does not have the strength of will sufficient to accept separation from the woman who has given him sexual identity and pointed the way to divine ecstasy. "Against his better knowledge" (IX.998), Adam perversely asserts his own self-sufficiency, in pride hoping to build out of his own flesh a love that comes only from God. Adam knows better, but the "Link of Nature" draws him on. Understandably: Adam has known God by loving Eve and that kind of learning has been significantly differ-ent from his experience of Nature and his discourse with the "sovereign Presence"; in consequence, he is reluctant to give up what God has instituted as a means of revelation, though the vessel has become unclean. One of the ironies of his existence (and ours) is to believe that what Adam thinks he feels along the nerves has its own integrity, whereas in truth it is given him by the Reason. In accepting Eve's sin as his own, Adam strives to preserve his own being, doomed though the effort is from the start. As we would say in our modern idiom, he resists the threat of isolation and

the collapse of his ego. But ironically, to pursue fallen Eve is to rush into
his own destruction.

The effect of the forbidden fruit on Adam and Eve is far otherwise than
the flight to divinity they feel capable of in their first intoxication:

> Carnal desire inflaming, hee on *Eve*
> Began to cast lascivious Eyes, she him
> As wantonly repaid; in Lust they burn:
> Till *Adam* thus 'gan *Eve* to dalliance move.
> (ix.1013–1016)

As Denis Saurat observed, "the first consequent of the Fall is sensuality. . . ."[90] In this, Milton is evidently following Saint Augustine: "They felt
a new motion in their flesh, which had become rebellious as a consequent
of their own rebellion. . . . Then it was that the flesh began to covet
against the spirit. . . . The motion of concupiscence is the consequence of
Sin."[91] The loss of love is the measure of the defeat of Reason. Physical
love, once an act of sanctity, is transformed into naked lust:

> . . . never did thy Beauty since the day
> I saw thee first and wedded thee, adorn'd
> With all perfections, so inflame my sense
> With ardor to enjoy thee, fairer now
> Than ever, bounty of this virtuous Tree.
> (ix.1029–1033)

In this riot of delusion, Adam does not yet realize that venereal desire has
obliterated his intellect. The joy he anticipates marks not the triumph of
the senses but the defeat of pleasure:[92]

> There they thir fill of Love and Love's disport
> Took largely, of thir mutual guilt the Seal,
> The solace of thir sin, till dewy sleep
> Oppress'd them, wearied with thir amorous play.
> (ix.1042–1045)

Unnatural fumes exhaling from the ingested fruit make their sleep "gross."
What was once pure is now diseased. And they awake "as from unrest,"
their minds darkened. Concupiscence has led them into dishonor, where
they are destitute of virtue. Unlike the "native Honor" they had enjoyed
before, their nakedness is now unbearable, but ironically their robes testify
to their shame and guilt. The union that was in love has given place to
isolation in lust. Each is trapped in the solitude of his own flesh. Their
coverings symbolize their withdrawal from each other, for they cannot
endure the distinctions. Though their bodies have remained the same, the

sign of "foul concupiscence" is written in their faces, in contrast to the love that was in their looks before. Sexual difference has not been abolished but set against itself; and instead of augmenting what is divine, it has now become self-denigrating, wherein the blessing of God is transformed into his burden.

The sad pass to which Adam and Eve have come is that each no longer exists for the other except as an object of narcissistic self-gratification, which ironically does not satisfy but frustrates. It is Eve's lesson at her pool played over, and more: Eve had provided unfallen Adam with a vision of beatitude and a glimpse into the Divine, but in their fallen natures they are spiritual impediments for each other. There is nothing in their corrupt relationship which can invoke God, and the creative joy they had found in their first "nuptial league" has degenerated into a hideous parody: "Love was not in thir looks, either to God / Or to each other . . ." (x.111–112). Sin, therefore, has violated love and impaired the capacity of our first parents to become one flesh. It has isolated them in personal guilt and denied them freedom from their own passions. To the extent that they are not free, they are diminished human beings, neither fully man nor fully woman.

It is entirely possible to say, as some have, that Adam and Eve become human only after the Fall. The idea of the Foutunate Fall is obviously cogent, though it may incorporate—perhaps unwittingly—a Pelagianism Milton would have resisted. What it means to be human needs clarification. On the one hand, we may argue that if we are human now, then prelapsarian man must have been something more than human. It follows that the knowledge, that is, experience, of evil is the single condition of being human. To be human is to be racked with lust as well as inspired with love. To this, there can hardly be any gainsaying. But on the other hand (and here we come to what I think Milton's point is), to be fully human is to be fully the *image* of God. And the image of God in man is the faculty of Reason empowered to embrace all that is good, everything from sexual intercourse to divine contemplation. As the hieroglyph of God, man is the image of perfect order in body and spirit. This, in turn, is the condition of our most exquisite pleasures. Anything less is a falling away from Reason and hence a falling away from manhood.

When Christ comes to judge the fallen pair, Adam pleads that whatever Eve did "seem'd to justify the deed" (x.142) and that he followed her into disobedience suspecting no ill from her hand. Adam, of course, has stooped to subtle duplicity. When he chose Eve instead of God, he did so not because he thought her judgment superior but because he was unwilling to give up conjugal love. Because sin has separated him from God, he, like Satan, has degenerated and his ability to tell the truth correspondingly diminished. Originally, he sinned with Eve out of a mistaken sense of honor; now, before Christ, he confesses her part in the crime because he fears that both "sin and punishment" will devolve to him. There is no reason to impute to Adam higher motives than Eve's when she, after eating the forbidden fruit, determines to murder her husband, if, after all, death is in disobedience. Nor has Adam learned not to flee God. That Adam's judgment is impaired is clearly shown in his assessment of the women on the plain, a troop of seeming goddesses who, "richly gay / In Gems and wanton dress," singing "amorous Ditties" and dancing to their harps, seduce the sons of Seth:

> . . . in the amorous Net
> Fast caught, they lik'd, and each his liking chose;
> And now of love they treat till th' Ev'ning Star
> Love's Harbinger appear'd; then all in heat
> They light the Nuptial Torch, and bid invoke
> *Hymen*, then first to marriage Rites invok't. . . .
>   (XI.586–591)

Adam delights in this vision of lasciviousness and judges that "Here Nature seems fulfill'd in all her ends" (XI.602). But Michael corrects him by saying that the women merely appear to practice "Arts that polish Life"; in truth, they are "Unmindful of thir Maker, though his Spirit / Taught them" (XI.611–612).

Adam also declares the Feminine a "novelty on Earth," unlike the "Spirits Masculine" in Heaven. Eve is a "defect / Of Nature," and Adam regrets that some other way to generate mankind had not been found. Lapsing into a cheap cynicism, he foresees that "innumerable / Disturbances on Earth through Female snares" will issue from "conjunction with this Sex" (X.896–898).

But Christ will not allow Adam to shift the blame to Eve and designates Adam's sin literally the resignation of his manhood (X.148). The "infirmer Sex" had been committed to his charge; her failure is therefore his failure, for which he must pay the forfeit. Michael corroborates this idea when he rejects Adam's declaration that "the tenor of Man's woe / Holds on the same, from Woman to begin" (XI.632–633). The death infused into the world proceeds instead from "Man's effeminate slackness" (XI.635). The crux of Adam's failure is sensuality, itself representative of man's failure to follow Reason, and his failure turns on the image of effeminacy which Milton transforms into the central action of his poem. Because the male principle is analogous to the Reason and to the principle of order and

authority, effeminacy associates with the principle of disorder. It is symbolically represented in sensuality, the figure of excess. Michelangel's
statue of Bacchus, now standing in the Bargello Museum, Florence, is an
iconographic representation of precisely these ideas and suggestive of how
thoroughly commonplace they were to the Renaissance mind. Thus, the
controlling image of *luxuria,* predominantly an expression of lust, becomes
the radical figure of postlapsarian man, whose evil travels all levels of
personal and civil discord:

> The brazen Throat of War had ceast to roar,
> All now was turn'd to jollity and game,
> To luxury and riot, feast and dance,
> Marrying or prostituting, as befell,
> Rape or Adultery, where passing fair
> Allur'd them; thence from Cups to civil Broils.
> (XI.713–718)

Until Christ restores what man has lost, intemperance is the manifest price
of surrendered manhood.

Eve, in fact, was first to sense that intemperance will assault the quiet
of their earlier and pure love: Adam may

> . . . judge it hard and difficult,
> Conversing, looking, loving, to abstain
> From Love's due Rites, Nuptial embraces sweet,
> And with desire to languish without hope,
> Before the present object languishing
> With like desire, which would be misery
> And torment less than none of what we dread. . . .
> (X.992–998)

Despairing, she proposes suicide as an alternative to unsatisfied desire.
Adam rejects her proposal of self-violence as well as her earlier determination to refrain from child bearing, both images of death and perversions of
natural fertility. Michael provides the true alternative: they must observe
the "rule of not too much, by temperance taught" (XI.531). And if, as
Adam says, the body is a "cumbrous charge," a judgment possible only
after the Fall, the burden can be relieved by living well "what thou liv'st"
(XI.553–554). Temperance, therefore, becomes the new covenant between
God and man; and Christ, who pays the blood ransom, will be the grand
exemplar.

Law supplies what nature cannot in the postlapsarian relationship between Adam and Eve: "to thy Husband's will," Christ decrees, "thine
shall submit, hee over thee shall rule" (X.195–196). The command to

procreation—"O voice once heard / Delightfully, *Increase and multiply*" (x.729-730)—becomes a curse of pain. But God's law is love still: it enables man and woman to be what they cannot be in their own inperfection. To Eve "pain only in Childbearing were foretold"; but bringing forth, she will soon be "recompens't with joy," the fruit of her womb (x.1050-91053). This, then, is the reason of the "Natural necessity" (x.765) with which Adam begets his sons, though not in choice but in desire to fill his own lack and to compensate for his self-abnegation in original sin. Although Eve laments her departure from the "nuptial Bower," she is consoled by Michael's words:

> Thy going is not lonely, with thee goes
> Thy husband, him to follow thou art bound;
> Where he abides, think there thy native soil.
>   (xi.290-292)

Christ's promise that her seed "shall all restore" (xii.623) revives Eve's flagging spirit: death shall turn to life. With that knowledge, a new life is possible; and Eve, having learned from her error, accepts her place in the order of nature. Eden yields to the "subjected Plain" but, as Eve to Adam,

> . . . with thee to go,
> Is to stay here; without thee here to stay,
> Is to go hence unwilling; thou to mee
> Art all things under Heav'n, all places thou . . .
>   (xii.615-618)

Eve is herself because Adam is the world. The final image of the poem— "They hand in hand with wand'ring steps and slow, / Through *Eden* took thir solitary way"—symbolizes the restored hope of man, the reconciliation of the eternal male and the eternal female. .

Like Milton as poet, we descend in the first books of *Paradise Lost* into rhetoric and semblance, through Chaos into Hell and Darkness so that we may ascend again into light and true knowledge. The descent overwhelms the imagination, wooing us to false belief as it lures us with the "trim disguises" of the father of lies. The verse itself persuades with its grandeur and in so doing indicts our Reason for misjudging appearances. It prepares us to accept the necessity and wisdom of Adam's admonition to Eve when she aspires to stand the test of her faith alone. The structural pattern of the epic thus rehearses the categories of life in which meaning and form co-inhere, acting out illusion and reality. It recreates the human dilemma of finding knowledge, makes our responses to literary artifice a parallel to the uncertainties of lived experience, and asks how and when we can be sure of our perception of truth.

The poem teaches us what love is and is not. It is, first and last, power— power to create, as God in Christ, the World out of Chaos and by extension the little world of ourselves. Evil creates nothing; it destroys. There is no knowledge in evil, for true knowledge is of good: it is virtue and wisdom, categories of a transcending Nature that reconciles all parochial limitations, a Nature that extends the reaches of our myopia. In love as a source of knowledge, we discover what creating power is. It leads us to clarity of vision, which is faith, the assurance of our capacity of acting instead of wishing (of doing instead of pretending). Satan, in Proust's words, "cannot emerge from himself" because he cannot, does not, love. He is obdurate in his pride and self-will, but ironically incapable of willing anything because the power of willing is of God.

Milton teaches that in a failure to love, we sin because we murder ourselves first and then others, as Satan, who, ruined, seeks to destroy the "new created World." Love assures meaning, relevance, identity, integrity: the unity of knowledge both existential and mystical. Less is to be impotent and ignorant, incapable of the authenticating potency of God's descent into man. Saint Teresa, in spite of her hysteria, confirmed the power of the Paraclete for all time, perhaps unknowingly testifying to the union of erotic and spiritual love:

In his [an angel's] hands I saw a great golden spear, and at the iron tip there appeared to be a point of fire. This he plunged into my heart several times so that it penetrated to my entrails. When he pulled it out, I felt that he took them with it, and left me utterly consumed by the great love of God. The pain was so severe that it made me utter several moans. The sweetness caused by this intense pain is so extreme that one cannot possibly wish it to cease, nor is one's soul then content with anything but God. This is not a physical but a spiritual pain, though the body has some share in it—even a considerable share. So gentle is this wooing which takes place between God and the soul that if anyone thinks I am lying, I pray God, in His goodness, to grant him some experience of it.[93]

Circumscribing erotic and divine love, her language—and Milton's in a lower key—posits transforming power. But erotic metaphor, because of its insufficiency, does no more than testify. It points the way to a higher truth. That truth, however, is for Milton neither occult nor "mythomystic," as Henry Reynolds (*Mythomystes,* 1632?) would put it. Erotic metaphor tells us what reality is *like,* only by association what it *is.* We assent to its assertion because its validity is ethical truth, measured only partly and not necessarily by the "factual" truth of Baconian empiricism. For

Milton the highest truth is the yield of faith, an act of the intuitive Reason, but we are moved to that knowledge by the kind of rational faith Spenser and Hooker practiced, echoed in turn by Milton himself when he wrote that "our understanding cannot in this body found it selfe but on sensible things, nor arrive so clearly to the knowledge of God and things invisible as by the orderly conning over the visible and inferior creature . . ." (*Prose*, II.368–369).

Satan, unlike Adam and Eve, is incapable of sacrificial love. Without oblation, selfless offering, there is no return of what God has given freely: "We love because he first loved us." God asks for adoration because such acts of love save. Milton saw it as law, inexorable, and his God demanded obedience because it was the one condition of being that could not be compromised. Incapable of reaching beyond his own possessiveness and into mystery, Satan—bereft of power and exiled—discovered that he had no dominion over even death, and because he could not learn that love was stronger than death, he became the first suicide.

Acknowledgments

I am indebted to the editors of the *Tulane Studies in English, Renaissance Papers 1967,* and *Renaissance Quarterly* for permission to use material that originally appeared in their journals. I am also grateful to the Tulane University Council on Research for a grant that allowed me to finish this monograph and to my colleague Marvin Morillo for reading it and making many valuable suggestions.

EGGOARCHICISM AND THE BIRD LORE
OF *FINNEGANS WAKE*

Grace Eckley

I. UNDER WHITESPREAD WINGS

A s Buck Mulligan maintains in the ballad of Joking Jesus ("My mother's a jew, my father's a bird," U19),[1] the eternal Spirit conceived of as wind or breath was early associated with those creatures which moved with outspread wings to catch the air. The particular theological significance of birds as either ascent to the holy spirit or symbols of that spirit generally ranks with another concept, that of egg as origin of life (compare the "roc's auk's egg" of Ulysses 737[2] and the Scandinavian world tree punned into "eggdrazzles" in the Wake 504.35) and therefore of the origin and continuing creation of the universe. In the Kalevala, for example, a duck "hovers over the waters," eventually lays seven eggs of which are formed the sun (yolk) and the moon (white) with the upper and lower halves of shell comprising the heaven and earth.[3] Of Egyptian cosmology, E. Wallis Budge writes, "The first act of creation began with the formation of an egg out of the primeval water, from which broke forth Rā, the immediate cause of all life upon earth."[4] In the Maya der indische Mythos, Joyce marked the passage in which the immortal Swan sings, "I am the Lord and I am the Swan. I brought forth the world out of myself."[5] He closes the Wake with Anna Livia's awaiting breathlessly the visitation of such a virile spirit "under whitespread wings like he'd come from Arkangels" (628.10).

In Ulysses Joyce included the blasphemous ballad of Joking Jesus in a work intended to develop the theme of the similarity of myth to contemporary existence. In Finnegans Wake—also a work famous for the mythical proportions of its characters—he rejects and ridicules many of these creation myths and much of popular bird lore (compare, for example, the satiric recitation of worldwide incidents of such birds' ubiquity, industriousness, and perseverance in 11.29-12.17). Nor is he so naive (as, indeed, the Egyptians were not) as to accept the concept of a cosmic goose without a fertilizing agent, hence the many references to ganders; the hen who finds the letter has a mate (12.5, 482.16), and King Mark, after the barnacle goose of Stephen's thoughts in *Ulysses* (*U* 50), is carefully designated a "barnacle gander" (399.10). Joyce, who is utterly cynical of legendary qualities of birds, barely touches serious acceptance of birds *per se* in the *Wake* but uses them extensively when, from nature, history, or myth, they can support his concept of time and his peculiar cosmology. More frequently he discredits their mythological significances when by doing so he can rail against known manuscripts and his anti-ego Shaun.

Since Joyce in the *Portrait* noted Swedenborg's phrase "on the correspondence of birds to things of the intellect" (*AP* 224), he was perhaps beginning then to distinguish the opposing characteristics of hawk and dove as well as to approach Swedenborg's representation of the natural man in the hawk as opposed to the spiritual man° and thus to distinguish Stephen from his associates. As rival of Stephen there is Heron; and Stephen's development is contingent upon his rejection of the dove of the Church (*AP* 149), which he sees reflected in the "dove's eyes" of the priest (*AP* 220), and his childhood sweetheart Emma, with her "bird's life" and bird's heart" (*AP* 216), though he accomplishes this last only with deep regret (*AP* 252). All these voices of "duties and despair" (*AP* 169) contrast

---

° See Ronald Bates, "The Correspondence of Birds to Things of the Intellect," *James Joyce Quarterly*, 2, no. 4 (1965), 281-290. In this excellent article, instead of Bates's statement, "the various birds in *A Portrait*, with the possible exception of the dove and the eagle, carry unpleasant, dangerous or destructive meanings," he should positively except only the eagle. The dove is associated both with Emma whose life Joyce describes as a "rosary of hours" (*AP* 216), and with the Roman Catholic Church, and both of these Stephen leaves behind him. Joyce's characterizations are never so ambivalent as they at first appear, though they may be confused in comparison with other sources. The *Portrait's* spiritual man has failed in regard to women (the *Les jupes* episode), language (the *tundish* eipsode), and sadism (the pandying episode); and this kind of spiritual man becomes the pharisaical Shaun of the *Wake*.

Joyce's artist as hawk should not be confused with Yeats's hawk in *On Baile's Strand*. On the broad lines of Yeats's power-knowledge polarity, the Cuchulain-hawk image contrasts with Conchabor-knowledge. Although Daniel Hoffman, in *Barbarous Knowledge*, insists Cuchulain is not to have druid knowledge (nor Conchobor either, for that matter), Joyce's Shem-hawk has the superior knowledge of the artist; and in the "Saint Patrick and the Archdruid" debate (*FW* pp. 609-613), Shem is the Archdruid while Shaun is Saint Patrick. Joyce does not make Shem a figure of physical power, as is Cuchulain, but only of intellectual power. True, Cuchulain refers to the people as "my chicks, my nestlings" and wipes his sword on chicken feathers after killing his son; and, since the people urge the battle with his son, the hawk-chicken contention may be discerned. Joyce's hawk-artist, however, is much different from Yeats's Cuchulain. For a discussion of Yeats's play, see Daniel Hoffman, *Barbarous Knowledge* (New York: Oxford University Press, 1967), pp. 97-104.

with the freedom of the hawk or eagle (*AP* 169) and the bird qualities of the inspirational girl in the stream (*AP* 171). The opening chapter of *Ulysses* features Buck Mulligan, who parodies Stephen's artistic aspirations at the same time he blasphemously assumes the pose of Jesus in the ballad ("What's bred in the bone cannot fail me to fly") and utters "birdlike cries" (*U* 19). So in the *Wake* Shaun—an elaborated Mulligan—assumes the pose of many divines and claims that he is a writer (421–425). Since Shaun-Kevin is associated with the hen (compare "that hen of Kaven's," 382.11), considering the ancient enmity between hawk and hen, the character of the hen further delineates Shaun and distinguishes him from his artistic brother—an extension of the *Portrait's* hawklike man—Shem.

The *Wake*'s use of ornithology and ornithomancy impinges upon certain concepts of creation and certain relationships among characters which are necessary to permit development into a unified whole. To digress, these may be briefly explained from an overview of the *Wake*.

Joyce in the *Wake* accepts the concept of creation out of primeval water, a thought represented in the female element Anna Livia (compare Genesis: "the Spirit of God moved upon the face of the waters"); and this concept begins with "riverrun" and "annadominant" and continues to the theological implications of the concluding "the,"* which circles once more to the beginning. Second, Joyce prefers a cosmology not completed and explained but essentially mysterious and ongoing; and Shem, the artist figure who as tree enjoys metaphorical union with the river Anna Livia (this "tree story" tells "How olave [Gaelic, *poet*], that firile, was aplantad in her liveside," 564.21–22), like his prototype Stephen in the *Portrait,* is a potential rather than accomplished artist.† Anna Livia and Shem remain mysterious in the construct of the novel through Joyce's technique of giving them small voice, or, as Michael Begnal explains of their contemporary (not archetypal) personalities, "both Shem and ALP are essentially passive characters who do not feel goaded to defend themselves. The opportunity is always available but they decline it, just as, oppositely, the stronger characters Shaun and HCE will leap to their own defense incessantly."[6] Third, while these factors develop the distinct characters of Shem and Shaun (Shem becomes the life principle in tree and Shaun the death principle in stone), Shaun exposes his character needlessly as he talks,

---

* Bernard Benstock writes that "the" is "a modulation from the strongest word in any language, the word for God, to the emasculated form which Joyce considered the weakest word in the English language." See Bernard Benstock, *Joyce-again's Wake* (Seattle: University of Washington Press, 1965), p. 113 n.

† This is true also of Gabriel in "The Dead" and Stephen in *Ulysses.*

appears with eggs dribbled on his vest (404.29), discovers the letter-manu-
script, and is identified with many creation myths which are preserved in
old manuscripts. Among these is the Egyptian *Book of the Dead,* from
which his character as Osiris is derived.* He must always take the form of
known gods, a contradiction of the concept of god as unnameable and
inscrutable and a contrast with the comparative silence of Shem. Fourth,
from this construct emerges some views on ancient manuscripts for which
the contemporary representative in the *Wake* is the mysterious unearthed
letter. Of the "structural" *Book of Kells,* James Atherton observes that
Joyce "suggests that the scribe was anti-Christian and is secretly mocking
at the text he transcribed.'"[7] Again, of the *Book of the Dead,* Budge points
to conflicting variations of creation myths in adjacent vertical columns on
papyri, plus the scribe's intrusion of his own views, plus (except for three
recensions) no mention of author or reviser.[8] The four commissioned
compilers of the authentic *Koran* destroyed all the rejected readings.[9]
Nevertheless, these ancient manuscripts, while penned by man, lost,
maimed, distorted, and expanded, are expected to reveal God and to
provide the means to eternal life; the *Wake*'s letter similarly baits its
seekers with promise of explanation of the crime and exoneration of HCE
but actually has many forms and several authors.† Joyce, said Atherton, in
the *Wake* attempts "to include references to all manuscripts, or at least to
all manuscripts which have been tainted by doubt or destiny."[10] But
because Joyce's creation must be always potential (like Shem's artistic
endeavors), completed manuscripts are associated with Shaun, who finds
but does not create. At the moment of completion, creation stops; the
created object becomes "dead." It will be remembered that Joyce per-
sisted in calling his own book a *Work in Progress* and kept its title secret
until publication.

The distinction between the living and the dead has been confused by a
"mergence of identity" viewpoint which scholars have advanced regarding
Shem and Shaun. In 1941 Harry Levin in his *James Joyce* wrote, "Sooner
or later these dichotomies [the opposite identities of the two brothers] 'by
the coincidence of their contraries reamalgamerge,' with the endless plas-

---

* As Budge states, *The Book of the Dead* contains no connected narrative of Osiris; but it
is derived from Plutarch's *De Iside et Osiride.* See E. A. Wallis Budge, *The Gods of the
Egyptians,* 2 vols. (London: Methuen, 1904), II, 123.

† For an analysis of the letter see Bernard Benstock, "Every Telling Has a Taling," *MFS,*
15 (Spring, 1969), 3-25. In the monologue, Anna imagines waiting with Earwicker to "watch
would the letter you're wanting be coming may be. And cast ashore" (623.29-30) while of
her own letter she says, "I wrote me hopes and buried the page when I heard Thy voice . . .
and left it to lie till a kissmiss coming" (624.4-6).

ticity of Ovid's *Metamorphoses* and the daft ingenuity of Walt Disney's
Silly Symphonies." In 1962 Clive Hart published his *Structure and Motif
in Finnegans Wake* in which he described the Shem-Shaun relationship in
this fashion: "When their orbits are in close proximity they war with each
other and—at a moment of exact equilibrium—even manage to amalga-
mate." In 1965 an elaboration of this concept appeared in Bernard Benstock's *Joyce-again's Wake* in which he asserts, "It logically then follows
that the sons in the *Wake* are at various instances unified into a single
figure, are themselves a pair, and are multiplied by Joyce's 'inflationary'
process into a trio."[11]

Because certain characteristics of Shem (he is the washerwoman Mrs.
Quickenough as well as the blind seer, the quick, the tree, Mercius, and
the hawk or eagle) and of Shaun (he is the washerwoman Miss Doddpeb-
ble as well as the deaf, the dead, the stone, Justius, and the hen) can be
discerned throughout the *Wake*, I do not agree that the characters blend
at any point before the *ricorso* (and in it they are often clearly distinguished). Nor do I agree with the view that Samuel Beckett's citing of the
danger "in the neatness of identifications,"[12] renders such identification
impossible. The smugness of Joyce's concluding phrase, "The keys to.
Given!" (628.15) counters such pedantic eagerness to elaborate the novel's
difficulties. Rather, Joyce's ambition to include all knowledge forces a
complexity of identifications because the sources overlap; often the diminished line between positive and negative is barely discernible. This can be
understood through examination of the use of creation myths, as already
explained; for although Joyce closes with positive connotations of "whitespread wings," he favors very few birds other than the phoenix and
rarely employs it as a resurrection symbol independent of other associations. A passage in Book III reveals the complexity of these attitudes in the
use of bird metaphors. When one of the Four Old Men urges Yaun, "Irise,
Osirises!" the imagery of a variant of the Prankquean riddle ("For why do
you lack a link of luck to poise a pont of perfect, peace?"—493.29–30)
plus the goddesses Isis and Iris and the god Osiris suggest the peace at the
dawn of creation; the cosmic goose from *The Book of the Dead* is there
("On the vignetto is a ragingoos," 493.30), and Anna Livia is summoned
with Yaun as spiritualist medium. Aside from Shaun's association with the
dead, this passage would appear innocent of condemnation of Shaun had
he not been, as early as Chapter 5, already committed to the hen, the most
popular bird of alectromancy. For this purpose, the "witlessness" of
chickens made them dependable, declares Ernest Ingersoll, and a fowl
propagated and kept in captivity "was merely the blank on which divine
intelligence was written,"[13] Shem's mind is never depicted with such

scathing abuse (except by Shaun). This is why, in the Joycean age of
sophistication when such reliance upon avian supersitition must provoke
skepticism, Joyce makes the hen not a brooding creative spirit but acci-
dental originative agent of one of the plots, that of the mysterious and
allegedly pivotal letter. For this reason Adaline Glasheen calls Chapter 5
the "Hen" chapter,[14] but the honor she thereby bestows upon Biddy the
Hen is largely undeserved; and Biddy's importance in the remainder of
the novel is actually minimal. In Chapter 5, however, there emerges the
designation of Shaun in relationship to the hen; and Shaun, who dominates
Book III, associates in various passages with other birds.

For an overall view of these developments in the *Wake*, Ovid's *Metamorphoses,* as well as Vico's cycles, proves helpful. In Book I of the
Metamorphoses, the Golden Age is succeeded by the Silver, the Bronze,
and the Iron Ages as man gravitates toward misuse of physical and
spiritual resources until Zeus at last sends a flood to punish mankind for its
wickedness. Then the new cycles must begin afresh. In parallel fashion,
Shaun, the epitome of the negative qualities of greed, lust, and gastronomy, presides over the third and declining phase of the *Wake*. But his
character is twofold, and he pharisaically strives toward sainthood while
he continually trips over his own tongue: "I never open momouth but I
pack mefood in it" (437.20) he utters as a Freudian slip, for throughout the
Wake he is characterized by both food and feet. Likewise, the kinds of
birds Shaun talks about and the kinds with which he is associated reveal
his characteristic greed and avarice. Last, to culminate the declining Ages
of the *Metamorphoses* (or the Viconian decline through Divine, Heroic,
and Civil Ages), in the *ricorso* at the end of the *Wake* some identities,
once apparently clear, become merged; hence the cycle may begin again
and the great questions be reexamined once more.

Central to the mystery of existence is the question of time and the
pertinence of all human endeavor—a compound philosophical question
aptly contained within the spherical and fragile shell of the germinal egg.
Joyce therefore begins and closes *Finnegans Wake* with the riddle of
Humpty Dumpty and sustains throughout the novel the analogy of Earwicker's form ("humptyhillhead," 3.20) and fall until Anna Livia as one
half of the presiding creative spirit awaits physical union, "humbly
dumbly" (628.11) with her counterpart.

And finally, the mystery of that seminal power, "under white-spread
wings like he'd come from Arkangels" (628.10), revives the question, not
of bird symbolism, but of symbolic birds. The phoenix, chief of these,
though it was mostly conceived of as red-gold, prevails almost universally
as a symbol of resurrection, exists as a stone carving atop a pillar in

Dublin's Phoenix Park,[15] nesting in flames functions as an emblem for Dublin's Phoenix beer, and graces the one penny piece of Irish currency— all of which, both preceding and succeeding the waking of Joyce's Finnegan, support the practical and local associations which Joyce offers.

II. A Parody's Bird

Because, in their appointing completed creation and subsequent events, creation myths defy the concept of continuing origin, they contradict a basic tenet of the *Wake*—the concept of potential creation. The chief bird of the *Wake*, Biddy the Hen, becomes, therefore, the chief agent for Joyce's satire of the myths he rejects. This "gnarlybird," a parody (compare "a parody's bird," 11.9) of the birds of creation, neither ascends nor creates but merely scratches among the cast-off refuse of life in the midden near Phoenix Park and unearths a mysterious letter, the product of another mind (and this, of course, consequently casts grave doubts upon the seriousness with which the letter is to be regarded). Joyce continues the parody by placing her, somewhat surreptitiously, at other strategic initial points (such as the beginning of the Butt and Taff episode, 338.8-9) in the novel, though she remains a minor figure at most.

The exact species of hen is not known until one of the Four Old Men identifies her as a "Guiney gagag" (482.19); but Joyce surrounds his guinea hen with a cluster of terms which fix her as a game hen and a member of the grouse family. The turkey hen (German, *Pute* and *Trut*) in "puteters" (111.1) and "trootabout" (113.12) as well as the expression "talk straight turkey" (113.26) and "gobbly-dumped turkery" (118.22) fix the general type, while such tantalizing expressions as "Noah Beery weighed stone thousand one when Hazel was a hen" (64.33-34) to describe HCE and the inclusion of the capercallzie (383.17) in the Tristan and Isolde story make a game of species designations. These are easy evolutionary steps, however, from the turkey hen to the black grouse or guinea fowl, while the hazel hen and capercailzie are also grouse. In the United States the ruffed grouse is often inaccurately called pheasant in the Mid-west and partridge in New England. The common distinctive characteristic among these species is the drumming courtship dance, and Shaun's character is linked with the partridge (301.30, 344.7, 447.27-28).

In Chapter 5, Shaun's hen when introduced has immediately one striking characteristic, her association with sterility. She is first seen when the visitors pass out of the Willingdone museyroom—a museum and musingroom of past persons and events. But rather than the inspirational directive of moving spirit, this scene's "wagrant wind" goes in circles, "awalt-'zaround the piltdowns" (10.29-30), with the latter place name suggesting the barrenness of a hoax. The place the hen inhabits, "A verytableland of bleakbardfields!" (10.34), confirms the absence of creativity (the bard) and introduces another aspect of bird symbolism, the sacrificial killing, by way of allusion to "Sing a Song of Sixpence."[16] The hen's running about on every "knollyrock" (10.31) connects her with the stone Shaun, and she appears propitiously during HCE's fallen state ("Under his seven wroth-schields lies one, Lumproar," 10.35).[*] The hen comes out only when the novel's prime creative force, Anna Livia or water, is not about (as they leave the Museyroom, "you mussna tell annaone," 10.26), and when there is no trace of the life-giving rain in the atmosphere, not even clouds (Latin *nubas*—"nubo") or fog (German *nebel*—"neblas"): "She niver comes out when Thon's [*Thom*—thunder] on shower or when Thon's flash with his Nixy girls [German *nixe*—water nymph] or when Thon's blowing toom-cracks down the gaels of Thon. No nubo no! Neblas on you liv!" (11.3-5). Like Chicken-Little (compare 10.32-34, in which the pattern of "Ten Little Indians" makes her "little" twelve times or all year round) who thought the sky was falling, "her would be too moochy afreet" (11.6). Her sensitivity to "such reasonable weather" (10.29) aligns her with those birds favored for prognostication of weather for which, according to John Cuthbert Lawson, "poultry serve better than the more dignified birds—perhaps because their movements on the ground are more easily ob-served—and by pluming themselves, by scratching a hole in which to dust themselves over, and by roosting on one leg or with their heads turned in some particular direction foretell rain, fine weather, or a change of wind."[17] With the hen's preference for favorable weather presented in Chapter 1, the effects of chill on her are obvious when she appears in Chapter 5: "As a strow will shaw she does the wind blague, recting to show the rudess of a robur [Latin, *strength*] curling and shewing the fansaties of a frizette [little curl]" (112,.34-36).

The first appearance of the hen, therefore, contrasts with the second, when the letter is found, in respect to time and weather conditions. On the second appearance the Thunderword (which logically equates with the feared "Thon's blowing toomcracks") announces the discovery of the letter, and this apparent cosmological perversity by contrast emphasizes

[*] The one-two-three motif here indicates the lapse of the quarrel after HCE's "de baccle." He is "one," while "Our pigeons pair are flewn for northcliffs. The three of crows have flapped it southenly" (10.36-11.1) marks the dispersion of the two temptresses and the three soldiers. See also, for example, 136.29-34.

the hen's divorcement from cosmic matters and insinuates the high-flying presence of the hawk-like artist. The hundred-letter word recalls the thunderbolt of the mythical cloud bird (in most mythologies, an eagle), and it unites varied divine and divinatory systems with the concept of thunder as the voice of God. In the beginning Osiris became the principle of creation by merely uttering his own name;[18] the *Bible* and the *Poetic Edda* offer parallels. The thunderword includes "sixdix" or sixteen, and as Alwyn and Brinley Rees state, "A division of the heavens into sixteen regions appears in the cosmic systems of the Greeks, the Romans and the Germans, and among the Etruscans these divisions were used for divinatory purposes. The Egyptians knew of sixteen giants who were closely connected with the celestial regions. Sixteen perfect lands were created by Ahura Mazda.[19] Thunderbirds of many species explained the natural phenomena of thunder and lightning for varied primitive cultures,[20] and at intervals Joyce repeats the association of Biddy the Hen with light. The hen, afraid of rain, remains a natural, rather than mythical creature; she is timid and only by fortunate coincidence assumes cosmic proportions. She is consistently a "parody's bird."

These matters of bird lore blend with Shaun's character when at her first appearance the hen demonstrates her association with Shaun through having "burrowed the coacher's headlight the better to pry" (11.17–18); Shaun as postman has a "belested loiternan's lamp" (299.16–17). Furthermore, the American bittern was once said to emit a light from its breast, "equal to the light of a common torch."[21] Joyce continues this association wherever the hen appears. In Chapter 1 she borrows the light; in Chapter 5 she is urged, "Lead, kindly fowl!" (112.9) in parody of "Lead Kindly Light"; in Chapter 11 the light is lightning at the beginning of the Butt and Taff episode ("All was flashing and krashning blurty moriartsky blutcherudd?"—338.8–9); and near the close of Chapter 11 Earwicker hears, "None of you, cock icy! You keep that henayearn and her fortycantle glim lookbehinder" (379.23–24). Finally in Chapter 16 she does indeed respond to the cock at dawn when she begins "in a kikkery key to laugh it off" (584.21).

Other details are primarily realistic. The time at the hen's second appearance is twelve o'clock noon (111.8), since it is daylight, and cold, for "Midwinter (fruur or kuur?) was in the offing and Premver [before green] a promise of a pril" (110.22–23). Although the weather has changed from warm to cold, the two appearances of the hen nevertheless coincide in one season; the winter solstice has not yet occurred in the latter appearance; in the former, HCE as nature king appropriately sleeps beneath the ground (compare Anna Livia's lament in which she is waiting for him "to wake himself out of his winter's doze," 201.11). The letter's expression of wishes "for a muddy kissmans" (11.14), therefore, is seasonal and, considering the ultimate "earthy" destination of the missive, gently ironical. Since Joyce seeks as freqently as possible to express the yearly cycle, the letter's date, "the last of the first" (111.10, and "31 Jan. 1132 A.D.," 420.20) indicates a lapse of nearly one year between its writing and its discovery, as does a similar lapse between the time of the hen's scratching up the letter (in the last month of the old year) and her scrutiny of it (in the first month of the new year). To emphasize Biddy the Hen's (and the letter's) siding with the death principle (Shaun), the attendant Divine Spirit, mysteriously present in the thunderword, is parodied on the human level in the unlikely form of the child Shaun-Kevin who gambles upon the letter's providing "a motive for future saintity" (110.34) and whose object in being there is food.

Joyce, then, utilizes in his description of hen and midden a variety of facts derived from nature, myth, and history to imply death. In the midden, with its refuse serving as the best example of the death principle, is the scrap of orange peel which facetiously revives the legends of plants and gems capable of magically opening rocks or mountains containing buried treasure; these connect with bird myths because the "stone" or "plant" dropped by the cloud-bird was the devastating lightning bolt. Also, the orange peel painfully recalls "the massacre . . . of most of the Jacobiters" (111.2–4) in the 1690 defeat of the Irish in the cause of James II. The desire for food (a Shaun characteristic which emphasizes consumption rather than creation) which drives Kevin to seek the "few spontaneous fragments of orangepeel" and accidentally discover the letter compares with an adult begging potatoes ("puteters," 111.1) who with a birdlike "pious clamour" discovered the Ardagh chalice (1868). Lunchtime ("An outdoor meal") for the unknown person who left the orange peel as evidence of affiliation with William III and lunchtime for child and hen ("the hour of klokking twelve") elaborates not only consumption but also elimination with the scatological tea stain as a complimentary close ("signing the page away," 111.21) and marks it "at the spout of the moment," with the familiar pun on chamber pot, as genuine Irish pottery (Shaun will repeat this allusion in the Book III bird passage, 448.34–450.33). Transmuting the child's game of hide and seek to the adult's character as a "sunseeker or placehider" (110.30–31) with a "mistridden" [German *Mist, dung*] past, Joyce expresses a combination of urgencies which have driven other esteemed persons, as well as birds, to dumps. Ornithologist Louis Halle, for example, reports an observation of birds descending to Parnassus because a by-product of the housing of tourists "at the top of the scarp" is "the garbage dumped over the edge." He adds, "The Delphic Oracle attracted a profitable business not altogether unlike that which the Delphi ruins attract today, and the birds must have shared in it then as now."[22]

Having discerned the attraction of birds to dumps—or established its Grecian precedent for his "parody's bird"—Joyce does not deny his midden creative potential. In it can be found a variety of ores and minerals ("pril" or prill, a virgin metal; "limon" or limonite, a yellowish-brown iron ore and limonene, a substance in orange oil; "sahatsong" or sahlite, a green mineral), while the song of birds ("kischabrigies sang life's old sahatsong") greet the perennial spring and a cluster of beach terms ("strandlooper," 110.31–32; "beachwalker," 110.36; "Now Sealand," 111.1)—though all imply scavenging from the sea and England's possession of New Zealand augments the William of Orange negativism—still mark the verge of creativity in water.[23] In other words, the midden presents the familiar Generation-Destruction theme, preserved from triteness by Joycean ingenuity and multiple associations, as in the example "goddam and biggod" (111.3).

The satire Joyce offers has a precedent in Aristophanes' drama *The Birds* (400 B.C.). In it are many of the bird qualities found in the *Wake*, including a precedent for the hen's finding of the letter. "None knows where my treasure lies, unless perchance it be some bird," says Pithetaerus, as he offers his version of a proverb to prove the discovery of buried treasure as one evidence of bird-power so important to his founding a bird republic.[24] Analogous to the hen's "nabsack" into which she gathers the remnants of civilization (11.18–27) is the capacious "bird's crop" described by a chorus leader. Slightly more obscure is the allusion to the Feast of the Pots in honor of Athena and her owl, which Joyce parodies in calling his hen a "peri potmother" (11.9) and in making the hen's discovery of lost records coincide with the dawn of a new era when "Dannamen gallous banged pan the bliddy duran" (14.20–21). So also our cosmologies are indeed "past postpropheticals" (11.30–31), contrived in the present in the form of prophecy from the past, "to will make us all lordy heirs and ladymaidesses of a pretty nice kettle of fruit" (11.31–32).

Further, in Joyce's paraphrase of *The Birds*, the second detailed description of the hen (110.22–113.23), in the sacred terms of Newman's hymn, summarizes her primal importance: "Lead, kindly fowl! They always did: ask the ages" (112.9). As proof that birds are older than the gods, the Leader of the Chorus offers his version of creation myths: "Firstly, black-winged Night laid a germless egg in the bosom of the infinite deeps of Erebus, and from this, after the revolution of long ages, sprang the graceful Eros with his glittering golden wings, swift as the whirlwinds of the tempest. He mated in deep Tartarus with dark Chaos, winged like himself, and thus hatched forth our race, which was the first to see the light. That of the Immortals did not exist until Eros had brought together all the ingredients of the world, and from their marriage Heaven, Ocean, Earth and the imperishable race of blessed gods sprang into being." Included in *The Birds* also is mention of the Aesopian fable in which the wren merits the title of "king of all birds" because he flew under the eagle's wing until the eagle became exhausted and then flew higher than the eagle. Familiar to readers of *Ulysses* from the "wren song" of Saint Stephen's Day, this appears in the *Wake* in the phrase "Wreneagle Almighty" (383.4); and Lina Eckenstein recalls the Grimm fairy tale in which "by a similar strategem [the wren] proved his superiority over [the beasts of the forest]. Consequently the kingship of the wren extended to the four-footed as well as to the feathered tribes."[25] Aristophanes' birds also build a wall. During the building process each bird exhibits his particular craft and, coincidentally, teaches it to mortals; he makes a catalog of species; the cock crows the world awake; and a new age is implied by the "Oracle Monger" when "the wolves and the white crows shall dwell together." This last alludes to the Golden Age or its equivalent which is the threat, the goal, and the dream of all mythologies (see, for example, Ovid's *Metamorphoses* and the "Voluspo" of the *Poetic Edda*). Joyce echoes it in "Let us auspice it! Yes, before all this has time to end the golden age must return with its vengeance. Man will become dirigible, Ague will be rejuvenated, woman with her ridiculous white burden will reach by one step sublime incubation, the manewanting human lioness with her dishorned discipular manram will lie down together publicly flank upon fleece" (112.18-23).

   The Birds won only a second prize for Aristophanes at the festival of the Great Dionysia in 414 B.C.; Joyce condescends to a parenthetical announcement of his "bird in the case" (111.5) as a "Terziis prize with Serni medal" (111.6); and, a pejorative of the Dionysia, it is only a Chapelizod-Cheeping Hen Exposition ("Cheepalizzy's Hane Exposition," 111.6-7) with "Hane" connoting the French *haine* (hate) and the German *Hahn* (cock). This hen does not intend to uncover earth's glass "diamonds" of art and literature ("postmantuam glasseries"—Mantua the birthplace of Virgil plus Tuami brooch and an implication of castration ["glasseries" as cuttings] of rabbits ["lapins"] and crickets ["grigs"]) but expects everyone to try to get ahead (113.2-9). This latter aggressive quality, like the hints of gems and animals and carnality, will be repeated by Shaun-Jaun in Book III; a typical expression of it is: "Did ye save any tin? says he. Did I what?

with a grin says she. And we all like a marriedann because she is merce-
nary" (12.5-7). The hen's age, "more than quinquegintarian" (111.5)
parodies the *hen* period of Egyptian history, a period of sixty years.[26] In
this manner the hen has acquired a formidable background by the time
the thunderword sounds and ushers in three cycles plus *ricorso:* "Mes-
daims, Marmouselles, Mescerfs! Silvapais!" (113.11). Analysis of such pre-
tentious and portentious cosmic efforts will, appropriately, be left to
scholars of origins, "old almeanium adamologists like Dariaumaurius and
Zovotrimaserovmeravmerouvian" (113.4-5).

Other than analogy with Shaun, because every aspect of the female half
of the world is represented in Anna Livia Plurabelle, and each female
partakes of some quality of the all-inclusive feminine principle, the hen's
character (like that of every other female creature in the *Wake*) bears
some resemblance to Anna Livia. The part of motherhood represented in
the hen's devotion to her children—"she knows, she just feels she was
kind of born to lay and love eggs (trust her to propagate the species and
hoosh her fluffballs safe through din and danger!"—112.13-15)—finds an
echo when the Earwicker children are called in at night: "And haste, 'tis
time for bairns ta hame. Chickchilds, comeho to roo. Comehome to roo,
wee chickchilds doo, when the wildworewolf's abroad" (244.9-11); all this
ends when "Gallus's hen has collared her pullets" (256.2). Also the hen's
busy efforts to provide for her household include frugality as well as
physical labor: "Though the length of the land lies under liquidation
(floote!) and there's nare a hairbrow nor an eyebush on this glaubrous
phace of Herrshuft Whatarwelter she'll loan a vesta and hire some peat
and sarch the shores her cockles to heat and she'll do all a turfwoman can
to piff the business on" (12.7-11). This compares with Anna's efforts,
during Earwicker's winter sleep, to keep her household going: *"Is there
irwell a lord of the manor or a knight of the shire at strike, I wonder,
that'd dip me a dace or two in cash for washing and darning his worship-
ful socks for him now we're run out of horsebrose and milk?"* (201.13-16).
This quality in the hen, evidenced in the "Did ye save any tin," which
begins the passage quoted above (12.5), merges with the implication of
sexuality, though she is never seen with her own egg or chicken. The
"night's duty" corresponds with that of Anna and HCE when the cock's
"treading her hump and hambledown" (584.18) coincides with the dawn
in Chapter 16. The analogy between the bird's crop and Anna's "zakbag"
is developed in connection with the scholarly wealth of the discovery:
"any of the Zingari shoolerim may pick a peck of kindlings yet from the
sack of auld hensyne" (112.7-8),[27] and the physiological fact that the first
and second primaries of the hen's wing are digital accounts for that

seemingly farfetched aspect of folk stories in which a little red hen carries
a sack (compare "with the hen in the storyaboot we start from scratch,"
336.17–18). And Anna is described "as proud as a peahen" (578.20).

Anna's wisdom throughout is parodied in "the sagacity of a lookmelittle
likemelong hen" (111.33), in this instance the "sagacity" of discovering the
letter. The letter and its finder, the hen, correspond with the letter's
paradigm, the *Book of Kells*, and the presumed writer of the letter, Anna
Livia. The newly discovered letter, as a key, provides numerous (and
humorous) possibilities for reinterpreting the *Book of Kells*, "since we
have heard from Cathay cyrcles how the hen is not mirely a tick or two
after the first fifth fourth of the second eighth twelfth" (119.22–24); and
all these numbers, regarding the mystical odd number, added to even
divisions of geography to provide a center,* and regarding cycles of time
(compare the *hen* period of Egyptian mythology), may be rearranged (add
the digits in the fractions 1/4 and 1/5 for 11; subtract digits of 12/16
divided by 5/4 for 32) to represent 1132. Earwicker explains how the
letter he thinks Anna has written should exonerate him because this
quality, a variation of the love of gossip, is expected of a wife: "And if my
litigimate was well to wrenn tigtag cackling about it, like the sally berd
she is, to abery ham in the Cutey Strict . . . dismissing mundamanu all the
riflings of her victuum gleaner (my old chuck! she drakes me druck!
turning out, gay at ninety!) and well shoving off a boastonmess like lots
wives does over her handpicked hunsbend, as she would be calling, well,
for further oil mircles upon all herwayferer gods and reanouncing my
deviltries" (364.29–365.2).

Although the egg riddle belongs to another chapter, HCE's Freudian
slip about the henpecked husband ("handpicked hunsbend") has important connotations regarding his own physique as well as his character and
that of Anna Livia. Eckenstein investigates the Humpty Dumpty rhyme
thoroughly and claims that "The word Humpty-Dumpty is allied to *hump*
and to *dump*, words which express roundness and shortness." Because
HCE is hump-backed and evidently failing in virility (and the letter was
found in a dump), Eckenstein's further comments are helpful:

---

* Regarding Ireland's four provinces (Ulster, Leinster, Munster, and Connacht) and its
center (Meath), Alwyn and Brinley Rees write, "Every ritual place or cult object is endowed
with what Professor M. Eliade has called 'the prestige of the Centre,' be it a local meeting-
hill, a pillar-stone, an inauguration tree, a sacred well, a grave or what it may." See Rees and
Rees, *Celtic Heritage*, p. 187. Venetia Newall cites the same tendency among the Romans:
" '*Numero Deus impare gaudet*,' says Virgil—the gods rejoice in uneven numbers." See *An
Egg at Easter: A Folklore Study* (Bloomington: Indiana University Press, 1971) p. 102.

The word Hoddy-Doddy in the sixteenth century was directly used to express "a short and dumpy person" (1553). It was also applied to a "henpecked man" (1598). The meaning of shortness and roundness is expressed also by the name of the foreign equivalents of Humpty-Dumpty. The German Hümpelken-Pümpelken, and probably Lille Bulle of Scandinavia convey the same idea. On the other hand, the names Wirgele-Wargele and Gigele-Gagele suggest instability. The Danish Lille Trille is allied to *lille trolle*, little troll, that is, a member of the earlier and stumpy race of men who, by a later age, were accounted dwarves. These were credited in folk-lore with sex-relations of a primitive kind, an allusion to which seems to linger in the word Hoddy-Doddy as applied to a hen-pecked man.[28]

Anna applies the same term, including the river Dodder in Ireland, when she refers to her husband as her *"old Dane hodder dodderer"* (201.8).

Appropriately, hen and egg close the third phase of the "vicociclometer" which precedes Anna's letter, when that "exprogressive process" of generation and records is ascertained, "as sure as herself pits hen to paper and there's scribings scrawled on eggs" (615.10). And Anna's description of the letter merges with the description of Joyce's book when she evokes hen imagery in saying she included "what scrips of nutsnolleges I pecked up me meself" (623.32–33).[*]

Joyce's assurance that fowls have always led us and his playful reiteration of their inauguration of the cycles ("What bird has done yesterday man may do next year, be it fly, be it moult, be it hatch, be it agreement in the nest," 112.9–11) derives from mythology, folklore, and ornithology. Birds were not only the first artisans, as in Aristophanes' *The Birds;* but also in the *Koran* birds were the first morticians; the raven taught the son of Adam to bury his dead brother (Surah V, 31). Joyce adds facetiously, "her socioscientific sense is sound as a bell" (112.11–12); but the serious undertones of such a statement are self-evident. Ornithologist Dean Amadon, speaking of one of those civil declines in the destruction of the Mayas, comments, "Birds are scarcely more than a pawn in these global reverberations," and, unaware of Viconian or other philosophical cycles, he recalls "the caged canaries once used to warn of poison gas in coal mines." Birds may well hover over our decline and our rejuvenation for, he continues, "we may by saving nature save mankind."[29] And Biddy the

---

[*] The "scraps of nutsnolleges" no doubt refers to Joyce's mania for including everything he knew in *Finnegans Wake*. Also, Robert Graves writes, "The nut in Celtic legend is always an emblem of concentrated wisdom: something sweet, compact and sustaining enclosed in a small hard shell—as we say: 'this is the matter in a nut-shell.' " See *The White Goddess* (New York: Noonday Press, 1966), p. 181.

Hen, witless as she is, functions at the beginning of things—discovery of the letter, the Butt and Taff episode, the dawn of day, and Anna's letter.

III. A WARBL IS A WORLD

Joyce sprinkles the *Wake* with many common expressions, derived from bird lore, such as "You is feeling like you was lost in the bush, boy?" (112.3)[30] and the history of human faults in "feathered foes' nests and fouled their own" (579.36-580.1).* Too many to list here, these expressions have familiar meanings which require no repetition, such as the caution implied in "Don't kill the goose that lays the golden egg" (see 394.27); but the esoteric meanings are less familiar. Originally derived from the myths of the golden egg of the sun, this latter cultural phenomenon appears in many folk tales, such as that of the giant's hen in "Jack the Giant Killer," which Joyce alludes to in "Fe fo fom!" (11.7). And while the current vocal reflections of such myths are often divorced from the original sacred or sacrificial intent, Joyce's use of them suggests his knowledge of their cultural history. When Joyce describes the "Greek ees awkwardlike perched there and here out of date like sick owls hawked back to Athens" (120.19-20) he may pun on the slang meaning of "hock," but the prevailing cultural allusion is to the owl of Athena and to the celebration of Apollo's birthday for which each year the Athenians sent a sacred ship to Delos. The return of the ship to Athens (for which Socrates' execution was delayed one month) meant that public executions could be resumed. That the owls were sick, Halle believes, refers to the dying of the old religion.[31] In other uses, Joyce strives to combine all cultural and linguistic possibilities and to invent even more, as in his telling of the courtship of Anna Livia.

Birds, of course, announce the new age and tender a prediction of Anna's marital future: wedding vows ("For mine ether duck I thee drake. And by my wildgaze I thee gander," 197.13-14); insurance ("Was his help inshored in the Stork and Pelican against bungelars, flu and third risk parties?"—197.18-20); lechery ("he raped her home . . . in a parakeet's cage," 197.21-22); gullibility ("Who sold you that jackalantern's tale? Pemmican's pasty pie!"—197.26-27, with an allusion to the blackbirds baked in a pie); Earwicker's Noah role ("he loosed two croakers from under his tilt," 197.30); and homing ("By the smell of her kelp they made

---

* Several species, including the cuckoo, steal other birds' nests. The hoopoe, for example, has a foul-smelling nest because the excretion of the young is not removed.

the pigeonhouse," 197.31–32). The parakeet's cage may parody the concept of souls kept in cages (see the story "The Soul Cages" in Yeats's *Irish
Fairy and Folk Tales*) and, to enforce HCE's godlike aspects, would
encourage reading of a pun on Paraclete, for which Bayley provides the
meaning of the Greek word as that of Fire of the Great God; in South
America the parakeetlike quezal means Light God.[32] The soul cages no
doubt have an origin in the concept of the holy spirit, or, as Stephen
ponders it, the "unseen Paraclete, Whose symbols were a dove and a
mighty wind" (*AP* 149). At the simple, narrative level, Earwicker protects
his catch, Anna Livia, in a proper ecological niche; for Amadon assures us
that the security of a cage may enable a songbird to live for twelve years
"while very few attain half that age in the wild."[33] As a songbird, however,
Anna fails: her voice would "bate the hen that crowed on the turrace of
Babbel" (199.30–31). And she imitates the famous hen of the midden
when she borrows from her son Shaun a "zakbag" (206.9), into which, like
the hen's crop, goes an amazing assortment of "gifts."

While creation itself is the major gift of the divine spirit, Joyce makes
certain that his birds preside over not only the beginning of the cycle but
all phases. In the postlude at the close of the Butt and Taff drama, he
returns to Judaic-Christian creation myths ("When old the wormd was a
gadden and Anthea first unfoiled her limbs," 354.22–23) to suggest, once
more, the ages of creation, but also the fall and resurrection. Here the
garrulous magpie recalls the sinful Tower succeeded by and opposed by
the black and white raven and dove discharged from Noah's ark: "there'll
be bright plinnyflowers in Calomella's cool bowers when the magpyre's
babble towers scorching and screeching from the ravenindove" (354.26–
28).[34] Moncure D. Conway suggests that "the raven sent out of the Ark
may typify the 'darkness of the face of the deep,' and the dove the 'spirit
of God' that 'moved upon the face of the waters.' "[35] Over all Butt and
Taff's epilogue, a capsule of history and myth, hover the gulls ("he'll be
buying buys and go gulling gells," 354.30–31). From the ancients, according to Thompson, "The Gulls are souls of disembodied fishermen, hence
their gentle and peaceable disposition";[36] and these next appear in the
Tristan and Mark chapter.

As Chapter 12 closes Book II of the second phase, birds are represented
singing the opening poem; and Joyce, with apparent perversity, announces
"birds of the sea" and proceeds to name, after seahawk and seagull, the
curlew and plover which are waders and the kestrel and capercallzie
which are land birds. Assuming Joyce knew the difference, this is a
realistic means of establishing popular and mythical analogies, since land
birds were frequently kept captive on board ship to be released at appro-

priate moments to guide the ship, by their flight, to land (hence the repetition of Noah's releasing the raven and dove from his ship *Ark*).[37] Joyce then uses the prophetic birds' call for narrative and theme.

From the twelfth century, appropriate to the *Wake*'s axial date (1132), comes the myth of Tristan and Isolde at a time when, writes Denis de Rougemont, "the leading caste was making a great effort to establish social and moral order."[38] Joyce's earliest draft of the Tristan episode, then, made Isolde a vain, facetious female practicing feminine wiles; and the final version retains the penetration imagery which amounts to the mere kiss in "All the birds of the sea they trolled out rightbold when they smacked the big kuss of Trustan with Usolde" (383.17–18) and in the consummation, when Tristan "druve the massive of virilvigtoury flshpst the both lines of forwards (Eburnea's down, boys!) rightjingbangshot into the goal of her gullet" (395.36–396.2). A short time later Joyce wrote a more cutting satire of the social order into his "Mamalujo" episode starring the Four Old Men and in 1938 combined it with the Tristan unit. Regarding the Tristan myth, David Hayman implies Joyce may have experienced a change of heart and suggests a connection with Wagner in 1923;[39] at approximately that time H. A. Guerber published the "story" of the opera with phrasing strikingly similar to the epigraph of the *Portrait*: "It was in 1854, when still an exile from his native land, that Wagner, weary of his long work, 'The Ring of the Niblungs,' . . . conceived the idea of using the legend of Tristan."[*]

In many versions of the legend Mark first learned of Isolde's existence when a bird brought him a golden hair; and four felon barons (true to the command of King Mark but "felon" in courtly love) unsuccessfully guarded the queen's virtue and revealed the adultery to the king. Joyce, however, apparently was not interested in retelling the details of the legend but only in its outline and symbolic aspects. De Rougemont stresses that everything in the tale is symbolical: "Everything holds together and is connected after the manner of a dream."[40] In this manner HCE, having drunk "more than the better part of a gill" (382.8–9) and "just slumped to throne" (382.26) at the close of Chapter 11, dreams

---

[*] H. A. Guerber, *Stories of The Wagner Opera* (New York: Dodd, Mead, 1924), p. 72. For comparison, see Levin's translation of the reason for Dedalus' resolution to "abandon his mind to obscure arts": he was "weary of his long exile and lured by the love of his natal soil." See Harry Levin, *James Joyce* (New York: New Directions, 1960), pp. 61–62. Wagner also applies the term *gander* to a failed hero in much the same sense Joyce calls Mark a gander. When Parsifal fails to ask the important Grail question, Gurnemanz cries, "Go find yourself a goose, you gander!" See Joseph Campbell, *The Masks of God: Creative Mythology* (New York: The Viking Press, 1968), p. 456.

about the ship bearing the lovers to Cornwall. The new insight which must have induced Joyce to discard much of the early draft, abandon the concept of it as a unit, and combine it with Mamalujo, de Rougemont may well have discerned; Wagner's version added a new depth to the old story. De Rougemont writes of Tristan and Isolde that "each loves the other *from the standpoint of self and not from the other's standpoint.* Their unhappiness thus originates in a false reciprocity, which disguises a twin narcissism. So much is this so that at times there pierces through their excessive passion a kind of hatred of the beloved. Long before Freud and modern psychology Wagner saw this."[41] Since HCE plays in the dream the role of old man Mark losing out to young man Tristan—and it is a "philosopher's passion to meditate in the act of swooning"[42]—his dream is not mere masochism but also vindication; his comfort is in the futility of their passion which leads to death. It is therefore important that at this stage in HCE's development he can have this dream. With it he relinquishes the major role to Shaun, who dominates Book III. The Four Old Men, while they speak in lecherous terms of desire and death by drowning, extend this futility and reveal their own natures in the same breath. Their confessions, plus the example of Tristan and Isolde, confirm, as de Rougemont insists, that no happy love exists in western literature; certainly none exists in Joyce's novel.°

The function of birds in this chapter emerges from such a background, and the birds have nothing flattering to convey regarding HCE. Joyce begins Chapter 12 at the point of beginning of Wagner's opera, on shipboard as they heave into sight of Cornwall (and this accounts for the presence of wading birds).† In clamorous chorus the birds of the opening song appeal to the "Wreneagle Almighty" while they blaspheme Mark's age and impotency; he is called an "old buzzard," "moulty Mark," and "the rummest old rooster." The tragedy that the love is undesired and unmerited emerges here: "Tristy's the spry young spark/ That'll tread her and wed her and bed her and red her/ Without ever winking the tail of a feather" (383.11–13).

The Encyclopedia Londonensis of the eighteenth century reported, "If a flock of various birds came flying about any man it was an excellent omen,"[43] but only in respect to a deathly love potion is luck on the side of

---

° When at last in bed with Anna, HCE is apparently too old for successful union: "Withdraw your member! . . . You never wet the tea!" (585.26–31).

† Of the wading birds curlew and plover, Ingersoll claims that in Chapter XXVII of the *Koran* the plover is said to have brought together Solomon and Sheba. See Ingersoll, *Birds in Legend,* p. 260. The bird, however, is the hoopoe in Pickthall's version. See Marmaduke Pickthall, *The Meaning of the Glorious Koran* (New York; Alfred A. Knopf, 1930), p. 387.

Tristan; rather the "shrillgleescreaming" of these birds represents a warning, commonly thought to be a warning of danger or of death.[44] Birds also were thought to represent the four winds, and hence the Four Old Men.[45] The choice of species—kestrel and capercallzie—somewhat reflects the carnal theme. The kestrel builds no nest; the capercallzie or capercallie was often called the cock of the woods, and Mark thinks he is "cock of the wark" (383.10). The male bird has a courtship dance which produces a drumming sound and after mating abandons both the female and the young. Thompson noted capercallzie's resemblance to the hazel hen and the guinea-fowl, or the hen which finds the letter.[46]

While the birds treat Mark-HCE disrespectfully, it may be observed that Joyce has no reverence for bird lore as fact, or for the appropriateness of the superstitions it generates. In his hands the procreation of the cosmic goose diminishes to the doggerel of nursery rhymes and, like the aged man ignored by his bride, represents discarded belief in an outmoded faith: "Ah, dearo dearo dear! Bozun braceth brythe hwen gooses gandered gamen" (389.31-32); and among "subjects being their passion grand" (394.24-25) ranks high for ridicule "that one too from Engrvakon saga abooth a gooth a gev a gotheny egg" (394.26-27). Belief in both romantic love and the old manuscripts of creation crumbles as Joyce follows the outline of the Tristan story even to Tristan's marriage with Isolde of the White Hand ("that was her knight of the truths thong plipping out of her chapell-ledeosy, after where he had gone and polped the questioned" (396.30-32). The brevity of the sexual spasm signals the death of desire: "volatile volupty, how brieved are thy lunguings!" (396.29).

The chapter's concluding poem moves through one week and gives in sequence the attraction of Mark's money (Stanza 1), Isolde's arrival Venus-like by sea (Stanza 2), rejection of age and marital security (Stanza 3), and the final perfidy of Isolde, her indifference to her lover (Stanza 4), *"Mick, Nick the Maggot or whatever your name is"* (399.26-27). Isolde unintentionally (and somewhat tritely) represents the amoral sexual thrust, but only because she swallowed a love potion; and she remains barren of offspring. Of her latest love, the balladeer says, a *"Grand goosegreasing we had entirely with an allnight eiderdown bed picnic to follow"* (399.23-24); and HCE, when reminiscing about his marriage, claims "goosegaze annoynted uns" (548.3-4). The goose myth in the concluding poem takes the brunt of Joyce's attack; he asks of the rejected Mark, *"Yerra, why would she bide with Sig Sloomysides or the grogram grey barnacle gander?"* (399.9-10). This recalls Stephen's thoughts in *Ulysses:* "God becomes man becomes fish becomes barnacle goose becomes featherbed mountain" (*U* 50). Again from the twelfth century (1187), according to Ingersoll, comes

Giraldus Cambrensis' condemnation of "the practice of eating barnacle geese in Lent on the plea that they are fish; and soon afterward Innocent III forbade it by decree." Related to the nonsensical belief that certain geese grow on trees, the confused myths were perpetuated in moralistic clerical literature and "the fable was reaffirmed in the *Philosophical Transactions* of the Scottish Royal Society for 1677."[47] Obviously because the *Branta bernicla* is realistically a bird of the littoral, Henry Lee in *Sea Fables Explained* (London, 1884) could offer two suppositions, one regarding trees which resembled willows that grew close to the sea and dropped fruit believed to contain the embryo of a goose, the other an absurdity regarding geese bred from fungus on floating wood. Ingersoll adds, "this fable sprang from the similitude to the wings of tiny birds of the feathery arms that sessile barnacles reach out from their shells to clutch from the water their microscopic food, and also to the remote likeness the naked heads and necks of young birds bear to stalked or 'whale' barnacles (Lepas)."[48] For Joyce, who enjoyed a bit of heresy now and then, the best religious intentions of one age may be mocked by the next whose profit from the dead goose (other than mere speculation about reincarnation)[49] consists of sexual grease and feather beds.

As Joyce moves through the cycles it is necessary that such a negative and sterile figure as King Mark become the focus of the third cycle of emasculated man, in keeping with the hen's augury quoted earlier. As Book III develops, then, Shaun will have Mark's sterile characteristics, will rail against sexuality while expressing lechery, and will continue the satire of the social order developed in the Tristan-Mamalujo episode.

Shaun imagines himself to have the bird qualities of song, astronomical height, and swift flight, as well as the creative potential of myths, all supported by his aspirations to divinity; and he combines bird lore with courtship of his sister Issy. He intends "to give the note and score" (448.36–449.1) and in parody of Jonathan Swift he imagines the birds *swift* and *swallow* aiding his love and leading the way to infinite vision: "his onsaturncast eyes in stellar attraction followed swift to an imaginary swellaw, O, the vanity of Vanissy! All ends vanishing!" (449.2–4). But he wants to hug close also the pleasures of earth, especially food and women, worth foregoing those celestial attributes, if he can "only spoonfind the nippy girl" to guide him by "gastronomy" (449.11). From a favorite location "in the birds' lodging, me pheasants among" (449.17–18) he imagines himself, godlike, naming the fish of the sea and the birds of the air and riding to the hounds—especially as all these occupations yield food. Confident of his excellent voice, he alters "poor old Balfe's" vassals and serfs and sings "I'll dreamt that I'll dwealth mid warblers' walls when

throstles and choughs to my sigh hiehied" (449.18-19)—stressing the
extended last note—and compares himself with the many saints who held
special communion with birds.* All the while the owl keeps time: "that
owledclock (fast cease to it!) has just gone twoohoo the hour" (449.24-25).

At this point one hesitates to add to David Hayman's extensive analysis
of the next sentence (449.26-450.2),[50] but additional bird lore develops
Shaun's character. "I could sit on safe side" (449.26-27) alludes to the
visitation of Athena in the form of a bird to Ulysses in the Calypso episode
of the *Odyssey*. Halle, apparently incorrectly, writes "Odysseus had
shared the danger of the Hoopoe in the trough of the wave";[51] according
to Thompson the αἴθυια of Book V, line 353 is clearly the shearwater,
though translators are notoriously careless of species. "I could sit on safe
side" also alludes to Shaun's deformity of the hip or foot, confirmed by
Anna Livia (620.13) and mentioned, like that of Jacob, when he names his
friend after himself, "Jacobus a Pershawm" (449.15). Of "the bark of Saint
Grouseus for hoopoe's hours" (449.27), since both "the boat of millions of
years" (479.26) and the hoopoe are solar emblems, "hoopoe's hours"
should be the daylight hours. The Joycean concoction "Saint Grouseus"
extends Shaun's combination of lechery and saintliness; the grouse family
of birds is notorious for their distinctive and trancelike courtship dances,
referred to in "the drummling of snipers" (449.29). Hayman has remarked
that "grenoulls" are frogs (449.33)[52] but the term implies the tawny frog-
mouth, a croaking nightbird in Australia, and when read as "green owls"
continues the religious associations; John Keane in 1887 published the
"superstition among the Mohammedans that the spirits of martyrs are
lodged in the crops of green birds, and partake of the fruit and drink of
the rivers of paradise."[53] Thompson remarks that "Horapollo brings the
Hoopoe and Hippopotamus together, the one signifying gentleness, and
the other the reverse,"[54] and this may partially explain the phrase "as
peacefed as a philopotamus" (449.32). Also, among many bird species
which perch on the backs of nearly submerged hippopotamuses to search
for food and therefore may be said to love (*philo-*) the animal, the ham-
merhead looks for frogs and may be, according to Hayman's reading, the
bird Shaun hears "crekking jugs at the grenoulls." With this sentence,
Shaun returns to his cosmic ambitions, though content now to rest on
earth and contemplate the sky with his "upfielded neviewscope" (449.34),

---

* These extend the concept of holy spirit as a bird and include Saint Francis, who
sermonized them, and Saint Kevin, into whose hand a blackbird dropped her eggs. This
worthy man held his arm rigid until the eggs were hatched. See Ingersoll, for many legends
of birds and the religious, *Birds in Legend*, pp. 253-269.

through which he will see the coming ages (compare "peeking into the focus," 452.11). The sounds he hears in the night are the mating calls of distinctive nightbirds—the owl, whippoorwill, and nightingale—and these sounds, "the wireless harps of sweet old Aerial and the mails across the nightrives (peepet! peepet!) and whippoor willy in the woody (moor park! moor park!) as peacefed as a philopotamus, and crekking jugs at the grenoulls" (449.29-33) will continue until the rising of the sun, "my nocturnal goosemother would lay her new golden sheegg for me down under in the shy orient" (449.36-450.2).

The morbidity insinuated by Shaun's bragging throughout the passage (448.34-450.33) does not find direct expression until near the close; but the wailing of invisible birds in the night, says Ingersoll, has long been of evil portent, even to the "Welsh conception of the Three Birds of Rhiannon that could sing the dead to life and the living into the sleep of death,"[55] and Joyce records his awareness of this in the next chapter when the ass hears "the mockingbird whose word is misfortune, so 'tis said, the bulbul [Arabic nightingale] down the wind" (476.1-2).[*] Shaun imagines what he would like to do if alone, "O twined me abower in L'Alouette's Tower, all Adelaide's naughtingerls juckjucking benighth me, I'd gamut my twittynice Dorian blackbudds chthonic solphia off my singasongapiccolo to pipe musicall airs" (450.16-19), but the ancient ritual of bird sacrifice was conducted with many types of birds killed—wren, lark, thrush, blackbird, magpie, robin—and, as in the example of *l'alouette,* plucked and divided up. Eckenstein explains, the spirit of the sacrificed bird "was held to be incarnate in other creatures of its kind; it therefore continued to be spoken of as alive."[56] In some versions, as in "Sing a Song of Sixpence," then, the bird continues to sing after it has been killed. Finally Shaun alludes to Socrates, to whom chiefly is attributed the fiction of the swan's dying song (swans cannot sing): "What's good for the gorse is a goad for the garden. Lethals lurk heimlocked in logans. Loathe laburnums. Dash the gaudy deathcup!" (450.30-32). In this way Joyce parodies Socrates' lament in the *Phaedo,* "It seems I appear to you no less prophetic than the swans who, when they perceive that they must die, though they have been used to singing before, sing then more than ever, rejoicing that they are about to depart to that deity whose servants they are" and his assertion "I am like the swans. I also belong to Apollo, and he has made me as clear-sighted as the birds, so that I depart this life in no less

[*] The Persian bulbul or nightingale was famed for its singing in pain against a rose thorn or for its singing the rose into bloom (see Byron, *The Giaour*). For discussion, see Ingersoll, *Birds in Legend,* pp. 48-50.

spirits than they."[57] The birds' song, regarded as art, marks the Platonic triumph of mind over matter, and this positive element shines through the "Dorian blackbudds" and other death songs or rituals. At the same time Shaun, like Socrates, imagines that he can sing like the birds or like John McCormack; his "voicical lilt too true" (450.24) projects a corresponding sexual desire: "For I sport a whatyoumacormack in the latcher part of my throughers. And the lark that I let fly (olala!) is as cockful of funantics as it's tune to my fork" (450.25-27). Shaun may well sing his swan song, preparatory to his death and rebirth in the next chapter (15). The many references to his bad voice and the associations with crows (choughs) make a possible pun on one of his names, Chuff.

With a passing reference to Biddy the Hen ("I don't want yous to be billowfighting your biddy moriarty duels, gobble gabble, over me" (453.3-4), Chapter 14 closes with more of the birds of creation, appropriate to Shaun's awakening as Yaun at the beginning of Chapter 15: "The phaynix rose a sun before Erebia sank his smother! Shoot up on that, bright Bennu bird! *Va faotre!* Eftsoon so too will our own sphoenix spark spirt his spyre and sunward stride the rampante flambe. . . . The silent cock shall crow at last" (473.16-22). Budge confirms Joyce's identification of the Bennu bird as the phoenix with its Egyptian, not Greek, symbolism. Disclaiming the glossing of Herodotus to the effect that the phoenix burnt itself to death and rose from its ashes, Budge explains, "All these fabulous stories are the result of misunderstandings of the Egyptian myth which declared that the renewed morning sun rose in the form of a Bennu, and of the belief which declared that this bird was the soul of Rā and also the living symbol of Osiris, and that it came forth from the very heart of the god. The sanctuary of the Bennu was the sanctuary of Rā and Osiris."[58]

Having been identified, through bird associations, with Osiris at the close of Chapter 14, Shaun, as Chapter 15 opens, is found awaking and shivering on the midden heap; and the Four Old Men who interrogate him hark back to that previous incident with the hen in this same location: "Hooshin hom to our regional's hin and the gander of Hayden. Would ye ken a young stepschuler of psychical chirography, the name of Keven, or (let outers pray) Evan Vaughan, of his Posthorn in the High Street, that was shooing a Guiney gagag, Poulepinter, that found the dogumen number one, I would suggest, an illegible downfumbed by an uneligible?" (482.16-21).

In addition to the species of the hen, many other associations, particularly of the ass and of Shaun, are clarified in this chapter. Shaun is again identified with the partridge, when he answers a query, "O mis padredges!" (478.34). In the earlier Butt and Taff episode, Taff exclaims to

Butt (an appropriate epithet), "Take the cawraidd's blow! Yia! Your
partridge's last!" (344.7). The partridge, known for lechery and thus
befitting Shaun's established character, connects, according to Robert
Graves, with Dionysus, the bull-footed god whose dislocation of a thigh
forced him to walk on his toes and wear the high-heeled boots called
buskins[59] which gave a seductive waggle to the hips. Shaun has "a bull-
ock's hoof in his buskin" (429.16-17), and in his role as washerwoman in
the ALP chapter is called "hobbledyhips" (214.21). The courtship dance
of the partridge resembles the gait and rituals of heel gods[60] when the
"cocks flutter around in circles with a hobbling gait, one heel always held
in readiness to strike at a rival's head."[61] Furthermore, the partridge had
gained disfavor in Ovid's *Metamorphoses* through drumming approval of
the death of Icarus, but even earlier than that incident it had derived its
character and attained its identity through contention with Daedalus.
Once an inventive apprentive to Daedalus, who through envy hurled him
from a high temple, the boy was preserved by Minerva and changed into
Perdix, the partridge. But he

> Never flies high, nor nests in trees, but flutters
> Close to the ground, and the eggs are laid in hedgerows.
> The bird, it seems, remembers, and is fearful
> Of all high places.[62]

Jaun claims, "I am perdrix and upon my pet ridge" (447.28-29), his
highest eminence not gained in flight but with the ground securely under
foot. In the Chapter 10 dispute, while Shem is "laying siege to goblin
castle" (301.27), Shaun is "lying sack to croakpartridge" (301.29-30)—
activities appropriate to Shem's reputed attacks on his country's reputation and Shaun's religious devotions (Croagh Patrick the mountain of
Easter time pilgrimage in Ireland). The partridge certainly polarizes
Shaun's character with that of the hawklike artist as known in the *Portrait*.

The uses to which avian associations may be put spills over to the grey
ass of the Four Old Men, to whom one of them speaks, "Whisht awhile,
greyleg! The duck is rising and you'll wake that stand of plover" (478.35-
36); he then proceeds to answer Shaun with mention of "guineagould"
(recalling the golden egg of the sun) and the curlew in "Tucurlugh"
(479.6), a portmanteau word combining the bird with direction, place, and
with Lugh, a god representing the light of the sun which was often
depicted as hawk or eagle. What comprehension the ass should have of
creation myths comes from the French in such works as *Le Testament de
L'Ane*, which is similar to the sacrificial bird ritual, "The Robin's Testament." Another dialogue piece, says Eckenstein, "describes how the she-

ass, conscious of the approach of death, bequeathed her feet and ears to her son, her skin to the drummer, her tail to the priest to make an aspergill, and her hole to the notary to make an inkpot"[63]—the last an appropriate Shemian addendum. But because of various revered biblical donkeys, the parts of the ass were also descriptive of the parts of the cathedral: "the four legs, its pillars—the heart and liver, its great lamps—the belly, its alms-box," and so on in a convincing fashion until Eckenstein punctures all speculation with the pronouncement that "the ass was not known in Western Europe till a comparatively late period in history. It has no common Aryan name."[64] To solve the mystery she proceeds to recite the many nicknames of the ass which are similar to bird names—jackass, jackdaw; betty-ass, magpie; jenny ass, jenny wren, for examples—so that "the ass in Western Europe somehow got mixed up with the birds."[65] The term *ass* in the *Wake*, used in conjunction with birds ("chicks," 20.25; "cockaded," 50.26; listening to birds, 475.35–476.2), also appears with religious terms (a ghostly appearance to one washerwoman, 214.33; Brahaam's ass," 441.25); and Joyce probably knew also that to the ancient Egyptians the ass was regarded as both god and devil.[66]

A third development of Chapter 15 is Shaun's connection with *The Book of the Dead.* One of the Four Old Men introduces the topic with bird augury, birds and dumps, and the claim that the midden constitutes all the creative potential of the Egyptian eternity: "Dunlin and turnstone [both common European birds] augur us where, how and when best as to burial of carcass, fuselage of dump and committal of noisance. But, since you invoke austers for the trailing of vixens, I would like to send a cormorant around this blue lagoon. Tell me now this. You told my larned friend rather previously, a moment since, about this mound or barrow. Now I suggest to you that ere there was this plagueburrow, as you seem to call it, there was a burialbattell, the boat of millions of years" (479.18–26). Shaun agrees, and the ship, now called *Pourquoi Pas* (one mythology is as good as another), blends with the *Nancy Hans* of Tristan and Isolde fame: "Her raven flag was out. . . . Crouch low, you pigeons three! Say, call that girl with the tan tress awn!" (480.1–4), for Tristan in his first acquaintance with Isolde sought to disguise his identity by calling himself Tantrist, and these boats—the Egyptian boat of millions of years, the *Pourquois Pas,* the *Nancy Hans*—blend with the Danish arrival of HCE, while the three pigeons recall the sin in the park.

While Joyce in this manner combines mythologies with his own several plot lines, he continues to employ elements of physical nature which lend verisimilitude to abstraction. From Plutarch comes the description of the intelligence, alertness, and speed of birds, so that birds were early designated the "heralds of the gods." Among the Greeks, singularity of habit, in addition to size, strength, and intelligence, made the vulture, hawk, raven, and crow early favorites of diviners. To this "canon of ornithological divination," writes John Cuthbert Lawson, were added in classical times the wren, the owl, and the woodpecker. Basic to divination was accurate identification of species—even distinction between the crow and the raven—plus observation of the bird's cry, flight, posture, and movement when settled.[67] The Old Man, while invoking the cosmological goose with Anna Livia, also invokes the Egyptian oceanic god Nu to proclaim her arrival with distinction of species and characteristics in a paraphrase of an ancient papyrus: "On the vignetto is a ragingoos. The overseer of the house of the oversire of the seas, Nu-Men, triumphant, sayeth: Fly as the hawk, cry as the corncrake, Ani Latch of the postern is thy name; shout!" (493.30-33).

How closely Joyce adheres to the old manuscripts he obviously treats with skepticism may be observed here, yet at the same time he strives toward euphony. Joyce may have seen Budge's illustration of the vignette, a goose, from Chapter XCV of the Papyrus of Userhat placed side by side with a different vignette from the same chapter of the Papyrus of Nu;[68] the text of all chapters begins with the invocation, "The Overseer of the house of the overseer of the seal, Nu, triumphant, saith," and the best-known recension, from the Papyrus of Ani (Chapter XVII), distinguishes species among careful listing of virtues: "I fly as a hawk, I cackle as a goose."[69] Joyce's variation not only has rhythm and rhyme and distinct species but also, by choosing a bird native to Ireland, Joyce enables Shaun to remain in the dialogue and continues the Shem-Shaun contention; the corncrake is a member of the crow family and, lowly of ambition like the partridge, builds its nest on the ground. For further Egyptian analogies, the soul as bird is implied; and Anna Livia's speaking through Shaun represents one of the portals through which the dead must pass, naming each portion as he goes, including the latch, as in Chapter CXXV of the Papyrus of Nu: " 'We will not let thee enter in through us,' say the bolts of this door, 'unless thou tellest our names'; 'Tongue [of the Balance] of the place of right and truth' is your name,"[70] a proper welcome for the loquacious Anna. Budge writes, "In the earliest time the goose, or rather gander, was associated with Seb, the *erpāt* of the gods, who is called in *The Book of the Dead* 'the Great Cackler' (Chapters LIV, LV)."[71] Since it is not Shaun in this passage proclaiming his divinity, but rather one of the Old Men speaking, the alteration from goose to corncrake seems a subtle means of depriving Shaun of his self-ascribed godliness.

And finally the birds appear in the Scandinavian world tree, for which

Shaun is called to give his "bard's highview, avis on valley!" (504.16), and since he is no bard he does so incorrectly. The "bird flamingans sweenyswinging fuglewards on the tipmast" (504.23) alludes to the Irish Mad Sweeney who lived in trees. But the bird's eating fruit at the top of the tree, as represented on ancient carvings of the world tree,[72] would scarcely be accomplished by the flamingo, whose hooked and troughlike bill is adapted for scooping and sifting water animals and algae. Having tested our credulity by placing this unlikely tropical and water-loving species in a northern tree, the poet then exclaims, "nobirdy aviar soar anywing to eagle it!" (505.17).

Joyce rightfully closes Chapter 16 and opens the *ricorso* with differing cock crows. Another universal symbol with slight variations, the cock crows the world awake not only to the new day but to the new era, both individually and culturally. The *Poetic Edda* alone features *Fjalar*, the cock whose crowing wakes the giants for the final struggle; *Gollinkambi*, who wakes the gods and heroes; and a third, the *rust-red bird* who awakes the people of Hel.[73] Biddy herself, having appeared at the beginning of the *Wake* (pp. 10–12), now closes this last cycle-chapter by mocking the sexual gaming of the old HCE and Anna Livia and apparently, with her cock, surpassing theirs. When the morning dawns, "the hen in the doran's shantyqueer began in a kikkery key to laugh it off, yeigh, yeigh, neigh, neigh, the way she was wuck to doodledoo by her gallows bird . . . at all times long past conquering cock of the morgans" (584.20–25). The crowing sound is fittingly Viconian: "Cocorico!" (584.27). Next, appropriate to the night's sleep, to the dawn, to the Sanskrit philosophical allusions, and also to the tradition of the Sandman of English nursery tales, the cock is a "friarbird" (though also this is a realistic species of New Guinea) who sounds "Conk a dook he'll doo. Svap" (595.30)° near the beginning of the *ricorso*. He announces, among other things, Shaun's elevation to the role of Saint Kevin. The Brahman creation, in which sound is important, is there also in "a flash from a future of maybe mahamayability through the windr of a wondr in a wildr is a weltr as a wirble of a warbl is a world" (597.28–29)—a statement encompassing the vast mystery of seeing in a flash, as if through a window, the imminent creation of the universe, symbolized not by the sight of but by the warble of a cosmic bird.

And Joyce fulfills the promise at the close of Chapter 15: "The silent

° According to Campbell and Robinson, *Svap* is Sanskrit for sleep. See Joseph Campbell and Henry Morton Robinson, *A Skeleton Key to "Finnegans Wake"* (New York: The Viking Press, 1961), p. 342.

cock shall crow at last" (473.22). Since the last is also the first, he crows twice.

The chief characteristic to be derived from the *Wake*'s variety of realistic birds is the singular application to the character of Shaun, since he is best known by the goose, the hen, the partridge, and the crow. The goose chiefly derives from the Egyptian *Book of the Dead*, designates Shaun an Osiris, and confirms his affinity with the death principle (as opposed to the tree, the life principle in Shem). The hen is that parody of creation myths which discovers, but does not write, letters. The partridge has the peculiar gait similar to that derived from a hip or foot injury, and, like the hen, finds the hawk a mortal enemy—the hen from physical circumstances, the partridge from mythological. All these are game birds and all remain close to the ground, while the crow's raucous voice reveals the real status of Shaun's vocal or artistic abilities. Having rather fully developed the idea of artist as hawklike man in the *Portrait,* Joyce keeps this a minor element in the *Wake*. Almost unobtrusively it appears at the close of the Anna Livia Plurabelle chapter when the telling and listening washerwomen, being gradually metamorphosed into tree and stone, are identified with hawk and bat. The artist-teller has poor eyesight but keen hearing; the listener-stone has keen eyesight but poor hearing. "Dark hawks hear us" (215.36) is spoken by the tree-Shem-artist and "Can't hear with bawk of bats" (215.33) by the stone-Shaun-public man.

The creative aspects of birds emerge, of course, with Anna Livia in the *ricorso*. The morning means the birds will "start their treestirm shindy" (621.35-36) and have a peculiar political good-luck significance when heard and seen high and white in the morning. "Look, there are yours off, high on high!" Anna imagines herself exclaiming to the sleeping Earwicker. "And cooshes, sweet good luck they're cawing you, Coole!"[4] You see, they're as white as the riven snae. For us. Next peaters poll you will be elicted or I'm not your elicitous bribe" (621.36-622.03). And because man may be degenerate but never unregenerate, Anna's last call to the freedom of spirit in the birds and to Earwicker has been a reminder that the dead past generates a new future: "the book of the depth is. Closed. Come! Step out of your shell!" (621.3-4).

IV. EGGOARCHICISM

Humphrey Chimpden Earwicker, mocked and reviled and beseiged in his Lough Neagh retreat, sustains himself with a dream of an ideal future society, "where the Meadow of Honey is guestfriendly and the Mountain of Joy receives, of a truly criminal stratum, Ham's cribcracking yeggs, thereby at last eliminating [much desultory delinquency] from all classes and masses" (76.4-6).° Such a paradise of acceptance, embracing at once the newly born and the fallen, exists in a timelessness like that of the *Wake's ricorso,* for here all events both end and begin, and here is the coexistence of opposites—the egg as new life plus the egg as fall (of Humpty Dumpty). In the *Wake's* conflationary style, "Ham's cribcracking egg" refers to the biblical Ham's sin in knowing his father,[75] plus creation as the original sin,[76] with the bringing forth of Eve from Adam's rib, and with the egg of creation myths plus the "crib" or cradle of all civilization. Venetia Newall has found a contemporary parallel: "The words *atyi akan,* meaning 'the hip egg,' still used by the Bulu people of the Cameroons to describe the bone in the hip, express the same idea [of a young creature suddenly breaking out of what seemed a lifeless object] and recall God creating Eve with a bone from Adam's rib."[77]

For Joyce, however, the end of life, or a fall, is merely the end of one phase of life and necessarily constitutes, with its altered circumstances, a new beginning. Contained in such phrases as "past postpropheticals" (11.30) it seeks not only to capture elusive time but also to keep it moving. It unites past, present, and future to demonstrate that today turns into yesterday and tomorrow turns into today, "If there is a future in every past that is present" (496.35-36). These two motions, represented in a diagram of overlapping circular lines in opposing directions, will always construct an egg in the center.

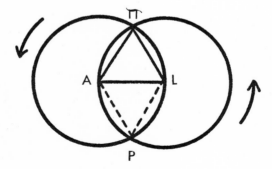

This egg of timelessness (uniting past and future in a constant present)

° The words in brackets in the quotation (76.6) are a correction of the *Wake* text. See James Blish, "Special Announcement: A *Wake* Appendix," *James Joyce Quarterly,* 9 no. 2 (Winter, 1971), 175.

was being formed in the *Portrait* when Stephen wrote into his journal, "The past is consumed in the present and the present is living only because it brings forth the future" (*AP* 251). In the *Wake* Joyce introduces the diagram of Anna Livia's vagina with a similar comment, "a poor soul is between shift and shift ere the death he has lived through becomes the life he is to die into" (293.2–5). Campbell and Robinson discerned the egg at the center of the diagram and wrote, "The figure the boys are drawing is the geometrical counterpart of the philosophers' stone,"[78] which is signalled by "the lazily eye of his lapis" (293.11). Dr. Newall confirms such an association, including the female object under discussion. She writes, regarding the philosophers and their work, "the vessel used, the *aludel* or retort, was egg-shaped. This was also in imitation of the universe, so that the stars would be sure to influence the operation. The miraculous substance that was supposed to emerge was often called the 'philosopher's egg,' and is depicted as such in early woodcuts. This creative aspect is emphasized by the word *Mutterschoss,* mother's womb, a common metallurgical term for a smelting kiln."[79] Shem calls his diagram "As round as the calf of an egg!" (294.11) and he challenges Shaun to "goaneggbetter" (298.3).

Both historical and generative, the paradox of that which remains the same while changing, that is, creating new life, occurs in such expressions as the "eternal geomater" (296.31) and "the constant of fluxion" (297.29). Bounded horizontally by the life principle itself, "A is for Anna like L is for liv" (293.18–19), the diagram is bounded vertically by the "tew tricklesome poinds where our twain of doubling bicirculars, mating approxemetely in their suite poi and poi, dunloop into eath the ocher" (295.30–33). That the generative process and its representation of the present has existed since the beginning of time appears in "it's the muddest thick that was ever heard dump since Eggsmather got smothered in the plap of the pfan" (296.20–22). Here the allusion is to the egg and the mud of the Nile as origin of life: "Khnum, a god of creation whose name signifies 'The Moulder,' formed the world egg from a lump of Nile mud on his potter's wheel."[80] The linguistic mutation from *oeuf* to *life* parallels the mythological and biological process, appropriate to the name *Anna Livia Plurabelle* and to the diagram egg as vagina of the eternal earth mother (compare the sexual allusions of Issy's remark, "There's a refond of eggsized coming to you out of me so mind you do me duty on me!"—457.16–17, and Anna's remark about HCE's "knowing the size of an eggcup," 616.20). Shem-Dolph delights in the eroticism of explaining the diagram's central egg and triangle, "bissyclitties and the three comeseekwenchers trundletrikes" (284.23–24) so that he creates a successful image of sexual penetration ("if this habby cyclic erdor be outraciously enviolated . . . the zitas runnind hare and dart with the yeggs in their muddle," 285.1-5). (The *egg and dart* in architecture is an instrument combining the shape of an egg alternated with another in the form of a dart to enrich the ovolo or circular molding, though for Joyce "enrichment" has additional sexual connotations.) Ultimately Joyce's timelessness is the "exprogressive process" of continually kindling cyclical life, involving the "vicociclometer" which he described elsewhere somewhat more philosophically as "eggburst, eggblend, eggburial and hatch-as-hatch can" (614.32-33), or the process of birth, marriage, death, and resurrection.

In mythology "eggburst"° generally describes many stories of world, cosmic, or solar eggs which explain all vital principles, including the rich ores within the earth and even the separate soul of man.† Most begin in primeval waters, and a number of myths allow for a bird which laid the egg; others do not. The common image of a god raising itself from water and the laying of a seminal egg no doubt account for Joyce's description of a detail of the Book of Kells as "very like a whale's egg farced with pemmican" (120.11). Since whales are mammals and bear live young, the obvious explanation is in mythology, of which the North American Indians offer a delightful story which combines egg, water, whale (the largest animal and capable of laying the largest cosmic egg), the changing seasons, and thunderbird:

Old Man South Wind was travelling north when he met a giantess and, since he was feeling hungry, she gave him a net to catch some fish. He caught a whale, but, instead of splitting it open' as she had told him, he cut it across and began to remove some pieces of blubber. At once the whale changed into the Thunderbird, so large that it hid the sun, the noise of its wings causing the earth to shake. The

---

° In Buddhist thought the same image serves for transcendence of the cycles of rebirth. The Buddhist teaches, "I alone, among all those who live in ignorance, and are as though enclosed and imprisoned in an egg, have burst through this shell of ignorance; I alone in this world have attained to the blessed, the universal dignity of Buddha." Quoted in Newall, *An Egg at Easter* pp. 32-33.

† Venetia Newall writes, "Time and again the universe egg appears from the waters of creation at the beginning of the world, preceding matter and existence. It contains all being, all life, and the creator god who is the soul of the world. The evolution of the universe serves as a pattern for the evolution of man, and a large group of myths also describe how the first ancestor appeared from an egg of this kind. If it is from this that life derived originally, in turn the egg appears to have become recognized as a possible seat of the soul.

"The idea that the soul could be separated from the body was in fact quite common. . . . So precious a thing needed careful guarding, and certain traditional stories describe magicians and sprites who had the power to enclose their soul within an egg. . . . The soul egg could be inside a number of other objects." See Newall, *An Egg at Easter*, pp. 104-105.

Thunderbird flew to Saddleback Mountain, near the mouth of the Columbia River, where it laid a nest of eggs upon the summit. The old giantess followed and threw all the eggs down into the valley where they broke and were changed into Indians. The Thunderbird and South Wind both looked for the giantess in order to punish her, but could not find her, although they travelled northwards every year.[81]

In the term "beaconegg" (382.11) Joyce optimistically aligns the hen with the most popular "eggoarchicism" [first egg] which has caught the fancy of numerous storytellers. Preserved in a common metaphor for the life of ease ("Don't kill the goose that lays the golden egg"), it establishes the round, yellow yolk of the egg as a symbol for the sun, because, like the mud of the Nile, the sun was thought also to bring forth life. This is one of the "subjects being their passion grand," the "gooth a gev a gotheny egg" (394.27) which makes a story more fabulous than that of Tristan and Isolde; and it is the "golden sheegg" (450.1) of Shaun's "shy orient." Such an analogy also offers at least one explanation of Issy's accounting for herself as "burned a rich egg" (527.14).

The very imaginative tale of the creation in the *Kalevala* allows for a "mother of the water" who raised her leg so that the "goldeneye" bird built its nest on her knee; when she moved, the bits of egg separated but retained their individual integrity:

> The bits were turned into fine things, the pieces into beautiful things:
> The lower half of one egg into the earth beneath,
> The top of another egg into the heavens above.
> The top half of one yolk gets to glow like the sun,
> The top half of one white gets to gleam palely as the moon;
> Any mottled things on an egg, those become stars in heaven,
> Anything black on an egg, those indeed become the clouds in the sky.[82]

The explosive moment of creation, when the goddess raised her knee as told in the *Kalevala* or the American thunderbird burst from the whale, in Joyce's mind is like the "celestial intemperance" or raging of the elements occasioned by what he satirically calls the "war-to-end war by Messrs a charitable government" (178.25–26). The timid Shem, therefore, emerges from hiding to test whether the earth has settled back to normalcy after the World War, "with an eachway hope in his shivering soul, as he prayed to the cloud Incertitude, of finding out for himself, on akkount of all the kules in Kroukaparka or oving ["owing" plus *ove*] to all the kodseoggs in Kalatavala, whether true conciliation was forging ahead or falling back after the celestious intemperance" (178.30–35).

The commonest mythical sources of life—water, egg, tree—frequently merge in a setting which offers all at once. *The Book of the Dead,* for example, contains instructions, accompanied with an explicit vignette, for the soul of the deceased to utter these words: "Hail, thou sycamore of the goddess Nut! Grant thou to me of the water and of the air which dwell in thee. I embrace the throne which is in Unnu (Heliopolis), and I watch and guard the egg of the Great Cackler."[83] One of two trees, presumably at eastern and western ends of the sky, Budge believes this sycamore was the one under which the Virgin Mary sat and rested during her flight to Egypt, for "many of the details about her wanderings in the Delta, which are recorded in the Apocryphal Gospels and in writings of a similar class, are borrowed from the old mythology of Egypt."[84] Similarly, Newall relates, "A Hindu symbol reproduced in *Les Religions de L'Antiquite* shows the Cosmic Tree growing up from the primeval egg which lies deep in the waters of creation."[85] Joyce, then, writes a magnificent description of a bisexual cosmic tree (504.20-505.13) teeming with life and representing all phases of existence (even the Kilmainham jail) and all philosophies (ending with a triumphant exclamation, "Evovae!"). The Scandinavian Yggdrasil, with its spring at the root, serves as model, while Joyce's specific reference to it marks the bird as origin of life with its egg representing the gold and white of sun and moon: "cock robins muchmore hatching most out of his missado eggdrazzles for him, the sun and moon pegging honeysuckle and white heather down" (504.34-505.1).

Joyce obviously knew of superstitions, as well as mythology, surrounding any small or unusual egg, for these merely glossed and overburdened the already portentous ovum and doubled in significance because the cock himself was credited with extraordinary powers, especially because he "shook the east awake." From a cock's egg might come supernatural demons and monsters such as the basilisk, and in 1474 at Basle a cock was convicted as sorcerer and actually burned at the stake with its egg.[86] Venetia Newall finds a natural basis for belief in a cock's egg: "Because of the cock's magic powers, misshapen eggs were attributed to it and greatly feared. In fact, the bodies of aged roosters sometimes contain a small, white egg-shaped globule, which may help to account for the superstition, particularly as it was only an aged rooster that was supposed to lay a 'cock's egg.' "[87] This is why Joyce's "cock robins" may hatch "missado eggdrazzles" and why the House That Jack Built—another cosmic metaphor—can contain the line, "that cribbed the Cabin that never was owned that cocked his leg and hennad his Egg" (205.35-36). HCE's name is punned into *"Hatches Cocks' Eggs"* (71.27); since mistaken sex may explain some of these phenomena, Jaun claims to have read a book entitled *"Egg Laid by Former Cock"* (440.20); "elacock eggs" are attributed to "provincials" (447.12); and Treacle Tom vows, "as sure as my briam eggs is on cockshot under noose" (524.33–34).

When cocks lay eggs in Joyce's cosmic tree, however, it merges with that one fatal to the peace of mind of Adam-Earwicker (see 506.4–8), who is also a man of nineteen names including "Egbert Yggdrasselmann" (88.21–23), or "Haroun Childeric Eggeberth" (4.32), or, with reference to his store, "Hennery Canterel—Cockran, eggotisters, limitated" (137.7–8), or "Hung Chung Egglyfella" (374.34). Here, in the example of the egg is the concept of creation as the original sin; and, in the example of the apple, the timelessness of paradise is broken. The connection with Humpty Dumpty, established in this manner, becomes explicit in the "football match song": *Broken Eggs will poursuive bitten Apples for where theirs is Will there's his Wall*" (175.19–20). Shem is observed to "get up" a "fowlhouse for the sake of akes" with the astute parenthetical judgment, "the umpple does not fall very far from the dumpertree" (184.13–14).

Since the first egg laid by a pullet had especial significance, the Scots had a term *eirack* for it,[88] and this puns nicely as a name for Earwicker who committed the prototypal sin. In the Mime he is "King Ericus of Schweden" who is "partially recovered from a recent impeachment due to egg everlasting," and the term combines with the *v* and *w* sound shift in "Ericus Vericus corrupted into ware eggs" (373.24). *Egged*, when used in the sense of *urged*, completes the sexual implications of the fall; many kinds of kings, like Earwicker, "were egged on by their supporters in the shape of betterwomen" (87.27), and a title for Anna Livia's "manifesto" reveals her part in the Edenic sin: *"It Was Me Egged Him on to the Stork Exchange and Lent my Dutiful Face to His Customs"* (106.17–19). The sin aspect of Earwicker's fall carries through his business activities, as seen in the Stock Exchange, and his ownership of a store makes him a butter and egg man, always with the emphasis on sex; as Humpty Dumpty, therefore, his fall becomes the collapse of Wall Street: "whiles eggs will fall cheapened all over the walled the Bure will be dear on the Brie" (163.27–28). In stuttering he reveals his anxiety when, during an attempt at self-defense, he renounces a fourth part in a "mouthless niggeress" (compare Anna Livia's—the Liffey's—"mouthless face" in 101.30) as "eggseggs excessively haroween to my feelimbs" (537.28–29). His being driven out of house and home in disgrace becomes "they provencials drollo eggspilled him out of his homety dometry narrowedknee domum" (230.4–6), and Mutt and Jute review the crime, "He was poached on in that eggtentical spot" (16.36), the Edenic-Phoenix Park spot where life began. Jaun rehashes the entire escapade to sermonize Issy on proper behavior: "Leg-before-Wicked lags-behind-Wall where here Mr Whicker whacked a great fall. Femorafamilla feeled it a candleliked but Hayes, Conyngham and Erobinson sware it's an egg" (434.10-13).

Earwicker's connection through Humpty Dumpty with the term *hoddy-doddy* has been already observed, and the parallels with his humpbacked physique and henpecked position. Eckenstein collects the Humpty Dumpty riddle rhymes,[89] and, tracing them back to a children's game in which girls roll with skirts clasped tightly at the feet, in imitation of an egg, accounts for the most bizarre element of the standard rhyme, "sitting on a wall, or a bank, or a ledge . . . or lying in a beck, which for an actual egg are impossible situations."[90] She concludes that the sport must be older than the rhyme. Interest in it may have been stimulated in the seventeenth century when the term *Humpty Dumpty* meant a drink consisting of ale boiled in brandy;[91] but the meaning sustained throughout the allusions to Earwicker is that of the original sun myth, even to the extent of the sun's power represented in the king who drove his horses across the sky. The Adversary in one *Wake* repetition of the primal sin is mistaken for Earwicker, "to whom the headandheelless chickenestegg bore some Michelangiolesque resemblance" (81.22-23), a reminder of the barrel vault of the Sistine ceiling; and in some riddle rhymes the egg is described "as a cask containing two kinds of beer."[92]

The implications of the fall of the sun egg, or the sin in the park, are endless and awe-inspiring, especially should the fall of the sun signal the end of the world; but this event, in Joyce's terms, could mean only the semination of the new. In a double sense, then, when Treacle Tom is accused ("Y'are absexed, so y'are, with makerglosia and mickroocyphyllicks") he replies, "Wait now, leixlep! I scent eggoarchicism" (525.8-10).* That the egg is present at the beginning, continues through all, and constitutes another new beginning, Joyce expressed in "the tantum ergons irruminate the quantum urge so that eggs is to whey as whay is to zeed" (167.7-8). The continuation of all seems inescapable, as evidenced in the ubiquitous hen: "even if Humpty shell fall frumpty times as awkward again in the beardsboosoloom of all our grand remonstrancers there'll be iggs for the brekkers come to mournhim, sunny side up with care" (12.12-15).

As usual, because Shem's meager diet consists of little more than eggs, Joyce employs the common food item to distinguish Shem from Shaun. In

---

* Perhaps a third meaning should be derived from the "absexed" charge. Venetia Newall writes, "In the sixteenth-century eggs, mussels, garlic and onion all symbolized debauchery, because of their supposed aphrodisiac properties." Ibid., p. 357.

a passage testing Shem's (or Joyce's) ingenuity, Joyce displays Shem's internationalism with a list of ten varieties of eggs. "Our low hero," he writes, "brooled and cocked and potched in an athanor, whites and yolks and yilks and whotes" (184.17-18); all these efforts provide "his oewfs à la Madame Gabrielle de l'Eglise, his avgs à la Mistress B. de B. Meinfelde, his eiers Usquadmala à la pomme de ciel, his uoves, oves and uves à la Sulphate de Soude, his ochiuri sowtay sowmmonay à la Monseigneur, his soufflosion of oogs with somekat on toyast à la Mere Puard, his Poggado-vies alla Fenella, his Frideggs à la Tricarême" (184.26-32). This explains why, among the litter in his house, are numerous "doubtful eggshells" (183.12) and why Shaun calls him peculiar, "that eggschicker" (423.19). Shem's near-starvation is part and parcel of his craft as a writer and an exile, "With harm and aches till farther alters!" (229.1) in contrast with his brother. Stanislaus Joyce wrote into his diary, "What use is all this writing to me when, for instance, there is no dinner in the house?"[93] And Shaun-Jaun paints a dreary picture of his brother Shem-Dave's appearance: "He is looking aged with his pebbled eyes, and johnnythin too, from livicking on pidgins' ifs [oeufs] with puffins' ands" (463.27-28). Since Shem stands for druidism as opposed to Shaun's Catholicism, Shem "druider would smilabit eggways" (288.5).

Shaun by contrast uses eggs as only a small part of his vast diet, but a worthy one. Fond of food, he announces "Stamp out bad eggs" (437.21) as his motto. As Shaun-Butt he knows the importance of character revealed in cooking eggs (339.3) and gives a gift of "meggs and teggs" (351.3). Because he is a sincere patriot, eggs dribbled on his vest help to deck him in the green, white, and orange of Ireland when he appears as Shaun the Post "with his motto through dear life embrothred over it in peas, rice, and yeggy-yolk" (404.28-29). Among a virtual catalog of foods he con-sumes at one sitting, eggs appear often with meat, "the half of a pint of becon with newled googs" (405.33-34), "with second course eyer and becon (the rich of) with broad beans, hig, steak, hag, pepper the diamond bone" (406.15-16), and in general "given prelove appetite and postlove pricing good coup, goodcheap, were it thermidor oogst or floreal may while the whistling prairial roysters play . . . he grubbed his tuck all right" (406.35-407.2). Finally in the role of holy Saint Kevin greeting the dawn he appears "with that smeoil like a grace of backoning over his egglips of the sunsoonshine" (603.1-2); apparently the young Stephen's resentment of the physical comfort of the clergy, exemplified in the "smiling well-dressed priest" (*AP* 84), continues into the wellfed clergy of the *Wake*.

Eggs as sustenance doubled in purpose and meaning with the spring-time egg festivals which originally in many instances clearly derived from fertility rites. Many of the Easter games of the past which have been discontinued or adulterated in contemporary custom were followed by egg feasts, some with contests for the person who could consume the largest number of eggs. While Joyce does not confuse Shaun's appetite with folklore, he does develop several aspects of the ancient Easter games. The children in the grammar lesson assert "The game [of life] goes on" (269.22), and they refer to the egg and spoon race in discussing whether "egg she active or spoon she passive" (269.28). The matching of boy and girl in some of the games implied their engagement, and often the feast at a local inn after the games provided an economic reason for their encouragement. In Issy's letter, therefore, she expresses mock indignation at "that espos of a Clancarbry," plus "you, Innkipper" (obviously HCE) and others "baiting at my Lord Ornery's, just becups they won the egg and spoon there so ovally provencial at Balldole" (144.5-10). Consciously seductive as Issy always is, she adds, "He is seeking an opening and means to be first with me as his belle alliance" (144.11-12). Some of the contests required hard eggs, for tossing, rolling, or tapping, because the winning egg survived with shell unbroken. Processes for strengthening the egg shell, such as soaking the egg in lime or alcohol for a week,[94] therefore gave great significance to the age of an egg. Some such awareness plus calendar changes seems to lend significance to the gift included in Anna's "zakbag," when she carries "a niester egg with a twicedated shell and a dynamight right for Pavl the Curate" (210.35-36). The game of egg hunting, with fertility overtones, appears in the list of games where it is called *"Eggs in the Bush"* (176.10), while sailing the shells, another common Easter game, helps Shaun to denounce the shamefulness of the famous letter: "An infant sailing eggshells on the floor of a wet day would have more sabby" (420.15-16). Easter rites combine with the forcefulness of HCE's incarceration for his crime when "he felt like sticking out his chest too far and tempting gracious providence by a stroll on the peoplade's eggday, unused as he was yet to being freely clodded" (69.27-29), with a reference to the annual throwing of eggs which sometimes resulted in brawls and to HCE's Easter-time resurrection. That HCE is enclosed in a place with an "applegate" (69.21) returns to the Edenic theme of the fall in association with Humpty Dumpty which is developed elsewhere, while the woman and fertility (or sexuality) theme is developed in "And let oggs be good old gaggles and Isther Estarr play Yesther Asterr" (69.13-14).

The possible disgrace of being clotted with eggs is only one aspect of Earwicker's character in association with them; clearly, Joyce insists, his eyes have the appearance of eggs just as Leopold Bloom remarked of Howard Parnell, "Poached eyes on ghost" (*U* 165). When the Wet Pinter answers questions at Festy King's trial, his features are described: "A crossgrained trapper with murty odd oogs [eyes], awflorated ares [ears], inquiline nase [nose] and a twithcherous mouph [mouth]?" (88.16-18). And in his midwinter decline, Anna Livia sees her husband with "his fringe combed over his eygs" (199.5-6). The same sort of disparagement, when Shaun speaks of Shem, can turn the Platonic parable to an accounting not at all flattering. Shaun remarks, "We were in one class of age like to two clots of egg" (489.19).

Like Joyce's use of birds and bird myths, his use of eggs and egg myths reveals a profound understanding of the fundamentals of myth at the same time he returns the abstraction to a basis in physical fact and to the purposes of his novel. Joyce's HCE is a hump-backed Humpty Dumpty who falls, in a manner analogous to the sun from the western sky, from the historic magazine wall or the serpentine wall of Phoenix Park and simultaneously commits the sin in the Park. Joyce diagrams the continuing egg of life at the center of Anna Livia's anatomy. His hen is expected to show her beaconegg but at dawn is preoccupied with sexual matters so that the cock has a sexual triumph, not a cosmic phenomenon, to crow about. The cock's egg of folk belief connects with HCE's store and the mysterious unconfirmed rumors about him. Eggs as food reflect the eternal brother conflict.

But regardless of how far civilization turns from its origins and its ancient customs or how skeptically Joyce turns the esoteric backward into the exoteric, he sees the eternal morning dawn, "Cockalooralooraloomenos" (615.8), in the vital principles of the origin of life and letters, "as sure as herself pits hen to paper and there's scribings scrawled on eggs" (615.9-10). Such introduces Anna Livia's closing monologue, where living becomes continual. Joyce has uttered the same prayer many times: "And let every crisscouple be so crosscomplimentary, little eggons, youlk and meelk, in a farbiger pancosmos" (613.10-12).

V. IT'S PHOENIX, DEAR

The witlessness of hens must have been apparent to James Joyce, since, in the midst of his long account of the letter found by the hen, like an armchair Thackeray he intrudes his editorial comment to jeer at his audience, "You most shouts out: Bethicket me for a stump of a beech if I have the poultriest notions what the farest he all means" (112.4-6). In the same manner, the hen's early morning activities of copulation with the unnamed rooster lack the dignity of cosmic proportions: "the hen in the doran's shantyqueer began in a kikkery key to laugh it off, yeigh, yeigh, neigh, neigh, the way she was wuck to doodledoo by her gallows bird (how's that? Noball, he carries his bat!) nine hundred and dirty too not out, at all times long past conquering cock of the morgans" (584.20–25). The narrator intrudes another comment, "How blame us?" (584.26) while the rooster, apparently not even distantly concerned with shaking the east awake, crows "Cocorico!" (584.27) about his sexual conquest. Just as the hen was frightened of water but powerless to avoid the peal of the thunderword, the sun of the new day rises in true Viconian fashion without her aid or cognizance. Joyce, then, retains to the end his early insistence that Biddy the Hen is merely "a parody's bird."

In doing so, Joyce avoids the errors surrounding mythologies of fabulous birds and remembers, as many persons did not, that the fabled birds were symbols—mere abstract expressions of physical phenomena—and not intended as physical realities in themselves. There are at least five principal varieties of the phoenix myth, primarily a sun myth,[95] which Budge claims derives from the Egyptian "Bennu": "According to the story which Herodotus heard at Heliopolis, the bird visited that place once every five hundred years, on its father's death; when it was five hundred, or fourteen hundred and sixty-one years old, it burnt itself to death. It was supposed to resemble an eagle, and to have red and gold feathers, and to come from Arabia; before its death it built a nest to which it gave the power of producing a new phoenix, though some thought that a worm crept out of its body before it died, and that from it the heat of the sun developed a new phoenix."[96] Since the bird was the symbol of Rā and Osiris, in Chapter LXXXII of *The Book of the Dead,* instructions were given for the "deceased to transform himself into a Bennu bird if he felt disposed to do so; in it he identifies himself with the god Khepera, and with Horus, the vanquisher of Set, and with Khensu."[97]

To the primitive mind, immortality meant resurrection; and this is the meaning Joyce intends when he uses the symbol of the phoenix in connection with HCE. The theme is announced early in the book: "Phall if you but will, rise you must; and none so soon either shall the pharce for the nunce come to a setdown secular phoenish" (4.15–17). When HCE is the giant Finn MacCool, the symbol reasserts HCE's resurrection at least three times over: "the phoenix be his pyre" (128.35); he was "comminxed under articles but phoenished a borgiess" (130.11–12); and "he crashed in the hollow of the park, trees down, as he soared in the vaguum of the phoenix, stones up" (136.33–35). The phoenix as a palm tree was "the only tree known to the ancients which never changed its leaves"[98] and remains a symbolic Tree of Life, but the annual life cycle of any tree makes it an appropriate symbol for all life, even to the extent of the death of the tree from whose decay new trees spring: "The oaks of ald now they lie in peat yet elms leap where askes lay" (4.14-15). HCE then becomes that tree as a symbol for all recurring life which whirls around it; his death is foretold in the destruction of the tree and his resurrection implied: "their convoy wheeled encirculingly abound the gigantig's lifetree, our fireleaved lover-lucky blomsterbohm, phoenix in our woodlessness, haughty, cacuminal, erubescent (repetition!) whose roots they be asches with lustres of peins" (55.26-30). HCE's list of nineteen names concluding with "Yggdrassel-mann" is then followed with the exclamation, "Holy Saint Eiffel, the very phoenix!" (88.23-24).

The flame of the phoenix, then, originally indicative of the flaming sun, appears in such expressions as "Pynix Park" (534.12) and essentially asserts resurrection rather than signals destruction: "the phoenix, his pyre, is still flaming away with trueprattight spirit" (265.8-10). The customers in the pub may malign ALP for apparent indifference during HCE's lapse, "As if ever she cared an assuan damm about her harpoons sticking all out of him whet between phoenix his calipers and that psourdonome sheath" (332.30-32), but the symbol sustains the certainty of resurrection. The phases glide one into another, so that the lyrical close of Chapter 14 stresses the emergence of the new before the old has perished: "The phaynix rose a sun before Erebia sank his smother! Shoot up on that, bright Bennu bird! *Va faotre!* Eftsoon so too will our own sphoenix spark spirt his spyre and sunward stride the rampante flambe" (473.16-19).

Wherever the "sphoenix spark" indicates the Phoenix Park, in addition to the particular incident of HCE's sin in the park, Joyce turns to local matters of management ("Touching our Phoenix Rangers' nuisance," 587. 25, the appointment in 1679 of two keepers and a ranger to supervise the park), of history of the city ("Fiendish park," 196.11; the "phaymix cup-plerts," 331.2, the Phoenix Park Murders of Lord Frederick Cavendish and T. H. Burke on May 6, 1882), the geographic representation of the legendary giant Finn MacCool ("Finn his park," 564.08; "Big Maester Finnykin with Phenicia Parkes," 576.28), and of the Park's reputation as "one of the largest and most magnificent city parks in Europe"[99] ("Finest Park," 461.10; and for his city and ALP, HCE builds "a Queen's garden of her phoenix," 553.24-25). This city pride then connects with the city motto, *"Obedientia Civium Urbis Felicitas,"* or "The obedience of the citizens is the good of the town," which Joyce rephrases in "the ubideintia of the savium is our ervics fenicitas" (610.7-8) and in "If you want to be felixed come and be parked" (454.34).

While the spelling of phoenix mutates toward both *felicitas* in the motto and "felix" in the repeated reference to the Edenic fall, "O felix culpa," the Phoenix Park, like the bird, becomes emblematic of both fall and rise, or death and resurrection—its positive Edenic connotations marred in history by the murder and in the novel by HCE's sin. The term provides, then, with obvious dubious intentions a culprit when applied to Kersse the tailor ("for finixed coulpure," 311.26) and a possible murderer of the Russian General, "Colporal Phailinx" (346.36). HCE's fall *is* the Edenic fall in "O foenix culprit!" (23.16), but because the exact nature of his sin remains a mystery, "he reddled a ruad to riddle a rede from the sphinxish pairc while Ede was a guardin" (324.6-7). The sin takes place where the letter is discovered, at the "filthdump near the Serpentine in Phornix Park" (80.6). Because all creation is in some form sexual and the Edenic sin is sometimes interpreted as sexual, as was reputedly HCE's crime, Phoenix and fornication blend humorously in "the feelmick's park" (520.1) and in "Let a prostitute be whoso stands before a door and winks or parks herself in the fornix near a makeussin wall (sinsin! sinsin!) and the curate one who brings strong waters (gingin! gingin!)" (116.16-19).

The curate as an assistant in a pub who brings whiskey or the Water of Life° therefore connects with the famed "Phoenix brewery stout" (382.04), or "a bottle of Phenice—Bruerie '98" (38.4); and Shaun drinks "her old phoenix portar" (406.10). That the fall is necessary to the rise, or the death to the resurrection, as implied in "O happy fault," becomes apparent when HCE's sin is known and discussed immediately after its commission in the "Phoenix Tavern" (205.25). All these references to the Tavern, the sexual delights in the Park, and the Water of Life which will awaken the fallen Finnegan combine in "Let be buttercup eve lit by night in the Phoenix! Music. And old lotts have funn at Flammagen's ball" (321.16-17). Just as the Phoenix Park is the setting for everything that happens in the novel, HCE's Tavern becomes a stage for all the world, according to the proclamation which opens Chapter 9 for the Mime of Mick, Nick, and the Maggies. "Every evening at lighting up o'clock sharp and until further notice in Feenichts Playhouse" (219.1-2).

In another sense, when Shem-Dolph seeks to bring the light of learning to Shaun-Kev in the Chapter 10 lessons, he is represented in the footnote as one of the many endangered and sequestered instructors of a forbidden

---

° Bayley explains, "The magic elixir revives the dead, awakes the sleeping, cures the sick, opens the eyes of the blind, restores the petrified to life, causes a vast accession of strength to the strong, and imparts immortal youth and loveliness." See *Lost Language*, I, 242. In the Song of Solomon, it is called the "best wine" in its form as the liquor of Wisdom. See *Last Language*, 252.

subject(sex): "What signifieth whole that but, be all the prowess of ten, 'tis as strange to relate he, nonparile to rede, rite and reckan, caught allmeals dullmarks for his nucleuds and alegobrew. They wouldn't took bearings no how anywheres. O them doddhunters and allanights, aabs and baas for agnomes, yees and zees for incognits, bate him up jerrybly!" (283.20-28). The footnote reads, "Slash-the-Pill lifts the pellet. Run, Phoenix, run!" (283, n. 3). Like a captured chicken, rather than the bird of flight, Shem should make his escape before the onslaught begins, before they can "bate him up jerrybly."

All these asseverations—which combine the light of life in the flaming sun myth, the Water of Life from the Phoenix brewery, the creative (sexual) aspects of the sin in the Phoenix Park, the lights of the Tavern stage, the light of Shem-Dolph's sexual knowledge—deny a contradiction implied in the usage of the term *phoenix* near the close of the *Wake*'s third book. Here HCE has just concluded an unproductive union with ALP; it is, by nature, certainly his last: "never again, by Phoenis, swore on him Lloyd's" (590.5). And the factual stability of Lloyd's of London lends credence to the vow, with the added insinuations of the famed insurers' having been burned out in 1838 and rebuilt, and of the phoenix as the emblem of a large American insurance company. All readers of the *Wake* realize, however, that HCE is certain to rearise. Since he is also a Phoenician sailor of the Ulysses type, the *ricorso* confirms, "the Phoenician wakes" (608.32).

Because Ireland in reality knew no such bird as the phoenix with its red and gold feathers descriptive of the sun, Joyce naturally attached his allusions and references to the phoenix myth to physical realities, such as Park and Brewery, befitting the typically Irish setting of the novel. Of native habitat are those birds which Anna Livia sees in her closing monologue as she imagines herself walking with HCE and watching the birds made famous by Yeats at Coole Park: "Look, there are yours off, high on high! And cooshes, sweet good luck they're cawing you, Coole! You see, they're as white as the riven snae. For us" (621.36-622.2). Colorless, rather than colorful, these white birds recall the swan maidens of Irish lore and the prophetic birds of the Nibelungen saga. In the last instance the singular bird of Anna Livia's passing out to sea appears like the Vedic "Swan out of Time and Space" in her hopeful thoughts, "If I seen him bearing down on me now under whitespread wings like he'd come from Arkangels, I sink I'd die down over his feet, humbly dumbly, only to washup" (628.9-11); the Swan out of Eternity should lay the new egg ("humpty dumpty") from which the new universe will be born. In this manner Joyce returns Anna's thoughts to a time preceding the creation of the phoenix-sun, just as Anna Livia, no longer a river, returns to the globe-encircling ocean. At the same time the gulls (628.13), like those which anciently led the sailors, bid her onward in her ocean voyage.

Having developed the hawklike man as an image of the artist in the *Portrait,* and having established Shem as artist in the *Wake,* Joyce devotes little space in the *Wake* to a repetition of the flight of the artist's swift intellect, or to his divinity as represented in a bird. On the other hand, Shaun's association with lowly ground birds—the goose, the guinea hen, the partridge, the corncrake—merits sufficient space to imply a distinction from Shem. Shaun, a poser all his life, assumes the pose of the gods whom many men have created. Shem, the mystical, creative force of the actual Unknowable god, does not pass through successive stages, as does Shaun, does not strike such affirmable poses, and remains essentially absent and mysterious. The insinuation of the god's presence at the discovery of the letter is in the sounding of the thunderword in defiance of the hen's established preference for dry weather. Although Joyce in mimic suggests her association with light, her inability to represent the cosmos, in contradiction of many cosmogonies in which the creative spirit is represented as a bird, continues to the end when her anticipated "beaconegg," the sun, rises independent of her efforts. The cosmos exists and its elements function in spite of, not because of, the hen.

In like proportion, Joyce's awareness of egg mythologies and egg rituals which survive to the present time only enable him to write his own version of these stories. His phoenix is securely attached to local places and conditions; at the same time the question "Which came first, the egg or its creator?" implies, as Venetia Newall states, "A magical procreative cycle."[100] And, just as Joyce wrote of Vico's cycles that he would not pay "overmuch attention to these theories, beyond using them for all they are worth,"[101] so he uses mythologies—for illustrative purposes—while he creates his own "farbiger pancosmos."

NOTES

1 Aage Brusendorff, *The Chaucer Tradition* (London and Copenhagen, 1924), p. 262 ff.; as I note later, Brusendorff himself accepts Furnivall's separation, but he persuasively supports the linking of the poems on the level of the so-called "personal allegory." See also Haldeen Braddy, *Chaucer and the French Poet Graunson* (Baton Rouge, La.: Louisiana State University Press, 1947), pp. 71 ff., for additional arguments of the latter sort in favor of the linking. G. H. Cowling, *Chaucer* (London, 1927), p. 63, points explicitly to the assumption underlying the theories they all hold: he says that whoever Mars and Venus may represent, the same persons are represented in both poems.

2 I follow the transcription given in Eleanor P. Hammond, *Chaucer: A Bibliographical Manual* (New York, 1933), p. 384. Hammond also summarizes the question of sources.

3 In his phrase "knight Savosyen" Shirley provides a key to another ironical statement in "Lenvoy": though Grandson wrote in French, he seldom "made" in what was known as France, but rather in Savoy, in England, or even in a Spanish prison. Grandson himself, in *Le songe Saint Valentin* (which was almost certainly known to Chaucer and may have provided the suggestion for *The Parliament of Fowls*), distinguishes his native Savoy from France; near the end of the poem, his dreamer expresses his pity for "tous amans,"

> Soyent englois ou alemens,
> De France né ou de Savoye . . .

—ll. 402-406, p. 322, in Arthur Piaget, *Oton de Grandson, sa vie et ses poésies,* (Lausanne, 1941). See Piaget's discussion of Grandson's life, pp. 11–20, and Braddy, *Chaucer and the French Poet Graunson,* pp. 22-37, for a description of the poet's career in England, Spain, and Savoy.

4 On Shirley's reliability see Brusendorff, *The Chaucer Tradition,* p. 231, where

he shows that ". . . the textual value of Shirley's copies is practically negligible in view of the many arbitrary changes he introduced into his text. . . ." On p. 234 he argues that Shirley's collections "have a real importance through their notes about the authors."

5 Chaucer, *Works,* ed. F. N. Robinson, textual notes, "Mars," p. 916; "Venus," p. 919. With respect to the latter, Robinson shows three groups, but the first of these (α) consists of two Shirley MSS, and in view of Brusendorff's remark quoted above, it seems improbable that we should ascribe any independent authority to this group. One of these Shirley MSS, moreover, is that (MS R. 3, 20) containing the rubrics discussed above, whose version of the "Mars" (according to Robinson) is in the same textual group (β) as both versions contained in Pepys 2006, Arch. Selden B. 24, and Harley 7333. The other is Ashmole 59, discussed below in the text; it is late and extremely unreliable. Robinson apparently derived his MS schemata from Heath in the Globe edition (London, 1898), p. xxxvi for the "Mars," and p. 1 for the "Venus." It should be noted here that Heath perpetuates the erroneous belief that Shirley's rubrics are responsible for suggesting the title of the "Venus" despite the fact that his own MS schema makes such contamination seem highly improbable, to say the least. It was no doubt merely a slip of the pen which made him go even further and say that Shirley gave "The Compleynt of Venus" this very title—for Shirley never once refers to the poem as a "compleynt."

It should perhaps be emphasized that in both branches of the MS tradition the two parts of the poem together form a single textual unit. Brusendorff's discussions of the "Hammond group" of MSS, including Fairfax 16 and Tanner 346, and of the "Tyrwhitt group," including both versions in Pepys 2006 and probably Notary's edition, make it clear that "Mars" and "Venus" occurred together in both of the "booklets" from which the respective traditions descend (Brusendorff, *The Chaucer Tradition,* pp. 183-198). Therefore, among significant MSS and prints (that is, those containing both complaints, except for Shirley's MS R. 3, 20) the division into textual groupings is the same. On the basis of Robinson's and Heath's schemata, we find the following groups for these MSS:

	"Mars"			"Venus"
α	Fairfax 16 Tanner 346 Thynne's edition	α (Robinson's β)	Fairfax 16 Tanner 346 Thynne's edition (not included in schemata, but Robinson says it "often agrees with β")	
β	Pepys 2006, Hand B Pepys 2006, Hand E Arch. Selden B.24 Notary's edition	β (Robinson's γ)	Pepys 2006, Hand B Pepys 2006, Hand E Arch. Selden B.24 Notary's edition	

As for MS R. 3, 20, Brusendorff's rejection of its independent authority as regards the "Venus" (together with Ashmole 59) is supplemented by his statement, p. 263 n, with regard to Shirley's versions, "From a textual point of view his copies of both poems are comparatively close to the Tyrwhitt group." In other words, Shirley's texts give no real basis for supposing that the complaints circulated independently before the late and unauthoritative copies, discussed further on in the text, were made.

6   This discussion draws on Hammond and Brusendorff as cited above. See also, on Longleat 258, Hammond's article in *MLN*, XX (1905), 77-79. Robbins describes the "Findern Anthology" in *PMLA*, LXIX (1954), 610-642.

7   Brusendorff, *The Chaucer Tradition*, pp. 178-207, "The Manuscript Collections."

8   See Robinson's notes to the "Mars," pp. 856-857, for the controversies over this "personal allegory," and the articles cited there.

9   Chauncey Wood, *Chaucer and the Country of the Stars* (Princeton, N.J., 1970), p. 104, suggests that Shirley's "doughter to the kyng of Spaygne" means John of Gaunt's daughter (thus Shirley would be mistaken in his rubric); Wood seems not to realize that Isabel Langley's father was indeed King of Spain. It seems highly unlikely that Shirley, writing several decades after Gaunt's failure to make good his claim to the Castilian throne (his second wife was Isabel's older sister Constance, but Pedro's brother Enrique had taken possession of the throne), would refer to the Duke by such a title, especially as he calls him "þe Duc Iohn of Lancaster" in the preceding rubric.

10   Cf. Wood, *Chaucer and the Country of the Stars*, p. 107; Brusendorff's discussion is also relevant here.

11   Braddy, *Chaucer and the French Poet Graunson*, pp. 71-80, discusses the matter at some length. Piaget, *Oton de Grandson*, pp. 156-164, suggests Isabel of Bavaria, Queen of France; N. R. Cartier, in *Romania*, LXXXV (1964), 1-16, prefers Isabel Countess of Neuchatel. These scholars have no real evidence to support their arguments, but simply theorize on the basis of the possibilities of Grandson's life. Shirley at least had access to authentic channels of information, as Braddy shows.

12   Chaucer, *Complete Works*, ed. W. W. Skeat, 6 vols. (Oxford, 1894), I, 87.

13   Piaget, "Oton de Granson et ses poésies," *Romania*, XIX (1890), 418-419; Paget Toynbee in *Academy*, XXXIX (1891), 442.

14   See Jean Seznec, *The Survival of the Pagan Gods*, trans. Barbara F. Sessions (New York, 1953), figs. 50 and 71, pp. 138 and 186, for representations of Jupiter with beard and spear; the miniaturist's comic realism is strikingly emphasized by the contrast between these figures, one majestic, the other seated on an eagle, and the fatherly moralist portrayed in the Fairfax painting. See the discussion of Apollo's attributes, Seznec, pp. 177-178. Wood's discussion occurs on pp. 132, 136, *Chaucer and the Country of the Stars*. It is worth mentioning, in relation to this discussion, that Troilus addresses Jove in terms like those used by Mars for "the God that sit so hye" in *Troilus and Criseyde*,

III,, 1016—"But O, thow Jove, O auctour of nature"—and reproaches him for injustice; just afterward he speaks of "heighe God that sit above" (III, 1027).

15   See Seznec, *Survival of the Pagan Gods*, figs. 74-78, pp. 190-192, for representations which emphasize the threatening rapacity of Mars' wolf. A comparison of the fully armed Mars of these pictures with the totally naked Mars shown in other illustrations of the story (cf. Wood, figs. 16 and 17) suggests the possibility that Mars' half-dressed condition in the Fairfax miniature results from the witty crossing of the two iconographical traditions, brought into correspondence with the comic "facts" of this treatment.

16   The grouping of the three women strongly resembles that of the Graces in the detail from the Tarocchi engravings reproduced in Edgar Wind, *Pagan Mysteries in the Renaissance*, enl. and rev. ed. (Harmondsworth, 1967), fig. 18. The Fairfax ladies, however, lack the attributes—loin cloth, flower, and flame—which signify Castitas, Pulchritudo, and Amor (p. 75). The comparison emphasizes the awkward postures and ungainly bodies of the Fairfax ladies, showing how the artist can use serious iconographic traditions to underline the comic realism of his—and Chaucer's—treatment of the story.

17   Once more Robinson, Hammond and Brusendorff are the sources for this discussion.

18   John Lydgate, *Fall of Princes*, ed. Henry Bergen, 4 vols. (London, 1924), I, 9-10: Prologue, ll. 320-329; discussed by Brusendorff, *The Chaucer Tradition*, pp. 261-262.

19   Scribal puzzlement over such "difficult" titles is evident in the analogous case of the poem printed by Robinson as "Fortune" (pp. 535-536), which is found in several manuscripts under the heading of "Balades de vilage sanz peinture." According to Hammond (p. 369), Henry Bradshaw first pointed out that the original title must have been "Balades de visage sanz peinture," referring to Book II, Prose I, of Boethius' *Consolation of Philosophy*. The "Pleintif" accuses Fortune of being a "fals dissimulour" who is now unmasked for him, and Fortune herself takes credit for showing him the difference between "Frend of effect, and frend of countenaunce" (l. 34). From two points of view, therefore, a visage has been stripped of its painting, so to speak. Chaucer's witty flattery consists in implying that the "beste frend" of Balade II has such an "unpainted" visage—and that therefore he may be relied on to help the "pleintif" to "atteyne" "som beter estat" (1. 79). Thus a title which seemingly applies only to points within a larger argument, and that in oblique and allusive fashion, really indicates the central intentions of the poem; for in the end the "pleintif's" heroic defiance of Fortune (he compares himself to Socrates) appears mere "peinture" for a begging poem—his "visage" is unmasked, like that of Fortune and of his false friends. Neither the original error in the title nor its transmission by uncomprehending scribes should surprise us, nor the tendency of scribes to drop it altogether in favor of more obvious headings, such as Shirley's "A compleynte of the Pleintyff against fortune."

20   Statius, *Thebaid,* trans. J. H. Manly (London and Cambridge, Mass.: Loeb
      Classical Library, 1961), pp. 414–416, Bk. II, ll. 266–305. The ME "broche" is
      simply a translation of the Latin *monile* (*Thebaid,* II, 266), which signifies a
      necklace or a jewel used as a pendant, not, as Robinson following Skeat says,
      a bracelet: Semele puts the harmful gift about her neck (*Thebaid,* II, 292–
      293). In *The Wife of Bath's Prologue,* ll. 740–746 (Robinson ed. p. 83), the
      Broche is referred to as "an ouche of golde" for which Eriphyle betrayed her
      husband Amphiaraus to the "Grekes" (cf. *Thebaid,* II, 299–305). The Prior-
      esse's "brooch" (*Gen. Prol.,* ll. 158–162, Robinson ed. p. 18) hangs on "A
      peire of bedes" around her arm, while the "broche" which reveals Criseyde's
      unfaithfulness to Troilus is fastened on "the coler . . . withinne" of a "cote-
      armure" captured from Diomede (*Troilus and Criseyde,* v, 1649–1665; Robin-
      son ed. p. 477). Its splendor, not how it was worn, makes the Broche of
      Thebes a notable jewel.

21   Neil C. Hultin, "Anti-courtly Elements in Chaucer's *Complaint of Mars,*"
      Annuale Mediaevale, IX (1968), 58–75, see especially pp. 63–66. Cf. also
      Wood, p. 159.

22   *Ad Herennium,* ed. and trans. Harry Caplan (London and Cambridge, Mass.:
      Loeb Classical Library, 1964), IV.xlix.62.

23   J. M. Manly, "On the Date and Interpretation of Chaucer's Complaint of
      Mars," *Harvard Studies and Notes in Philology and Literature,* V (Boston,
      1896), 124.

24   J. D. North, "Kalenderes Enlumyned Ben They: Some Astronomical Themes
      in Chaucer," *RES,* XX (1969), 137–142 (on the date and accuracy of the
      "Mars").

25   Gardiner Stillwell, "Convention and Individuality in Chaucer's *Complaint of
      Mars,*" *Ph Q,* XXXV (1956), 82. Stillwell's article provides a good discussion
      of the comic aspects of "The Complaint of Mars," relating it to the *aubade*
      convention, discussing the *Ovide Moralisé* as a possible source of the astrolog-
      ical machinery, and considering the poem as belonging to the "Valentine
      tradition" stretching from Grandson to Charles d'Orléans.

26   Nancy Dean, "Chaucer's *Complaint,* A Genre Descended from the Her-
      oides," *CL,* XIX (1967), 1–27; see especially p. 19.

27   Stillwell notes ("Convention and Individuality," p. 72) the comic incongruity
      of the song with its festive occasion: "Chaucer's fun is that of telling lovers
      exactly the opposite of what they ought to be told or hope to be told on St.
      Valentine's Day."

28   Without mentioning Stillwell, however, Dean in "Chaucer's *Complaint,*"
      pp.20, 25, has pushed his suggestion to an unjustified extreme: she takes
      Venus' reception by "Cilenius" as "his frend ful dere" as a certain sign of her
      infidelity to Mars and later says that she "is making merry with Cilenius and
      in ɤ ? affray.'" I do not deny the ambiguous possibility in "frend ful dere,"
      but the poem simply does not allow such an unequivocal conclusion. We hear
      nothing whatever about Venus' response to Cilenius. This second conjunction

is presented as one of friendship and consolation in need, not of passion. If the situation reminds us of Criseyde's reception by Diomede, it should also remind us that Criseyde thanks the Greek only for "his frendshipe" (*Troilus and Criseyde*, V, 185); she is not swept off her feet immediately, and we feel that her sorrow at leaving Troilus is genuine. Moreover, Dean herself stresses the mythical background, which has nothing to suggest this lightning transference of Venus' affections. Such a travesty of sexual love would take away from both of the following complaints all the seriousness of their comment on earthly affections. The fact that Venus has been "rescued" by Cilenius is quite enough to define ironically the subjectivity of Mars' complaint for his lady's distress.

29   See Cicero, *Topica*, in *De Inventione, De Optimo Genere Oratorum, Topica*, ed. H. M. Hubbell (London and Cambridge, Mass.: Loeb Classical Library, 1960), XXVI. 97, for a discussion of the use of the topics to accomplish the respective ends of each part of the oration. The division here corresponds to that of Aristotle, *Rhetoric*, 3.13 (1414a), and it is taken up by Fortunatian; see Edgar de Bruyne, *Etudes d'esthétique médiévale*, 3 vols. (Bruges, 1946), I, 49, quoting *Chirii Fortunatiani Artis Rhetoricae libri tres*, ed. Halm, p. 111. Elsewhere is found a division into six parts, *exordium, narratio, partitio* (or *divisio*), *confirmatio, refutatio* (or *reprehensio*), and *peroratio* (or *conclusio*); cf. Cicero, *De Inventione*, I, 19; and *Ad Herennium*, I.iii.4. The enormous influence of the *Topica* is well known; in any case there seems little practical value in looking for a six-part division in Mars' complaint.

30   Cf. *The Squire's Tale*, 1. 596 (Robinson ed., p. 134), and Lydgate's *Compleynt of a Loveres Lyfe*, stanza 2, where its use is probably an imitation of Chaucer's bird (see John Norton-Smith's edition of *John Lydgate: Poems*, Oxford, 1966, p. 47, and n. to l. 12, p. 163).

31   *Ad Herennium, interrogatio*, IV.xv.22; *repetitio*, IV.xii.19; *ratiocinatio*, IV.xvi.23.

32   Ibid., III.xiv.24.

33   Hultin's references (pp. 70–71) are as follows: Ovid, *Artis Amatoriae*, I, 393; Cicero, *De Senectute*, XIII, 44; Isidore, *Etymologiarum*, x, 5 ff.; D. W. Robertson, "The Subject of the 'De Amore' of Andreas Capellanus," *MP*, L (1952–53), 158; ". . . a luytel Sarmond þat is of good edificacioun," *The Minor Poems of the Vernon Manuscript*, ed. F. J. Furnivall, 2 vols. (London, 1901), II, 477–478.

34   Hultin cites Augustine in *Patrologiae cursus completus: series latina*, ed. J. P. Migne, 221 vols. (Paris, 1844–80), XXXV, 1700, and Andreas Capellanus in *The Art of Courtly Love*, trans. J. J. Perry (New York, 1959), p. 195. He also quotes Lydgate, *Fall of Princes*, II, 373–374 [Bk. III, ll. 1611–1638], which speaks of the "dominacioun" of women by their casting out of the "hookis" of sensuality—which, says Hultin, is precisely Mars' situation; in submitting to Venus "he abjures his masculine role." As I have suggested, we are not altogether sorry to see Mars lose his wonted ferocity, in spite of the comic

helplessness to which it leads, and thus we are allowed to see something positive in his love for Venus.

35 Gerard Manley Hopkins, *Poems,* third edition, ed. W. H. Gardner (Oxford, 1948), pp. 103–104; ll. 1–2, 12–14 of "To what serves Mortal Beauty?"

36 Grandson's *Cinq balades ensuivans* are printed in Piaget's edition, pp. 209–213. The first, fourth, and fifth of the balades are printed by Skeat in the Oxford Chaucer, I, 400–404, and by Braddy, pp. 61–63.

37 Paget Toynbee (*Academy,* xxxix, 442) suggested that "Pleye" in l. 31 of all the manuscripts should be "Pleyne," translating "Plaindre" in the French; and editors have unfortunately accepted this flat-footed destruction of Chaucer's game of translation. Venus and Mars have just been described as meeting for such nocturnal activities as "Pleye in slepyng" suggests, and "pleyne" here would not only be repetitious after l. 28, it would also suit the reversing of proprieties less well than "Pleye": when lovers should be dreaming, they play; when they should be playing (*i.e.,* dancing), they dream.

38 Needless to say, "Jealousy" as a personification is very common in the tradition of love literature to which the "Venus" (and *The Broche of Thebes* as a whole) contributes, and its inherited meanings might help us to understand its use here. We might look at the *Roman de la Rose,* for example, where it plays a very large part. What I am assuming here is that every time Jealousy appears as a personification, it does so in relation to a specific context, a particular psychological situation, and that its real force may be obscured rather than illuminated by too quick a recourse to "convention." We must see above all that Venus is attempting to handle the complex of emotions and interfering social circumstances which we call "jealousy" by projecting a person, more specifically a woman, for whose swift demise she can energetically wish. What she "objectively" refers to is less important: in the text I allude to the circumstances, both in the narrative and in the mythic background, which give rise to "jealousy," or which justify a fear of it. More important, perhaps, than these particular conditions is the reader's general knowledge of the word and of the social or emotional circumstances which it signifies. He does not need to know the *Roman de la Rose* or any other specific literary work in order to grasp the word itself, though of course such knowledge may increase his sense of its complexity. The same thing in substance is true of Love. We must grasp the way in which it is personified, and the speaker's emotional or rhetorical reasons for personifying it in his particular circumstances. This whole matter is obviously of central importance to our understanding of the courtly love lyric. I have discussed it at greater length in my unpublished dissertation, "Formal Elements in the Late Medieval Courtly Love Lyric" (Stanford, 1970), pp. 180–216.

39 *OED,* s.v. *on:* "The preposition expressing primarily the relation of contact with or proximity to the surface of anything, and so that of being supported or upheld by it; also, from the earliest times expressing motion to or towards such a position. . . . In ME, the distinction of case disappeared, but *on* contin-

ued in both uses, the sense being generally indicated by the accompanying verb . . . though *not infrequently with ambiguity"* [emphasis mine]. This ambiguity combines with the ambiguity in *wente* (the modern sense of *go* is probably secondary to "walked" in this context, but it is common enough in Chaucer) to produce the ambiguity noted in the text. Context also is of considerable importance: if we had to do with a merely earthly lover, we should almost certainly read "wente" simply as "walked," but we take account of Mars' celestial status in the second meaning. Finally, Chaucer uses *in* with *erthe* to signify mere location, in all the other cases I have found: e.g., *ABC,* l. 54, "So have I doon in erthe, allas the while!" See also *Romaunt of the Rose,* ll. 6547–6548, "That Crist, ne his apostlis dere, / While that they walkide in erthe heere" (probably non-Chaucerian, but nevertheless a useful indication).

40   See Dean, "Chaucer's *Complaint,*" pp. 2–3, for a discussion of this terminology. She thinks this line exemplifies the merging of the two genres in Deschamps and Chaucer, though she admits that elsewhere Chaucer, like Machaut, clearly considers "complaint" and "lay" as different genres. I personally think that this is a terminological game very characteristic of Chaucer; both Shirley and Skeat, we saw earlier, are so confused by the poem's form that they consider the work a "balade" (in the first case) or "balades" (in the second). Compare Prol. LGW, G 201–202, where the ladies in the God of Love's train "songen, as it were in carole-wyse, / This balade, which that I shal yow devyse"—and indeed the balade which follows seems to share its public and ceremonial nature with the carol, as against the more private or meditative character of most balades. Chaucer was concerned for strict generic definitions only as they contributed to the literary game, and here I think he is playing on our sense of the distinction between "complaint" and "lay."

41   Rosemary Woolf's discussion of the medieval lyrics on "Christ the lover-knight" makes it apparent that the readers of Chaucer's poem would be very well prepared to perceive and respond to the application of Venus' first balade to Christ. The second chapter of her *English Religious Lyric in the Middle Ages* (Oxford, 1968), pp. 19–66, describing how the Bernardine emphasis on the spiritual utility of ordinary human feelings influenced the writing of English religious lyrics, is relevant to the present poem. Not only is devotion to Christ almost diagrammatically compared with the profane love of Venus, but the religious love begins with human emotion toward Christ as incarnate (in his "manhod") and rises through recognition and acceptance of pain to a more spiritual love. On Christ as lover-knight, see especially Woolf, pp. 45–66. From this point of view, Chaucer's poem constitutes the transfiguration and illumination of the linguistic ambivalence apparent in Thomas of Hales's "Love-Ron" (*English Lyrics of the XIIIth Century,* ed. Carleton Brown, Oxford, 1932, pp. 68–74) and many other devotional poems which exploit courtly language by pointing out, in effect, that Christ alone fulfills the

hyperboles inspired by the lover's desire. A song contemporary with the "Venus" provides a striking parallel, in that it acknowledges the pain which must accompany this high love:

> I Hafe set my hert so hye
> me likyt no loue þat lowere ys;
> And alle þe paynes þat y may drye,
> me þenk hyt do me good y-wys.
> For on that Lorde þat louid vs alle,
> So hertely haue i set my þowȝt,
> yt ys my Ioie on hym to calle,
> for loue me haþ in balus browȝt.
>   Me   þenk yt do ⟨me good⟩ Iwys.

—*Religious Lyrics of the XIVth Century,* ed. Carleton Brown, 2d ed. rev. by G. V. Smithers (Oxford, 1952), p. 229.

42 Sister M. Madeleva, *Pearl: A Study in Spiritual Dryness* (New York and London, 1925), pp. 24–25.

43 Richard Rolle, *The Fire of Love* and *The Mending of Life* or *The Rule of Living,* trans. Richard Misyn, ed. Ralph Harvey, *EETS,* o.s. 106 (1896), 18.

44 Ramon Lull, *The Book of the Lover and the Beloved,* trans. E. Allison Peers (London, 1923), No. 71, p. 37; No. 78, p. 39; No. 103, p. 45.

45 *Purgatorio,* cantos xvi, ll. 67–105, xvii, ll. 91–139, and xviii, ll. 16–75.

1   See William Malleville Haller, "The Puritan Art of Love," *HLQ*, V (1942),
    235-272; William Haller, "Hail Wedded Love," *ELH*, XIII (1946), 79-97;
    and Roland Mushat Frye, "The Teachings of Classical Puritanism on Conjugal
    Love," *SRen*, II (1955), 148-159. C. A. Patrides' chapter on "The Christian
    Idea of Love," in *Milton and the Christian Tradition* (London, 1966), is also
    indispensable.

2   I concur in many of John Halkett's views expressed in *Milton and the Idea of
    Marriage* (New Haven, Conn., 1970), a book that has just come to hand as this
    essay is finished; but our views tend to diverge when he remarks on "the
    absence in *Paradise Lost* of an elaborate discussion of the mystical way or of
    spiritual ascent through love," and observes that in Book VIII, especially,
    Milton "shuns an opportunity which Dante might have handsomely ex-
    ploited" (pp. 122-123). Michael Lieb's *The Dialectics of Creation: Patterns of
    Birth & Regeneration in "Paradise Lost"* (Amherst, Mass., 1970), also recently
    to hand, is from start to finish a careful exploration of "creativity as it
    manifests itself both in a positive and in a negative manner" (p. 34); and
    although Lieb's dialectical approach is markedly different from my point of
    view, his method frequently yields insights that richly complement my own
    conclusions.

3   Denis Saurat, *Milton: Man and Thinker* (London, 1925), pp. 155-56.

4   W. B. C. Watkins, *An Anatomy of Milton's Verse* (Baton Rouge, La., 1955),
    pp. 61-62.

5   Joseph H. Summers, *The Muse's Method* (Cambridge, Mass., 1962), pp. 96
    and 109.

6   "Similitudo proportio dicitur, Græce ferè *analogia* & similia proportionalia,
    Græcè *analoga*. Proportio autem nihil aliud est quàm duaram rationum simili-

196

tudo: ratio autem est duorum inter se terminorum sive rerum callatio." *Artis Logica*, in *Works*, XI, 192, 194.

7 Ibid., p. 197.

8 All quotations from *Paradise Lost* are from Merritt Y. Hughes's edition of the *Complete Poems and Major Prose* (New York, 1957), hereafter cited as *Hughes*. Milton's prose to 1655 is cited from the *Complete Prose Works*, ed. Don M. Wolfe and others, 4 vols. (New Haven, Conn., 1953–66), cited as *Prose*. Quotations from Milton's later prose, including *De doctrina Christiana* (cited as *CD*), are from *The Works of John Milton*, ed. Frank Allen Patterson and others, 18 vols. (New York, 1931–38), hereafter cited as *Works*.

9 Ll. 55–60. Trans. in *Hughes*: "The reviving earth throws off her hated old age and craves thy embraces, O Phoebus. She craves them and she is worthy of them; for what is lovelier than she as she voluptously bares her fertile breast and breathes the perfume of Arabian harvest and pours sweet spices and the scent of Paphian roses from her lovely lips?"

10 William Madsen argues forcefully against a Neoplatonic interpretation of Raphael's speech—especially the meaning of *shadow*—and would substitute instead "its familiar Christian sense of "foreshadowing' or 'adumbration' "(*From Shadowy Types to Truth: Studies in Milton's Symbolism* [New Haven, Conn., 1968], pp. 88 ff.). Even if I fully agreed with Madsen, I do not see how his view necessarily excludes a Neoplatonic interpretation.

11 Cf. Aristotle, *Metaphysics* A5.986a.22 ff. Here, in the Pythagorean Table of Opposites, Aristotle doubtless synthesizes both old and new views of polarity. He identifies ten pairs of opposite principles: limit and unlimited, odd and even, one and plurality, right and left, male and female, at rest and moving, straight and curved, light and darkness, good and evil, and square and oblong. Some pairs are formed from observation of natural events, while others are created by symbolic association. G. E. R. Lloyd has pointed out that in this scheme of polarity one of the terms is positive while the other is privative (*Polarity and Analogy* [Cambridge, 1966], pp. 16 ff.). Saint Augustine's definition of evil as the privation of good may be traced to these early beginnings of philosophical speculation. Aristotle's commentary on the Table of Opposites established a predisposition of mind and attitude (as, for example, the superiority of right over left, male over female) that did not substantially change until the New Science of the Renaissance.

12 Benjamin Jowett, trans., *The Dialogues of Plato*, 5 vols. (New York, 1892), III, 390.

13 Plato, *Timaeus*, in Jowett, *The Dialogues of Plato*, III, 29C. Subsequent references to this translation will be given in the text.

14 Milton says in *CD*, *Works*, XIV, 31, 32, that "to know God as he really is, far transcends the powers of man's thoughts, much more of his perception," and that the "literal and figurative descriptions of God" in the Scriptures exhibit him "not as he really is, but in such a manner as may be within the scope of

our comprehensions" and whereby God has "accommodate[d] himself to our capacities." The idea expressed here can be traced to Saint Hilary of Poitiers and was affirmed by Saint Augustine, Saint Thomas Aquinas, Calvin and numerous Renaissance writers. See C. A. Patrides, "*Paradise Lost* and the Theory of Accommodation", *TSLL*, V (1963), 58–63.

15   *Artis Logica*, trans. in *Works*, XI, 17.

16   Ibid.

17   Origen, *The Song of Songs, Commentary and Homilies*, trans. R. P. Lawson, Ancient Christian Writers No. 26 (Westminster, Md., 1957).

18   "To the Most Blessed Pope Damasus," Prologue to the *Homilies*, in Lawson, *The Song of Songs, Commentary and Homilies*. Origen owes a considerable debt to Philo, especially when he says that allegory is the soul of the sacred text and that the literal meaning is only its body.

19   Ibid., pp. 74 and 218.

20   Sir Henry Vane "To the Reader," in *The Retired Mans Meditations* (1655), p. 1. It should be noted here that the concept of the *logos* (John 1:1 ff.) adds to the general authority of Vane's argument. Milton mentions the *logos* by name twice in *CD*, where he is concerned to explain the relationship of the Father to the Son, and he seems to be aware of the traditional meanings associated with the term. As the universal Reason or divine Law, the concept originated in Heraclitus and was identified with the Johannine Logos by Justin Martyr (*1 Apology 46* and *2 Apology 10*), who was very likely influenced by the thinking of Philo Judaeus a century before. Philo described the logos as the intermediary between God and the World and thus a functional means of revelation. The fourth Gospel shows the very considerable influence of Philo and the Jewish-Alexandria logos-philosophy, and so far as the logos-philosophy can be extended to the Word of God in general (cf. John 5:38; 8:55; 17:6; and Luke 8:11), it bears on the authority of language as a vehicle of revelation.

21   Serious students of the Renaissance have long recognized the importance of Ficino (1433–1499) as one of the chief architects of the Elizabethan world view. His Latin translation of Plato (printed 1484) was the first complete translation into any Western language. It included a commentary on each of the Platonic dialogues. The *Marsilio Ficini opera* were published at Basle in two volumes in 1576. Sears Jayne edited and translated the *De amore*, University of Missouri Studies, XIX (1943). A better edition, with a French translation, is that by Raymond Marcel (Paris, 1956). See also Paul O. Kristeller, *The Philosophy of Marsilio Ficino*, trans. Virginia Conant (New York, 1943), and for a general history of the movement, Nesca A. Robb, *Neoplatonism in the Italian Renaissance* (New York, 1935). Leonard Nathanson provides a summary of "The Platonic Context" in *The Strategy of Truth: A Study of Sir Thomas Browne* (Chicago, 1967).

22   Sir Henry Vane, *The Retired Mans Meditations*, p. 37.

23   The idea that God was both male and female was not, of course, unknown among the Church Fathers. Saint Augustine, for example, cites Valerius

Soranus (first century B.C.), by way of Varro's treatise *On the Worship of the Gods:* "Jupiter, Lord over kings, over things, over gods, / Father and Mother of gods, he is one, he is all." According to Saint Augustine, Varro says Soranus is right "since Jupiter is the world and therefore both puts forth and takes back all things that grow just as a father emits seed and a mother receives them" *(The City of God,* VIII.7, The Fathers of the Church [New York, 1950], VII, 356).

Lantanitus rejected the belief of Orpheus (cf. *Orphica,* fragment 21a4) that "God is both male and female, because He could not generate otherwise unless He had the power of both sexes, as though He came together with Himself or without coition He could not have procreated," along with the opinion of Hermes that God was "self-fathered" *(autopatora)* and "self-mothered" *(autometora) (The Divine Institutes,* IV.8, The Fathers of the Church [New York, 1964], XLIX, 259-260). Cf. Cicero, *On the Nature of the Gods,* 3.22.56; also Tertullian, *Apology,* c. 21.

24   *De generatione animalium,* trans. Arthur Platt, in *The Works of Aristotle,* 12 vols. (Oxford, 1908-31), V, 716a5. Subsequent references to Platt's translation will be given in the text.

25   Strictly speaking, Aristotle's male and female principles are not contraries in that they are not equal, the female being a lack of the male; but the tradition of alchemy, which has been greatly underestimated in Renaissance thought, held that the two reciprocal principles of nature—usually depicted as active and passive, or male and female—expressed the fundamental natural law of procreation. In this tradition, the Sun was male and the Moon was female, suggesting another authority for Milton's making both the Earth and Moon female and thus a cosmological figure for Eve. See John Read, *Prelude to Chemistry* (London, 1936).

26   As a scientist, Dr. Platt (trans. *De generatione animalium*) analyses this passage in a wholly physiological sense, to say that the sex distinction is deeply rooted in the organism and that any variation of hormone balance will affect the whole organism. But Aristotle, I think, goes a good deal further and may even anticipate Freud, who said that primordial principles of biology determine patterns of psychological behavior. Aristotle's point is that the distinct psychologies of the male and female answer to anatomical sexuality.

27   The metaphysical implication of this statement is based on what Aristotle believed to be the natural reasons for the separation of the sexes in the higher animals. He holds that the female parent "provides all the *material* for the body of the offspring" and that the male parent, "in the act of fertilization provides no material, but supplies the initial impulse . . . which leads to the working up of this material into a fresh living creature." See A. E. Taylor, *A Commentary on Plato's Timaeus* (Oxford, 1928), p. 636.

28   Taylor (pp. 636-637) points out that in Empedocles' cosmology Eros is the sexual impulse and said to be the cosmic force that men know in themselves as the sexual attraction that draws male and female together. In the second

book of Parmenides' didactic poem in hexameters, *On Nature*, Eros is the first of the gods to be formed. In his *Theogony*, Hesiod makes his primitive figures Chaos, Earth, Tartarus, and Eros. Phaedrus, in the *Symposium*, quotes the appropriate lines from Parmenides and Hesiod.

29   I'son colui che ne' prim'anni tuoi
                      gli occhi tuoi infermi volsi alla beltate
                      che dalla terra al ciel vivo conduce.

—Michelangiolo Buonarroti, *Rime*, Scrittori D'Italia, N. 217 (Bari, 1960), p. 20.

30 Quoted in *Hughes*, pp. 425–26, n. 807.

31 Walter Clyde Curry, *Milton's Ontology, Cosmogony, and Physics* (Lexington, Ky., 1957). Proclus (410–485), although a pagan and opposed to Christianity, had considerable impact on Christian thought through the works of Dionysius the Areopagite, often called the Pseudo-Dionysius. E. R. Dodds argues Proclus' influence at considerable length in his introduction to *The Elements of Theology* (Oxford, 1933), and points to the long succession of commentaries on the works of the Pseudo-Dionysius beginning with that of Maximus the Confessor and including those by Erigena, Hugh of Saint Victor, Robert Grosseteste, Albertus Magnus, and Saint Thomas Aquinas.

Of considerable historical importance is the *Liber de causis*, thought in the Middle Ages to be the work of Aristotle but recognized by Aquinas to be a translation of an Arabic work based on Proclus' *Elements of Theology*. Gerhard of Cremona translated the original Arabic book into Latin sometime between 1167 and 1187; it was, in turn, consistently cited as an authority for Alanus ab Insulis' (fl. late twelfth century) *De planctu naturae*.

Proclus was introduced directly to the West in 1268 when William of Moerbeke, a Dominican and friend of Aquinas, produced a Latin version of the *Elements*. The full significance of this and other translations of Proclus can be appreciated only if we recall that in thirteenth-century Europe both Plotinus and Plato (except for the *Phaedo*, the *Meno*, and part of the *Timaeus*) were unknown in Latin translations.

Although the Alexandrine Neoplatonists studied Proclus very little, the Florentine Neoplatonists evidently regarded him highly, perhaps because he had succeeded Plato in the headship of the Platonic Academy. There are over forty known copies of works by Proclus surviving from the fifteenth and sixteenth centuries, a certain indication of his popularity. Cardinal Bessarion had at least three manuscripts of the *Elements;* Pico della Mirandola owned another; and Ficino, still another. Patrizzi printed a Latin translation of the *Elements* in 1583, with the Greek text following in 1618. Proclus' most mature and complete work is *The Platonic Theology*, Greek text with Latin translation by A. Portus (Hamburg, 1618); first English translation by Thomas Taylor (London, 1816).

32   *The Six Books of Proclus . . . on the Theology of Plato,* trans. Thomas Taylor, 2 vols. (London, 1816), II, 194. Subsequent references to this translation will be given in the text.

33   This is especially true of the first book of the *Corpus Hermeticum.* I have used the English translation by Walter Scott, *Hermetica,* 4 vols. (Oxford, 1924). Passages are identified by Stephanus numbers rather than page numbers in order to facilitate comparison with the standard text established by A. D. Nock and translated into French by A. J. Festugiere (Paris: Societe d'Edition "Les Belles Lettres," 1960). Ficino's Latin translation of Corp. I–XIV was printed in 1471 and was enormously popular, as indicated by the fact that between the time it was first published and 1641, it went through twenty-two editions. The first Greek text was printed in Paris in 1554; a French translation appeared in 1557; and an English translation by the Reverend John Everard in 1650 (second edition, 1657).

34   Watkins, *An Anatomy of Milton's Verse,* p. 59, is right to note that "only in connection with the moon, with her mysterious power over tides and women, is light ever female in Milton." Light is characteristically masculine and the fertilizing agent of all life. Cf. *PL,* III. 585–586; IV.671–673; V.300–302; VII.95–97.

35   Curry, *Milton's Ontology,* p. 53.

36   A second edition of the *Zohar* was published at Cremona in 1590 and a third at Lublin in 1623. Milton, of course, could have read the Hebrew text, and he may well have done so considering the widespread interest in Cabala during the seventeenth century, as Henry More's *Conjectura Cabbalistica* (1654) suggests. The English translation of the *Zohar* cited here is that by Harry Sperling and Maurice Simon, 5 vols. (London, 1933), I, 176. Milton may also have been attracted to the use of Cabala in Pico della Mirandola's effort to synthesize a universal system of thought from all the philosophies he knew. Pico's nine hundred theses included forty-seven drawn from Hebrew cabalistic sources and seventy-two conclusions based on the cabalistic theses. But Pico did not know the *Zohar* as Milton could have, since the chief source of Pico's cabalistic knowledge was the Bible commentary of Menahem ben Benjamine of Recanati (c. 1290–c. 1350). For a detailed study of the transmission of cabalistic influence, see Joseph Leon Blau, *The Christian Interpretation of the Cabala in the Renaissance* (New York, 1944).

37   Blossom Feinstein follows an occult Eastern tradition which teaches the importance of chaos in ancient Egyptian and Babylonian cosmologies and finds that Spenser and other Renaissance poets used the idea sympathetically, "*The Faerie Queene* and Cosmogonies of the Near East," *JHI,* XXXIX (1968), 531–550.

38   Quoted in Kester Svendsen, *Milton and Science* (Cambridge, Mass., 1956), p. 163.

39   See Edgar Wind, *Pagan Mysteries in the Renaissance* (London, 1958), fig. 20, and his comment, p. 108.

40   Cf. Wylie Sypher, *Four Stages of Renaissance Style* (New York, 1955), p. 184.

41 *Odyssey,* VI, 230-232. Cited in *Hughes,* p. 285, n.301.

42 *Commentary on the "Symposium",* tr. Sears Jayne, University of Missouri Studies, XIX (Columbia, Mo., 1943), p. 160.

43 It has become almost a cliché in Milton criticism—certainly among traditionalists—to point to A. J. Waldock as having been wrongheaded in much of what he said about *Paradise Lost.* I take, for instance, his treatment of the Fall in *"Paradise Lost" and Its Critics* (Cambridge, 1962) as representative of those critics who regard Milton's treatment of Paradisal sexuality as a failure because they will not grant Milton his philosophical prerogatives. C. S. Lewis, however, is not among them, though for other reasons he too objects in *A Preface to Paradise Lost* (Oxford, 1960), pp. 123-124, to Milton's handling of prelapsarian love. In answer to these objections, one begins by citing the battery of evidence in support of Christian love collected by C. A. Patrides, *Milton and the Christian Tradition,* pp. 153-186.

44 Porphyry collected and published the writings of Plotinus (A.D.205-270) rather arbitrarily as the *Enneads.* The Greek text of the *Enneads* was first printed by P. Perna (Basle, 1580), together with Marsilio Ficino's Latin translation, which had already appeared in Florence (1492). My citations are to the Stephen MacKenna and B. S. Page translation (Chicago, 1952), augmented by the translation of Joseph Katz, *The Philosophy of Plotinus* (New York, 1950).

45 The "disposition" of the will, Ficino says in a letter following the *De amore,* operates so that we are compelled to love. Both willing and loving, according to Ficino (following Saint Augustine, who thought in turn he was following Plotinus), are inner longings for the true knowledge of God. For Renaissance Neoplatonists—and here we come full circle—the knowledge of God was the highest act of contemplation and the end of the soul's spiritual ascent. The systems of will and love, closely connected if not identical, were therefore essential phenomena in the soul's drive toward beatitude. See Kristeller, *The Philosophy of Marsilio Ficino,* pp. 256-288.

46 There are two stages of emanation from The First, which has always existed and is eternal: (1) Intelligence (or Mind) and (2) Soul. The Intelligence, or father of all things, contains all the archetypal Ideas, and like The First (whose nature it is to emanate) emanates a second stage called the Soul, which contains the reasons that act as the efficient cause of all things. All levels of emanation from The First are coeternal, hence outside of Time. The analysis of coeternal emanation, however, creates a vertical pattern that progresses downward from the One, thus describing a linear movement from unity to multiplicity. Emanation stops at the level of soul and creates Our World by sowing seeds of reason (*rationes seminales*) into matter, which is by definition incapable of final perfection or ultimate Form (complete Being). In general, Saint Augustine adopts Plotinus' system to explain the nature of evil in a God created universe: God creates the best possible world out of matter, but the nature of matter does not admit of absolute perfection. Thus the

world, because of its constituent matter, is necessarily imperfect. Evil, in consequence, is the lack of Being or, in its Neoplatonic context, the privation of Good. Cf. Bruno Switalski, *Neoplatonism and the Ethics of St. Augustine* (New York, 1946).

47 Plotinus is explicit about the function of sexual symbols as a means of perceiving transcendental forms of reality. "We speak," he says, "of eternal things metaphorically, in terms of generation. . . ." The purpose of these metaphors is to indicate the causal relations between higher and lower forms of being and to suggest their "systematic order" (*En*.i.iii.6). Sexual metaphors are therefore a way of knowing, an epistemology, predicated on a belief in the intrinsic soundness of analogy.

48 See two essays that have stood the test of print and time, J. B. Fletcher, "Benivieni's 'Ode of Love' and Spenser's 'Fowre Hymnes,' " *MP*, VIII (1911), 545–560; and "Spenser's 'Fowre Hymnes,' " *PMLA*, XXVI (1911), 466–475. Cf. Robert Ellrodt, *Neoplatonism in the Poetry of Edmund Spenser* (Geneva, 1960), and William Nelson, *The Poetry of Edmund Spenser* (New York, 1963). For general background, see also John C. Nelson, *Renassance Theory of Love* (New York, 1958).

49 See Rensselaer W. Lee, "Castiglione's Influence on Spenser's Early Hymns." *PQ*, VII (1928), 65–77.

50 *An Hymne in Honour of Love*, in *The Works of Edmund Spenser: The Minor Poems*, ed. Charles Grosvenor Osgood and Henry Gibbons Lotspeich, 2 vols. (Baltimore, Md., 1943), I. i. 100. Subsequent references to the *Foure Hymnes* will be indicated by roman numerals, followed by line number: i for *An Hymne in Honour of Love*, ii for *An Hymne in Honour of Beautie*, and iv for *An Hymne of Heavenly Beautie*.

51 My citations are to Sears Jayne's translation of the *De amore*. See Chapter I, p. 14.

52 Ficino's analysis of the two Venuses is clearly a redaction of Plotinus. Of the two kinds of love Plotinus distinguishes, one is the "commonplace" love "here below"; the other is the celestial love in the "world above" (*En*. vi.ix. 9). But like Ficino, Plotinus is of two minds about the nature of earthly love, and in another place modifies his evaluation of the twofold Aphrodite. Daughter of Ouranos or Heaven, the Heavenly Aphrodite is not born of a mother and has no part in marriages. The other Aphrodite is the daughter of Zeus and Dione and presides over earthly unions. Whereas the Heavenly Aphrodite has no part of matter and is ever intent upon the Divine Mind, the Earthly Aphrodite, though of this world, partakes of the "upward desire" and in varying degrees leads every soul toward love of the divine. All loves that serve the ends of nature are good, and those that do not are "merely accidents attending on perversion" (*En*. iv.viii.2). "Every soul is an Aphrodite," Plotinus says and thus gives philosophical authority to all the symbolic Beatrices and Lauras to follow (*En*. vi.x.9).

When earthly love remains free of lust, it shows the tendency of the soul toward pure beauty; and its sexual or copulative expression proceeds from the will to beget beauty. Because earthly beauty can lead to the "memory" of beauty in a higher realm, we are to cherish earthly love as an image of the divine (*En.* iii.v.1). The heavenly archetype of true love and beauty is thus the source of attraction between men and women.

53   *The Faerie Queene*, III, xii, 31. Citation from *Works: A Variorum Edition*, ed. Edwin Greenlaw and others, 9 vols. (Baltimore, Md., 1931-1949).

54   C. S. Lewis, *Spenser's Images of Life*, ed. Alastair Fowler (Cambridge, 1967), p. 25.

55   Edwin Greenlaw, "A Better Teacher than Aquinas," *SP*, XIV (1917), 196-217; see p. 206.

56   "When you love me," Ficino says, "you contemplate me, and as I love you, I find myself in your contemplation of me. . . . I keep a grasp on myself only through you as a mediator" (Sears Jayne's trans. of *De amore*, p. 145). In reciprocated love, a lover lives in his beloved, exchanging, as it were, mutual identities (p. 144). He becomes his true self only insofar as he finds himself in another, which is not a matter of reconciling opposites so much as it is the discovery of one's own likeness. Likeness generates love (p. 146).

57   Torquato Tasso, *Conclusioni Considerazioni*. Cited in A. J. Smith, "The Metaphysic of Love," *RES*, n.s. IX (1958), 368.

58   Summers, *The Muse's Method*, p. 99.

59   Cf. Patrides, *Milton and the Christian Tradition*, pp. 15-22, and articles by William B . Hunter, Jr., which Patrides cites.

60   Genesis 2:23-24; Matthew 19:4-6; and Mark 10:6-8.

61   Cleanth Brooks, "Eve's Awakening," in *Essays in Honor of Walter Clyde Curry* (Nashville, Tenn., 1954), p. 285.

62   Barbara Lewalski traces the main outlines of Aristotle's idea of magnanimity (*Nicomachean Ethics*, iv.ii.1123b), in relation to Milton's Christ, in *Milton's Brief Epic: The Genre, Meaning, and Art of "Paradise Regained"* (Providence, R. I., 1966), pp. 243-249. Milton, himself, as Mrs. Lewalski notes, derives (with some modification) his own definition of the concept from Aristotle. "MAGNANIMITY," he says in *De doctrina*, "is shown, when in the seeking or avoiding, the acceptance or refusal of riches, advantages, or honors, we are actuated by a regard to our own dignity, rightly understood." One might also cite Spenser's poetic rendering of the idea in *The Faerie Queene:*

> The noble hart, that harbours vertuous thought,
> And is with child of glorious great intent,
> Can never rest, until it forth have brought
> Th' eternall brood of glorie excellent (i.v.i.).

63   See Spenser's *Ecologues*, "April," 109-114; "June," 25-28; and *The Faerie Queene*, i.i.48; vi.x.14-15.

64   Pico della Mirandola, for example, speaks in his *Conclusiones* of a profound

"unity of Venus ... unfolded in the trinity of the Graces." By symbolic extension, the Graces became a perfect figure of the triadic relationship of co-eternal emanation (emanatio, raptio, and remeatio) which descends from God, inspires rapture, and returns to its source. The sequence conforms precisely with Seneca's description of the Graces as a circle of giving, accepting, and returning. Thus the Neoplatonists, inspired by Proclus' dictum that the whole was in every part, made the Graces a trichotomous image of the attributes of Venus and with notorious ease transformed pagan figures into a Christian theme. Ficino, for instance, identified the Graces by turns with any of the triadic formulas of Neoplatonic thought: the logical triad of species-numerus-modus, the theological triad of Mercury-Apollo-Venus; the moral triad of Veritas-Concordia-Pulchritudo; as well as the sequences animus-corpus-fortuna and sapientia-eloquentia-probitas. But the most characteristic interpretation of the Graces may be seen in the trinitarian philosophy of Neoplatonic love: pulchritudo-amor-voluptas. This sequence, in fact, is the inscription around a representation of the Graces on a commemorative medal cast for Pico. Interestingly enough, the triad does not appear anywhere in Pico's work, but it does occur literally in Ficino's Commentary on the Symposium: Circulus ... prout in Deo incipit et allicit, pulchritude: prout in mundum transiens ipsum rapit, amor; prout in auctorem remeans ipsi suum opus coniungit, voluptas. Amor igitur in voluptatem a pulchritudine desinit. See Edgar Wind, Pagan Mysteries in the Renaissance (London, 1958), pp. 32 ff. Jayne translates Ficino's Latin text in De amore, p. 134: "This single circle ... begins in God and attracts to Him, it is Beauty; inasmuch as, going across into the world, it captivates the world, we call it Love; and inasmuch as it returns to its source and with Him joins its labors, then we call it Pleasure. In this way Love begins in Beauty and ends in Pleasure."

65   Watkins, An Anatomy of Milton's Verse, p. 128, detects in Milton's "though terror be in Love" a sexual meaning of orgastic helplessness and loss of control.

66   See Paul Turner, "Woman and the Fall of Man," ES, XXIX (1948), 1–18; cf. Dorothy D. Miller, "Eve," JEGP, LXI (1962), 524–547.

67   In this section, I owe a considerable debt to Watkins' chapter on "Creation" in An Anatomy of Milton's Verse and to Summers' chapter on "Satan, Sin, and Death" in The Muse's Method.

68   Edward Topsell, Historie of Serpents (1608), p. 390, nn. 507–510.

69   Kester Svendsen, Milton and Science, pp. 169–170.

70   Jackson I. Cope, The Metaphoric Structure of "Paradise Lost" (Baltimore, Md., 1962), pp. 80–81.

71   Plutarch's Moralia, according to Feinstein, was the "most widely cited source of Egyptian knowledge in the Renaissance" (p. 534, n. 13).

72   Cf. Feinstein, "The Faerie Queen and Cosmogonies of the Near East," who traces the positive serpent lore through Near Eastern sources and shows its transmission and survival in European Literature.

73 My references are to the translation by Frank Cole Babbitt, Loeb Classical Library (Cambridge, Mass., 1936), V. 3–191.

74 Macrobius knew that the symbolism of a serpent entwined in a circle and biting its tail went back as far as the Phoenicians, who used it as a sacred image of the world or heaven feeding upon itself and turning upon itself (*Saturnalia*,i,9).

75 Cf. Howard Schultz, "Satan's Serenade," *PQ*, XXVII (1948), 17–26, who shows that Satan is one of the "vulgar amorists" mentioned in the *Reason of Church Government* and that Satan's argument is the "shallow, tinny song of a Cavalier seducer."

76 Cf. Jeremiah 7:18; 1 Kings 11:4–5; and 2 Kings 23:13.

77 Cited in *Hughes,* p. 222, n. 447.

78 J. B. Broadbent, *"Milton's Hell,"* ELH, XXI (1954), 161–192; see p. 175.

79 Cf. also the banquet Satan prepares for Christ in *Paradise Regained* (II.320 ff.). This invitation to eat is Satan's temptation to intemperance. The banquet scene, moreover, is a nonscriptural elaboration of Satan's earlier temptation to turn the stones in the wilderness into bread, and it serves to amplify Christ's rejoinder: "Man lives not by Bread only, but each Word / Proceeding from the mouth of God . . ." (I.349–350). Word and food imagery are thus significantly linked. The Word is the source of spiritual life just as human food sustains physical life. The denial of reason (i.e., Satan's "lying") is the sustenance and food of alienation (I.429). See Lee Sheridan Cox, "Food-Word Imagery in *Paradise Regained,"* ELH, XXVIII (1961), 225–243.

80 *Hughes,* p. 259, n. 70–73.

81 *Bellum Judaicum,* IV, 483, trans. H. St. J. Thackeray, Loeb Classical Library (New York, 1928). Kester Svendsen, *Milton and Science,* pp. 28–29, traces references to Josephus' story in popular Renaissance encyclopedias, especially in Swan's *Speculum Mundi* and Caxton's *Mirrour of the World.*

82 Matthew 10:15; cf. Jude 5:7 and 2 Peter 2:6.

83 Cf. Authorized Version, Deut. 23:17 with that of the Bishop's Bible.

84 Cf. I Kings 14:24; I Kings 15:12; 2 Kings 23:7.

85 Cope, *The Metaphoric Structure of "Paradise Lost,"* p. 82.

86 C. S. Lewis explains this Renaissance commonplace in *The Disgarded Image* (Cambridge, 1964), pp. 152–165, and cites Trevisa (1398), who translates the thirteenth-century *De proprietatibus rerum* of Bartholomaeus Anglicus: there are "thre manere soulis . . . *vegetabilis* that geveth lif and no feling, *sensibilis* that geveth lif and feling and nat resound, *racionalis* that geveth lif, feling, and resoun."

87 "A Valediction: Forbidding Mourning," ll. 13–16.

88 Lewis, *A Preface to Paradise Lost,* p. 125.

89 Greenlaw, "A Better Teacher than Aquinas," p. 201.

90 Saurat, *Milton: Man and Thinker,* p. 152.

91 *De civitate Dei,* xiii–xiv. Quoted in Saurat, *Milton: Man and Thinker,* p. 152.

92 Lewis (*A Preface to Paradise Lost,* p. 128) thinks the lines describing Adam

and Eve's lusting (ix.1022–1059) are "one of Milton's failures." But I agree with Professor Summers, who thinks that they are one of Milton's "extraordinary successes" (*The Muse's Method*, p. 105). And rather than the Homeric catalogue of flowers being, as Lewis claims, "wide of the mark," it is there, as Summers says, "not only because of Homer but because it provides a major measure of the loss" (p. 105). The contrast is clearly functional: "Everything about their love has changed utterly except the couch of flowers . . ." (p. 105).

93 *The Life of St. Teresa,* trans. J. M. Cohen (Baltimore, Md., 1957), p. 210.

ECKLEY: EGGOARCHICISM AND THE BIRD LORE OF "FIN-
NEGANS WAKE"

1 Page numbers for primary sources in the text are from these editions of
works by James Joyce: *AP, A Portrait of the Artist as a Young Man* (New
York: The Viking Press, 1964); *U, Ulysses* (New York: Random House,
1961); *FW, Finnegans Wake* (New York: The Viking Press, 1939). *FW* is not
so designated in parentheses, but by numbers for page and line numbers.

2 Joyce associates the roc and the auk, apparently because the roc, like the
phoenix, represents the sun, and the auk in Indian mythology was said to
have swallowed the sun. In the Eskimo tradition of Greenland a giant auk
appears in connection with totemism. For discussion of fabulous birds, see
Ernest Ingersoll, *Birds in Legend, Fable, and Folklore* (New York: Long-
mans, Green, 1923), pp. 191-211.

3 Harold Bayley, *The Lost Language of Symbolism*, 2 vols. (New York: Barnes
and Noble, 1912), I, 208.

4 E. A. Wallis Budge, *The Egyptian Book of the Dead* (New York: Dover,
1967), p. xcviii.

5 Heinrich Zimmer, *Maya der indische Mythos* (Berlin: Deutsche Verlags-
Anstalt, 1936), trans. Kurt P. Tauber, quoted in Thomas E. Connolly, *The
Personal Library of James Joyce* (Buffalo, N.Y.: The University of Buffalo,
1955), p. 43.

6 Michael Begnal, "The Narrator of *Finnegans Wake*," *Eire-Ireland*, 4. no. 3
(Autumn, 1969), 38-49.

7 James Atherton, *The Books at the Wake* (London: Faber and Faber, 1959),
p. 64.

8 E. A. Wallis Budge, *Books on Egypt and Chaldea: The Book of the Dead*
(London: Routledge & Kegan Paul, 1956), p. l.

9 Ibid., p. xxxii.

10 Atherton, *Books at the Wake*, p. 67.

11 Harry Levin, *James Joyce* (New York: New Directions, 1960), p. 144; Clive Hart, *Structure and Motif in Finnegans Wake* (Evanston, Ill.: Northwestern University Press, 1962), p. 130; Benstock, *Joyce-again's Wake*, pp. 11-25.

12 Samuel Beckett, *Our Examination* (New York: New Directions, 1939), p. 3, and quoted in Begnal, "The Narrator of *Finnegans Wake*," 48-49.

13 Ingersoll, *Birds in Legend*, p. 223.

14 Adaline Glasheen, *A Second Census of Finnegans Wake* (Evanston, Ill.: Northwestern University Press, 1963), p. xxxii.

15 The name Phoenix Park derives from the name given a seventeenth century viceregal country residence, The Phoenix, on the lands of the priory of Kilmainham, North of the Liffey. "Close to the main road-junction of the park is the beautiful Phoenix Column, erected by Lord Chesterfield in 1747." See Lord Killanin and Michael V. Duignan, *The Shell Guide to Ireland* (New York: Norton, 1967), pp. 258-259.

16 See Matthew J. C. Hodgart and Mabel P. Worthington, *Song in the Works of James Joyce* (New York: Columbia University, 1959), p. 86.See also Lina Eckenstein, *Comparative Studies in Nursery Rhymes* (London: Duckworth, 1906), p. 190.

17 John Cuthbert Lawson, *Modern Greek Folklore and Ancient Greek Religion* (New York: University Books, 1964), p. 312.

18 Budge, *The Gods of the Egyptians*, I, p. 301.

19 Alwin Rees and Brinley Rees, *Celtic Heritage* (London: Thames and Hudson, 1961), p. 198.

20 See Ingersoll, *Birds in Legend*, pp. 242-252.

21 In 1834 the *Magazine of Natural History* (London, Volume VI) criticized Wilson's *American Ornithology* for overlooking this amazing power of the American bittern. Quoted in Ingersoll, *Birds in Legend*, pp. 79-80.

22 Louis Halle, *The Storm Petrel and the Owl of Athena* (Princeton, N.J.: Princeton University Press, 1970), p. 235.

23 For an alternate view of this passage, see Nathan Halper, "Joyce and Eliot: A Tale of Shem & Shaun," *The Nation*, 200 (31 May, 1965), 590-595.

24 Aristophanes, "The Birds," in Whitney J. Oates and Eugene O'Neill, Jr., eds., trans, anon., *The Complete Greek Drama*, 2 vols. (New York: Random House, 1938), II, 759-762. All quotations are from this edition.

25 Eckenstein, *Comparative Studies in Nursery Rhymes*, p. 173.

26 See Budge, *The Gods of the Egyptians*, I, 298.

27 Dounia Bunis Christiani writes, "One of the most delightful puns in the *Wake*, this is unfortunately impossible to translate so as to convey its wit. *Hensyn*—compounded of *hen*, towards, and *syn*, vision—means regard or consideration, and in this context may be read as 'for the sake of.' But while it serves in a mimic 'Auld Lang Syne,' it figures contextfully as 'old hen's vision.'" See *Scandinavian Elements of Finnegans Wake* (Evanston, Ill.: Northwestern University Press, 1965), p. 117.

28 Eckenstein, *Comparative Studies in Nursery Rhymes,* pp. 111–112.

29 Dean Amadon, *Birds Around the World* (New York: The Natural History Press, 1966), p. 71.

30 Atherton believes "lost in the bush" applies to Samuel Beckett's lack of comprehension of the *Wake.* See Atherton, *Books at the Wake,* p. 16. For many varieties of the world-wide proverb, "A bird in the hand is worth two in the bush," see Archer Taylor, *The Proverb* (Hatboro, Pa.: Folklore Associates, 1962), pp. 22–24.

31 Halle, *Stormy Petrel and the Owl of Athens,* p. 239.

32 Bayley, *Lost Language,* I, 311.

33 Amadon, *Birds Around the World,* pp. 56–57.

34 For explanation of this allusion to the Quinet motif, see Hart, *Structure and Motif in Finnegans Wake,* p. 198.

35 From Conway's *The Wandering Jew.* Quoted in Ingersoll, *Birds in Legend,* p. 172.

36 D'Arcy Thompson, *A Glossary of Greek Birds* (London: Oxford University Press, 1936), p. 193.

37 See Ingersoll, *Birds in Legend,* pp. 161–162.

38 Denis de Rougemont, *Love in the Western World* (New York: Doubleday, 1957), p. 10.

39 For early drafts of Tristan and Mamalujo, as well as this note (p. 210, n.), see David Hayman, *A First Draft Version of Finnegans Wake* (Austin: University of Texas Press, 1963), pp. 208–219.

40 De Rougemont, *Love in the Western World,* p. 26.

41 Ibid., p. 44.

42 Ibid., p. 27.

43 Ingersoll, *Birds in Legend,* p. 213.

44 Ibid., pp. 63–64.

45 Ibid., pp. 203–204.

46 Thompson, *Glossary of Greek Birds,* p. 283.

47 Ingersoll, *Birds in Legend,* pp. 65–66.

48 Ibid., p. 66.

49 See Weldon Thornton, *Allusions in Ulysses* (Chapel Hill: University of North Carolina Press, 1961), pp. 65–66.

50 David Hayman, "From FW: A Sentence in Progress," in *Bibliography and Textual Criticism: English and American Literature, 1700 to the Present,* ed. O. M. Brack, Jr., and Warner Barnes (Chicago and London: University of Chicago Press, 1969), 256–294.

51 Halle, *Stormy Petrel and the Owl of Athens,* p. 245.

52 Hayman, *From FW,* p. 280.

53 Ingersoll, *Birds in Legend,* p. 15.

54 Thompson, *Glossary of Greek Birds,* p. 53.

55 Ingersoll, *Birds in Legend,* p. 14.

56 Eckenstein, *Comparative Studies in Nursery Rhymes,* p. 171.

57 Quoted in Lillian Grace Paca, *The Royal Birds* (New York: St. Martin's Press, 1963), p. 136.

58 Budge, *Gods of the Egyptians*, II, 96–97.

59 Robert Graves, *The White Goddess* (New York: The Noonday Press, 1966), p. 325.

60 Ibid., p. 303.

61 Ibid., p. 327.

62 Ovid, *Metamorphoses*, trans., Rolfe Humphries (Bloomington: Indiana University Press, 1968), p. 189.

63 Eckenstein, *Comparative Studies in Nursery Rhymes*, p. 194.

64 Ibid., pp. 195–196.

65 Ibid., p. 198.

66 Budge, *Gods of the Egyptians*, II, 253–254.

67 Lawson, *Modern Greek Folklore*, pp. 309–311.

68 Budge, *The Book of the Dead*, p. 291.

69 Ibid., p. 106.

70 Ibid., p. 375.

71 Budge, *Gods of the Egyptians*, II, 374.

72 For illustration, see John Arnott MacCulloch, *Eddic Mythology*, in *Mythology of All Races*, ed. John Arnott MacCulloch et al., 13 vols. (New York: Cooper Square, 1964), II, 334.

73 Henry Adams Bellows, trans., *The Poetic Edda* (New York: Biblo and Tannen, 1969), p. 19.

74 No doubt a reference to the poetry of William Butler Yeats, as in "The Wild Swans at Coole."

75 See Benstock, *Joyce-again's Wake*, pp. 29–30.

76 See Atherton, *Books at the Wake*, p. 31.

77 Newall, *An Egg at Easter*, p. 2.

78 Joseph Campbell and Henry Morton Robinson, *A Skeleton Key to "Finnegans Wake"* (New York: The Viking Press, 1944), p. 184.

79 Newall, *An Egg at Easter*, p. 16.

80 Ibid.

81 Ibid., p. 7.

82 Ibid., p. 9.

83 Budge, *Gods of the Egyptians*, II, 107.

84 Ibid.

85 Newall, *An Egg at Easter*, p. 13.

86 Ibid., pp. 69–77.

87 Ibid., p. 71.

88 Ibid., p. 63.

89 See Eckenstein, *Comparative Studies in Nursery Rhymes*, pp. 104–115.

90 Ibid., p. 110.

91 Ibid., p. 109.

92 Ibid., p. 108.

93 *The Complete Dublin Diary of Stanislaus Joyce,* ed. George H. Healey (Ithaca, N.Y., and London: Cornell University Press, 1971), p. 62.

94 Newall, *An Egg at Easter,* p. 346.

95 Ingersoll, *Birds in Legend,* pp. 191–199.

96 Budge, *Gods of the Egyptians,* II, p. 96.

97 Ibid., p. 97.

98 Bayley, *Lost Language,* II, 276.

99 *Shell Guide to Ireland,* p. 258.

100 Newall, *An Egg at Easter,* p. 111.

101 Letter to Harriet Shaw Weaver, May 21, 1926. See *Letters of James Joyce,* ed. Stuart Gilbert (New York: The Viking Press, 1957), p. 241.